J. F. Broderick
55 Chelfield Rd.
Glenside, PA 19038-1401

DESPERATE
ENGAGEMENT

ALSO BY MARC LEEPSON

Flag: An American Biography

*Saving Monticello: The Levy Family's Epic
Quest to Rescue the House That Jefferson Built*

Webster's New World Dictionary of the Vietnam War (editor)

DESPERATE ENGAGEMENT

How a Little-Known Civil War Battle
Saved Washington, D.C., and Changed
the Course of American History

MARC LEEPSON

Thomas Dunne Books
St. Martin's Press   New York

THOMAS DUNNE BOOKS.
An imprint of St. Martin's Press.

www.thomasdunnebooks.com
www.stmartins.com

Design by Phil Mazzone

Library of Congress Cataloging-in-Publication Data

Leepson, Marc, 1945–
    Desperate engagement : how a little-known Civil War battle saved Washington, D.C.,
and changed American history / Marc Leepson.—1st ed.
        p. cm.
    Includes bibliographical references and index.
    ISBN-13: 978-0-312-36364-2
    ISBN-10: 0-312-36364-8
    1. Monocacy, Battle of, Md., 1864. 2. Washington (D.C.)—History—Civil War,
1861–1865. I. Title
    E476.66.L44 2007
    973.7'36—dc22

                                                                2007011562

First Edition: July 2007

10 9 8 7 6 5 4 3 2 1

To my beloved aunt Sally Sherman
and
in memory of my parents,
Selma and Arthur Leepson

Contents

Acknowledgments

The idea for this book came from the fertile mind of my literary agent, Joseph Brendan Vallely. Once again Joe was with me every step of the way in the publishing process, giving me much-needed (and nearly always on-the-money) advice when he wasn't giving me my fair share of abuse for various book biz missteps.

I am extremely happy and grateful that I again had the opportunity to work with Pete Wolverton, the associate publisher at Thomas Dunne Books. He saw the merit in this book and guided me expertly through the bookmaking process. That also goes for assistant editor Katie Gilligan. Thanks to both of you for helping me make this book, as well as to copyeditor Paul Montazzoli.

I was warmly welcomed and given exceptional assistance by the staff at the Monocacy National Battlefield. Thanks to Susan W. Trail, the superintendent; Brett Spaulding, park ranger and volunteer coordinator; Cathy Keeler, chief of resource education and visitor services; and to volunteer Mary Ann Heddleson.

Special thanks to Gail Stephens at Monocacy, who took the time to do an amazingly thorough job of reading and critiquing the first draft of this book and whose every suggested change (and correction) I gratefully made. Gail has done extremely valuable work collecting archival information on the battle and on Early's Shenandoah Valley Campaign at libraries and archives across the nation. Her knowledge of the Monocacy battlefield and her willingness to share that information are unsurpassed and immensely appreciated.

Gloria Swift, the curator at Ford's Theatre National Historic Site in Washington, who spent many years at Monocacy, also shared her extensive knowledge of the battle, as well as the bigger picture. I am very much in debt to Gloria and Gail for providing me with excellent tours of the battlefield. And to the eminent Civil War historian James McPherson for his guidance on the bigger picture issues.

Thanks also to Douglas K. Harvey, the museum director for the Lynchburg Museum System in Virginia, who, with the Battle of Lynchburg expert Van Naisawald, kindly critiqued my section on that engagement. And to Scott H. Harris, the director of the New Market Battlefield State Historical Park in Virginia, who read the section on that battle and events before and after.

I depended heavily on the expertise and assistance of many librarians and archivists, all of whom came up with materials that I never could have found on my own. Thanks to John M. Coski, the historian and director of library and research, and Ruth Ann Coski, the library manager, who did a thorough search of their extensive archives at the Museum of the Confederacy in Richmond.

My everlasting gratitude goes to the terrific staff at the Middleburg (Virginia) Library: Sheila Whetzel, Dorothy Donahoe, Heather Eickmeyer, and Tina Thomas; and to my support group at the Loudoun County (Virginia) Public Library, especially Mary Lou Demeo, Linda Holstslander, Cindy Tufts, Doug Henderson, and ILL wizard Robert Boley.

I had the always excellent advice and assistance of my friends at the Library of Virginia in Richmond: Tom Camden, the manager of special collections; Audrey C. Johnson, the senior rare book librarian; Conley Edwards, the state archivist; Tom Crew and Minor Weisiger, archives research services; Nolan Yelich, the librarian of Virginia; Sandy Treadway, the deputy librarian; and Jan Hathcock, the public relations manager.

Special thanks to Mary Beth McIntire, the executive director of the Library of Virginia Foundation, and her capable and helpful staff: Joseph Papa, Rick Golembowski, and Elizabeth Weakley.

Other librarians, archivists, and academicians who helped me include: Alexandra Gressitt and Mary Fischback at the Thomas Balch Library in Leesburg, Virginia; John Miller of the Emmitsburg (Maryland) Historical Society; Roger C. Adams, the rare books librarian, special collections, at the Hale Library at Kansas State University; James Owens, professor of history at Lynchburg (Virginia) College; Len Latkovski, professor of history and chair of the history department at Hood (Maryland) College; Peggy Stillman, the Chesapeake (Virginia) Public Library director; and Bruce A. Thompson, professor of history at Frederick (Maryland) Community College.

Also: Elisabeth A. Proffen, the special collections librarian, and Francis P. O'Neill, reference librarian at the Maryland Historical Society's H. Furlong Baldwin Library in Baltimore; Mary K. Mannix, Maryland Room manager at the C. Burr Artz Central Library in Frederick County, Maryland; David Hostetter, director of research and programs at the Robert C. Byrd Center for Legislative Studies at Shepherd University in West Virginia; Rodney Davis, codirector of the Lincoln Studies Center at Knox College in Illinois; and Dr. John R. Sellers of the Library of Congress's Manuscript Division reference staff.

Many friends have helped me with the book with ideas, information, and with just plain support. Thanks to: Xande Anderer, Cliff Boyle, Bernie and Linda Brien, Amoret Bruguiere, Childs Burden, Shane Chalke, Bob Corolla, Larry Cushman, John Czaplewski, Diane Deitz, Tommy and Marianne Dodson, Benton Downer, Pat Duncan, Russell Duncan, Dale Dye, Bill Ehrhart, Carol Engle, Bill and Sue Ferster, Randy Fertel, Bill Fogarty, Gail Guttman, Sgt. Rob Gwynn, Billy Hendon, John R. Hoffecker, Peter Horan, Tom Jewell, Ava Jones, Wayne Karlin, Michael Keating, and Michael (M-60) Kelley.

And Evan Leepson, Peter and Ellen Leepson, Treavor Lord, Hunt Lyman, Glenn Maravetz, Dave Miller, Rick Moock, Dan Murphy, Katherine Neville, Tom and Ann Northrup, Angus Paul, Mokie Porter, Mike Powers, Susan and Gray Price, Gomer Pyles, Dan and Margie Radovsky, Pat and Barbara Rhodes, Moses Robbins, Margo Sherman, Richard Strother, Dave Tarrant, Susan and Fraser Wallace, David Willson, Bob and Martha Wilson, and Susan and Saul Zucker.

Special thanks to Liz Nelson Weaver for indulging me with the constant changes on the three excellent maps she created.

I humbly thank my biggest cheerleader and the best proofreader I know, my precious aunt Sally Sherman, and my loving family—my wife, Janna, and my children, Devin and Cara—for putting up with me during the research and writing of this book.

Thank you, too, Cara, for thoughtfully tacking the following hand-lettered sign to my office door, without which it is doubtful that I would have been able to complete this book: DO NOT INTERRUPT ME. OTHERWISE I WILL GET REAL ANGRY. COME BACK IN 15–20 MINUTES.

This was one of the sharpest and most bloody fights of the war and our Brigade lost fully one half of the men that went into action, including several of our best officers.

—Confederate captain William J. Seymour of the First Louisiana Brigade on the July 9, 1864, Battle of Monocacy

Now began a desperate engagement. . . . In no other engagement of our three years' service did we witness so many acts of individual valor and daring. . . .

—Union private Thomas H. Scott of company B, 122nd New York Volunteer Infantry Regiment, on the fighting outside Fort Stevens in Washington, D.C., on July 11, 1864

DESPERATE
ENGAGEMENT

Prologue

On the blisteringly hot afternoon of Monday, July 11, 1864, the bold, battle-hardened Confederate general Jubal Anderson Early sat astride his horse outside the gates of Fort Stevens in the upper northwestern fringe of Washington, D.C. The enigmatic forty-seven-year-old Early, a veteran of Gettysburg, Antietam, the Wilderness, Cold Harbor, and a dozen other bloody battles, was about to make one of the Civil War's most fateful, portentous decisions: whether or not to order his ten thousand veteran rebel troops to invade the nation's capital.

Almost exactly a month earlier, Early's commanding general, the gentlemanly Robert E. Lee, had made a bold, risky decision. He'd ordered Early's Second Corps to cut itself out of Lee's Army of Northern Virginia, which had hunkered down outside Richmond awaiting the next move by Union army commander U. S. Grant, who had massed an unprecedented number of troops outside the capital of the Confederacy.

In the predawn hours of June 13, Early marched his men out of their Richmond-area encampment and into Virginia's Shenandoah Valley.

Lee had ordered Early to wreak havoc on Yankee troops in the valley, then to move north and invade Maryland. Lee envisioned an audacious mission: to free some fifteen thousand Confederate prisoners at the Point Lookout POW camp east of Washington in southern Maryland, and, if Early found the conditions right, to take the war for the first time into President Lincoln's front yard. Also on Lee's agenda: forcing Grant to release a good number of troops from the stranglehold he had built around Richmond.

Early followed Lee's orders. He swiftly and stealthily moved his men through the valley and on July 5 crossed the Potomac into Maryland. Then he slowly moved east. There was panic in the streets of Washington—and in Baltimore thirty-five miles to the north—when word reached the citizenry that Early's troops were heading in their direction. Washington, although it was ringed by an impressive array of interconnected forts and fortifications, was drastically underdefended in July of 1864.

Once manned by tens of thousands of experienced troops, the city's defenses were in the hands of a ragtag collection of walking-wounded Union soldiers grouped in a unit called the Veteran Reserve Corps, formerly known by the inglorious name the Invalid Corps, along with so-called hundred days' men from Ohio—raw recruits who had joined the Union army to serve as temporary, rear-echelon troops in the North.

Help was on the way. Grant, doing what Lee had hoped he would, at the eleventh hour had ordered thousands of battle-tested Union troops from his Sixth Corps north to Washington. This came only after a series of desperate telegrams from Maj. Gen. Henry Halleck, the U.S. Army chief of staff in Washington, Secretary of War Edwin Stanton, and President Lincoln himself. Their pleas convinced Grant to part with a large contingent of seasoned troops taking part in his ongoing siege of Richmond and Petersburg, the linchpin of Grant's plan for the final defeat of Lee's army.

It was now up to the crusty, tobacco-chewing, foul-mouthed, hard-drinking Early whether or not to pull the trigger outside of Fort Stevens.

Consider the political and military ramifications of his next move, as Early did as he stared through his field glasses at the U.S. Capitol dome at high noon on that hot July day. If he broke through the ring of forts surrounding the city, Confederate veterans would be running loose on the streets of Washington, D.C. The U.S. Treasury, virtually undefended, was sitting ready for looting. Tons upon tons of brand-new, desperately needed war supplies, from blankets to rifles, were there for the taking. The president himself was a target of opportunity, not to mention the U.S. Capitol and dozens of other government buildings. And there was the releasing of what amounted to an entire corps of imprisoned Southern troops at Point Lookout.

Would Lincoln, even if he escaped Early's men (a ship docked on the Potomac near the White House waited to spirit him out of town), have had even a chance of convincing war-weary Northern voters to reelect him in the upcoming presidential election?

Would Early's raid lead to a Democrat—maybe even a pro-Southern Copperhead—winning the White House in November?

Would the fact that—regardless of what Early did at the gates of Washington—Grant was forced to take a large number of troops away from Richmond for weeks, if not months, delay what the Union high command envisioned as a massive, war-ending battle?

Would a Confederate advance into the heart of Washington finally convince England and France to back the Southern cause economically and militarily?

A "rebel occupation of Washington for however brief a time," former secretary of the Senate George C. Gorham later wrote, would have brought about "serious consequences." One of them "would almost certainly have embraced the recognition of the Southern Confederacy by France and England, both of which governments were understood to be extremely desirous of even a slight pretext for such action."

With Washington "in the hands of the enemy, it would have been impossible to prophesy the foreign complications," then secretary of the Treasury Leslie M. Shaw said in 1902, "to say nothing of the demoralization of the people of the United States."

Widespread demoralization—and any one of the other scenarios—surely would have brought about Union war concessions, including some sort of compromise peace plan that included giving the South the states' rights it fought for. That included the No. 1 right in the minds of nearly all Southern politicians, the institution of slavery.

What follows is a recounting of four short, but pivotal, weeks in the long American Civil War, beginning on June 13 when Jubal Early left Richmond, reaching their apogee on July 11 when he stood at the gates of the nation's capital prepared to invade Washington. What took place during those four weeks had an underappreciated, but very significant, impact on the course of the Civil War—and upon American history.

ONE

The River with Many Bends

The past is never dead. It's not even past.
—William Faulkner, *Requiem for a Nun*

The Monocacy River begins near the Maryland-Pennsylvania border just west of the small town of Harney, Maryland, six miles due south of Gettysburg, Pennsylvania. The river, the largest Maryland tributary to the Potomac, meanders southeast for about sixty miles. It flows a few miles east of the city of Frederick before emptying out into the Potomac about fifty miles northwest of Washington, D.C. The sixty-odd-mile swath of gently rolling woodlands and fertile farm fields surrounding the river in the western Maryland Piedmont Plateau is known as the Monocacy Valley.

Archaeologists have found evidence that bands of nomadic Native American hunters inhabited the Monocacy Valley as early as the year 2000 BC. While there seem to have been few, if any, permanent Indian settlements, the valley was a favorite hunting ground for several tribes, including the Algonquian-language Piscataway and Nanticokes, which had settled in Maryland and Virginia's eastern coastal regions. The Monocacy River became an important source of transportation for the Indians, who also cut a series of trails through the densely wooded valley.

When the first Europeans came to western Maryland in the 1630s, they found the warlike Susquehannock living in settlements in the valley and to the north and east. During the next ninety years several other tribes—the Algonkian Shawnee, the Delaware, the Catawba, and the Tuscarora—either set up settlements or traveled through the area on hunting expeditions.

The settlers and Indians were drawn by a pristine river valley just east of the two-thousand-foot Catoctin Mountain (and current-day U.S. Route 15) overflowing with chestnut, hickory, and oak forests abounding with deer, buffalo, black bears, muskrats, elk, caribou, and turkey—along with extremely fertile soil. The river itself and its tributaries teemed with fish, turtles, and terrapins.

By the late 1720s, however, the Indian tribes were gone. They had fled west in the wake of a flood of European settlers, mainly Scots/Irish from Northern Ireland, English land speculators, and emigrants from the Palatinate region of the Rhine in Germany. Many of the latter arrived from heavily German Pennsylvania via what was known as the Monocacy Road. That road began near York, cut southwesterly through Pennsylvania into Maryland through the Monocacy Valley, and then crossed the Potomac River and into Virginia's Shenandoah Valley.

The Indians who lived in the Monocacy Valley may have disappeared by the late 1720s, but they left behind their name for the river and its surrounding area. The Seneca called the river Cheneoow-quoquey. The earliest European settlers in the 1720s called it Quattaro and Coturki, names that also were sometimes given to the nearby Potomac. The name that stuck, Monocacy, is a variant of the Shawnee word "Monnockkesey," roughly translated as "river with many bends."

There may have been a village called Monocacy established by German-speaking settlers from Pennsylvania around 1729 located about fifteen miles north of Frederick, near the current-day town of Creagerstown. It is the site of the first German church, known as the Log Church, erected in Maryland. Archaeological and historical evidence that the little village did, in fact, exist, however, is inconclusive.

What we do know for certain is that John Thomas Schley (1712–89), the leader of a group of some one hundred Palatinate Germans, founded the city of Frederick (then called Frederick Town) near the midpoint of the Monocacy Valley in 1745. Schley, historians believe, chose the name in honor of Frederick Calvert (1731–71), the sixth (and last) Lord Baltimore, who had inherited (but never set foot in) the English province of Maryland in 1751. The city of Frederick, standing as it did as a crossroads between the growing cities of the east and the frontier to the west, soon blossomed and became the largest city in western Maryland.

It was here in 1755, a year after the start of the French and Indian War, that British major general Edward Braddock, the commander in chief of all British forces in North America, met with Benjamin Franklin (then a member of the Pennsylvania Assembly) and Braddock's trusted military aide George Washington. They came to Frederick to plan Braddock's next move—what turned out to be a disastrous expedition to try to take the French-held Fort Duquesne in what today is downtown Pittsburgh.

Ten years later, in 1765, Frederick was the scene of a heated protest over the British Stamp Act. Twelve Frederick County judges issued a statement on November 23, condemning that much reviled taxation-without-representation legislation.

One of the judges, Thomas Johnson (1732–1819), became the state of Maryland's first elected governor and later an associate justice of the U.S. Supreme Court. Two other famed early American lawyers also called Frederick home: Francis Scott Key (1779–1843), best known as the author of "The Star-Spangled Banner," and his brother-in-law, Roger Brooke Taney (1777–1864), the fifth chief justice of the United States, best known for issuing the 1857 Supreme Court Dred Scott decision, which denied citizenship to all African Americans, whether they were slaves or freemen.

By 1860, on the eve of the Civil War, the city of Frederick's population reached 8,143, and the surrounding Frederick County was home to some 40,000 people. Frederick grew, in large part, because of its geographic location as a natural east-west and north-south transportation hub and crossroads. The Baltimore Pike (also known as the National Road) connected Frederick with Maryland's largest port city to the east. The Georgetown Pike linked Frederick to the nation's capital some forty miles to the southeast.

The Baltimore and Ohio Railroad (B&O), the nation's first chartered passenger and freight railway, began construction in Baltimore in 1828. It reached the outskirts of Frederick in 1831. Like the Monocacy River, the B&O skirted Frederick about four miles to the southeast of the city. After protests from the city's fathers, the B&O laid tracks from a spot at the western bank of the Monocacy River and built a 3.5-mile spur into the city.

The triangular piece of land, officially known as Frederick Junction, was commonly referred to as Monocacy Junction. The B&O erected a wooden bridge to span the Monocacy at the junction, then replaced it with a more-sturdy (and expensive) iron suspension bridge.

Maryland, sitting as it does below the Mason-Dixon line, was a slave state. But it was also a geographically and socially divided border state. Tobacco planta-tions, which depended heavily on slave labor, dominated southern Maryland. The state's northern and western regions, on the other hand, had few slave-holding families and, in fact, were home to many freed blacks.

When Fort Sumter fell on April 13, 1861, and the Civil War began, Maryland's citizens were nearly equally divided among those who supported the Union and those whose sympathies lay with the Confederate States of America (CSA). When troops of the Sixth Massachusetts Volunteers ar-rived in Baltimore by train on April 19 on the way to Washington, a prose-cessionist mob attacked them. That urban skirmish resulted in the deaths of four soldiers and twelve civilians. Fearing that unrest would spread through-out Maryland, President Lincoln sent Gen. Benjamin Franklin Butler to oc-cupy the capital of Annapolis on April 22.

On that day Gov. Thomas Holliday Hicks called a special session of the Maryland General Assembly to discuss where the state's loyalty would go. In-stead of meeting in Annapolis, which was strongly pro-Confederate, Hicks, a member of the Native American Party (known as the Know-Nothings), took the legislature to Frederick, where sympathies strongly favored the Union. The General Assembly did not vote to secede, nor did it strongly support the Union. The legislators' goal seemed to be neutrality.

On September 17, when the General Assembly gathered after a six-week adjournment, federal troops and Baltimore police officers arrived in Freder-ick to arrest prosecessionist members. That act ended the official movement in Maryland to align the state with the Confederacy. But it did not end Maryland's direct involvement in the war. Much of that involvement cen-tered on Frederick because of its location as both a north-south and an east-west crossroads.

Contingents of Union troops bivouacked in the city and its surrounding areas, including Monocacy Junction, beginning in the summer of 1861. These included units assigned to guard the Monocacy Bridge and the railroad throughout much of the next four years. There were also large bands of Union and Confederate forces that moved into and out of Frederick and its environs during the war. Most of that action took place during the South's three invasions of the North: in September 1862, in July 1863, and in July 1864.

Robert E. Lee's forty-five-thousand-man Army of Northern Virginia began crossing the Potomac near Leesburg, Virginia, on September 4, 1862, in the South's first invasion of the North. Three days later Lee's troops marched into Frederick. They promptly took possession of the city without a shot being fired. Lee had hoped that he would be warmly greeted by pro-Confederates in Frederick. But his reception was lukewarm at best, a state of affairs memorialized in the (most likely apocryphal) poem "Barbara Frietschie" by John Greenleaf Whittier.

In that much-recited poem, Whittier describes how the townspeople of Frederick had taken down their American flags just before Lee's army marched through the city. The patriotic Frietschie, then ninety-five years old, according to Whittier (who heard the story secondhand), bravely flew the flag from her dormer window. When famed Confederate general Thomas J. Stonewall Jackson rode by, he ordered his men to shoot the flag down.

The determined Barbara Frietschie responded by saying, "Shoot, if you must, this old gray head, but spare your country's flag." Her outspokenness shamed Jackson, who then told his men not to touch "a hair of yon gray head."

That story may not be true, but it illustrates the pro-Union sentiment in the city, and gives the flavor of the reception that greeted Lee's men.

Following the march through Frederick, Lee made his headquarters at what was then known as South Hermitage Farm, three miles south of the city and a stone's throw from Monocacy Junction and the Georgetown Pike (today's Route 355). Lee's troops arrived just after the departure of the recently formed Fourteenth New Jersey Volunteer Infantry Regiment, which had been sent to the junction to guard the B&O Railroad Bridge over the Monocacy River. Lee's army pitched tents in the fields, and Confederate soldiers used the river to bathe and wash their uniforms.

It was at that spot on September 8 that Lee drew up his "Proclamation to the People of Maryland," a plea for Marylanders to join the Confederacy. It had little effect in pro-Union western Maryland. Lee abandoned his camp and moved his troops west of Frederick on September 10.

The day before Lee had written—and his assistant adjutant general Robert Chilton drew up—Special Orders No. 191, a ten-part document outlining the operational details of Lee's plan. The order provided specific instructions to Lee's lieutenants, including Stonewall Jackson, James Longstreet, J. E. B. Stuart, and Daniel Harvey Hill.

Chilton made copies of the order and sent them to each of Lee's generals, including Hill. When he received his copy of the order, Stuart had another copy made and sent to Hill because he had been under Jackson's command. That copy—or the original—never made it to Hill, probably because the courier carrying the document somehow lost it. Hill, of course, did not realize that fact since he had received one copy of the order and was not expecting another.

On September 13 troops from the Union army's Twelfth Corps set up camp on the same site where Hill had camped a few days earlier. That day two soldiers of the Twenty-seventh Indiana—accounts differ as to their identity—happened upon a strange package sitting in the tall grass: three cigars wrapped in paper. When the men looked at the paper wrapper, they were startled to see the label "Headquarters, Army of Northern Virginia, Special Orders, No. 191," signed by Robert Chilton. They had stumbled upon one of the copies of the order that was supposed to go to Hill.

The Union troops turned the order over to their superiors, and it made its way to Gen. George B. McClellan at his headquarters nearby. McClellan realized the value of the order; but, true to his usual method of operations, was slow to act on the startling intelligence, delaying his march from Frederick. Meanwhile, Lee learned through a Confederate sympathizer who happened to be in McClellan's camp when the order arrived that the enemy knew his battle plan.

The day before, on September 12, McClellan's troops had crossed the Monocacy and followed Lee into Frederick, where the populace greeted his army enthusiastically. "Our troops were wildly welcomed," the pro-Union *Harper's Weekly* reported the following week. "The three stone bridges across the Monocacy were found uninjured, though the fine iron railroad bridge was destroyed."

Troops from the Fourteenth New Jersey, which would return to Monocacy to fight in the big July 9, 1864, battle there, joined railroad workers who had begun replacing the bridge on September 17, the same day that the infamous slaughter took place at the Battle of Antietam just outside Sharpsburg, Maryland, about fifteen miles west of Frederick.

At Antietam, McClellan's 80,000-man Army of the Potomac went head-to-head with Lee's army in what has the unhappy distinction of being the bloodiest one day in American history. Nearly 22,000 Americans were killed, wounded, or went missing in that day of fighting. That included 2,100 dead and 9,550 wounded Union troops and 1,550 dead and 7,750 wounded Confederate soldiers. The Battle of Antietam ended in a stalemate, but one that forced Lee to retreat to Virginia.

McClellan famously did not pursue Lee into Virginia, a tactical error of such magnitude that Lincoln would strip him of his command on November 5. In early October Lee took advantage of McClellan's inaction by ordering some eighteen hundred Confederate cavalry troops with four pieces of horse artillery under Maj. Gen. J. E. B. Stuart to go back across the Potomac. At daylight on October 10, Stuart and his raiding party crossed the river near Williamsport, Maryland, and proceeded to raid the nearby Pennsylvania cities of Mercersburg and Chambersburg. Stuart's men then moved southeast into Maryland, through Emmittsburg, Liberty, New Market, Hyattstown, and Barnesville.

When he reached White's Ford, below the mouth of the Monocacy, Lee later reported, Stuart had made "a complete circuit of the enemy's position." After a short rest at Urbana, just south of Monocacy Junction, Stuart headed back to Virginia. "On approaching the Potomac he was opposed by the enemy's cavalry, under General Stoneman, but drove them back, and put to flight the infantry stationed on the bluff at White's Ford," Lee noted. Stuart then returned to Virginia. The "expedition," Lee said, "was eminently successful, and accomplished without other loss than the wounding of 1 man."

Stuart's evaluation of the raid was even more laudatory. "The results of this expedition, in a moral and political point of view, can hardly be estimated," he said a week later, "and the consternation among property holders in Pennsylvania beggars description."

Eight months later, Lee launched his second invasion of the North. Following up on his smashing victory at Chancellorsville early in May of 1863, Lee devised a plan to take his seventy-five-thousand-man Army of Northern Virginia northward again. The aim this time was to resupply his troops; get the Union army to leave Virginia; and perhaps threaten Philadelphia, Baltimore, and the national capital in Washington.

After victories at Winchester and Martinsburg, Virginia, Gen. Richard S. Ewell's Second Corps crossed the Potomac on June 15. By June 20 Ewell's forces had reached South Mountain to the west of Frederick. By the end of June, some seventy-five thousand Confederate troops were scattered throughout southeastern Pennsylvania in an arc to the north and west of the small town of Gettysburg.

The Union army soon met the challenge, moving the nearly one-hundred-thousand-man-strong Army of the Potomac from Virginia into Maryland. On

June 28, when Gen. George G. Meade took over as commander of the Army of the Potomac, a large percentage of his troops had set up camp in the area around Monocacy Junction. Those men began moving out at 6:00 a.m. on June 29. They marched east across the Monocacy River bridges, and the next day moved north, crossing the Pennsylvania line into Gettysburg. There the Union and Confederate forces engaged in what many consider the turning point of the Civil War.

The battle began on July 1 and lasted for three long days. When it was over, an astounding fifty-one thousand men had been killed or wounded, making Gettysburg the bloodiest battle in American history. At great cost the Union army held off Lee's troops, forcing them to retreat on the afternoon of July 4. Meade, although victorious, emulated the disgraced McClellan and did not pursue Lee's defeated army into Virginia.

By bringing the war into Pennsylvania, Lee had hoped to intimidate Union political leaders into negotiating for peace. That dream shattered after his army was decimated and forced to retreat from Gettysburg.

Meade's failure to capitalize also cost him. On the same day, July 4, 1863, that Lee retreated to Virginia, Union major general Ulysses S. Grant marched triumphantly into the city of Vicksburg, Mississippi. Grant had just won a hard-fought victory that cost the Confederacy its last important stronghold on the Mississippi River. As Meade's star plummeted, Grant's rose.

Early in March of 1864, Abraham Lincoln summoned Grant to Washington, where the embattled president conferred upon Grant the rank of lieutenant general in a White House ceremony. That rank, which had been authorized by Congress, made Grant the highest-ranking Union commander and gave him command of all Union armies, including Meade's Army of the Potomac.

On March 10 Grant met Meade at his winter camp near Brandy Station in Virginia's Culpeper County, some sixty-five miles south of Washington and about eighty miles north of Richmond. It was there that Grant unveiled his strategy for ending the war—a strategy that put in motion the events that would lead to the third Confederate invasion of the North in July, the Battle of Monocacy, and Jubal Early's march on Washington.

That sequence of events had a direct impact on the course of the Civil War, beginning when Grant put his plan into place in the early spring. If all went according to plan, Grant's strategy was designed to end the war, perhaps in a matter of months. As we are about to see, all did not go according to plan.

TWO

Grant's Grand Campaign
to End the War

It is well that war is so terrible: We should grow too fond of it.
—ROBERT E. LEE, DECEMBER 13, 1862

. . . I do not calculate on very good results. . . .
—U. S. GRANT TO W. T. SHERMAN, APRIL 4, 1864, ON UNION ARMY
OPERATIONS IN THE DEPARTMENT OF WEST VIRGINIA

Lee worried about being too fond of war. Grant practiced total
war as the best way to end it quickly. He put in motion an aggressive plan
that would unleash warfare at its most terrible throughout the South. Grant
cooked up an uncompromising, five-part plan that he believed would pummel the Confederate army and bring the war to an end.

Part I: German-born major general Franz Sigel, the commander of the
Union army's Department of West Virginia, would move out and take the
key cities of Staunton in the Shenandoah Valley and Lynchburg to the east
across the Blue Ridge Mountains. The main objective: to cut off Lee's Army
of Northern Virginia from the bulk of its food supply by blocking the railroad lines.

Part II: Maj. Gen. William Tecumseh Sherman, Grant's war friend and
ally who had succeeded him as commander of the Union's Western Theater
and was occupying Chattanooga, would go south, destroy Joseph E. Johnston's
Confederate Army of Tennessee's ability to fight, and then take Atlanta.

Part III: Department of the Gulf commander, Maj. Gen. Nathaniel P.

Banks—the political general who had been speaker of the House of Representatives and governor of Massachusetts before the war—would move east from New Orleans and take Mobile, Alabama, a Confederate stronghold and a crucial cog in the South's blockade-running operation.

Part IV: George Meade would take his Army of the Potomac from Fort Monroe near Hampton Roads, and pin down Lee's army in the southern capital of Richmond.

Part V: Benjamin F. Butler, acting independently, would move up the James River, cut the rail line between Richmond and Petersburg, and threaten the Confederate capital from the south.

The plan was bold; the generals chosen to carry it out—with the notable exception of Sherman—however, ranged from undistinguished to incompetent. Butler, a Massachusetts politician with big ambitions, turned out to be one of the dimmest stars in the Union military firmament. He had made such a mess of things as military governor of New Orleans in 1862 that Lincoln relieved him of his command after Butler imposed draconian conditions on the city, including hanging a man who had torn down an American flag.

In May 1864 Butler, nicknamed the "Beast of New Orleans," never made it past Bermuda Hundred, a small village on a neck of land between the James and Appomattox Rivers, about twenty miles southeast of Richmond and ten miles northeast of Petersburg. Astonishingly, Butler's army of some thirty-six thousand men was stopped in its tracks and bottled up there by a Confederate force under Brig. Gen. P. G. T. Beauregard that started out with fewer than eighteen thousand troops. Not only did Butler start out with a two-to-one advantage (Beauregard soon had the help of reinforcements from North Carolina), but some of the Confederate troops were bottom-of-the-barrel teenagers and old men recruited at Petersburg and Richmond at the eleventh hour.

Banks, who had lost badly to Stonewall Jackson in the Shenandoah Valley in 1862, ignored Grant's order to move east. Instead, with approval from Washington, Banks turned west and embarked on his ill-fated Red River Campaign, which ended in a humiliating defeat and led to Banks's being removed from his field command.

At the same time that Butler and Banks took their forces out of the picture, Grant himself took charge of the centerpiece of his strategy, destroying Lee's army in Virginia. "Lee, with the capital of the Confederacy, was the main end to which all were working," Grant pointed out in his memoirs.

Ulysses S. Grant, the Union army commanding general, did not count on having to defend Washington from a Confederate attack when he instituted his final plan to end the war in the spring of 1864. *Credit: The Library of Virginia*

Grant called the effort his Grand Campaign. Historians later dubbed it Grant's Wilderness Campaign and the Overland Campaign. Grant personally directed Meade's 118,700-strong army in his Grand Campaign against Lee's 64,000 soldiers in what would be some of the bloodiest fighting of the bloody Civil War. During that forty-day span in May and June 1864, Grant and his commanders suffered an almost unimaginable 60,000 casualties and Lee about 35,000.

The campaign started on May 4 when the Army of the Potomac, with Grant leading the way, crossed the Rapidan River west of Fredericksburg. He clashed with Lee the next day at the vicious, two-day Battle of the Wilderness, one of the worst bloodlettings in American history. Intense fighting raged in unseasonably and brutally hot weather in a heavily forested rural area about eighteen miles west of the city of Fredericksburg.

Lee outdueled Grant at the Wilderness. The Union suffered some eighteen thousand killed and wounded; Confederate losses were around eleven thousand. Eighteen thousand dead and wounded did not deter U. S. Grant though. He promptly moved his troops southeast toward Richmond.

About fifteen miles down the road, Grant and his men ran into Lee's entrenched troops at Spotsylvania Court House. Lee and Grant once again butted heads. The battle waxed and waned over twelve days and included eighteen hours of vicious hand-to-hand combat at the infamous "Bloody Angle." Grant finally had enough, and pulled his troops out on May 20. The final grim tally: some eighteen thousand Union dead and wounded versus some ten thousand Confederate casualties.

Still Grant pushed on, driving the Union army south and east around the Confederate lines toward Richmond. After ten days of sporadic skirmishing, the Union troops arrived at Cold Harbor about ten miles northeast of Richmond on May 31. The final battle of the vicious and ill-fated Overland Campaign began that day with a cavalry engagement at Cold Harbor led by Union major general Philip Sheridan against Confederate major general Fitzhugh Lee, a nephew of the Confederate commander.

The battle picked up steam on June 1; again the fighting ebbed and flowed. On June 3 some fifty thousand Union troops attacked Lee's well-entrenched men. By the following day, June 4, the fight turned into a siege, with sporadic skirmishing and the trading of artillery rounds.

Finally, on June 12, Grant called off the fighting after suffering some twelve thousand killed, wounded, missing, or captured. Lee's casualties in this, his last big field victory of the Civil War, stood at some four thousand.

Cold Harbor proved to be a turning point. The huge losses caused Grant to reassess his Grand Campaign strategy. He decided not to move directly against Richmond. Instead, Grant took his troops south. The aim now was to cross the James River to Petersburg, the large city about twenty miles south of Richmond that served as the capital city's rail hub, and to cut off Richmond's last rail connections to what was left of the Confederacy.

Grant also hoped to threaten the Confederate capital as a means of drawing Lee into battle—a fight that Grant was confident he would win because he vastly outnumbered Lee and because his army was much better supplied and equipped.

While Grant absorbed unimaginable losses in the Wilderness Campaign, Sigel was not doing much better in the Shenandoah Valley. The famed valley between the Blue Ridge Mountains to the east and the Appalachian Mountains to the west stretches from the Potomac River at the present-day Maryland–West Virginia border to Lexington, Virginia, 160 miles to the southwest.

The scene of Stonewall Jackson's daring 1862 exploits, the valley had been in Confederate control since the war had begun three years earlier. A land of famed scenic beauty, the valley also was a rich farmland that produced abundant food supplies that Lee's army heavily depended on.

Sigel, who was born near Heidelberg, Germany, in 1824, had immigrated to the United States in 1852, after an undistinguished, at best, military career. He became a public school official in St. Louis and a leader of that city's sizeable German community. When the Civil War broke out he organized the Third Missouri Infantry.

Commissioned as a colonel, Sigel was promoted to major general in March 1862 following his uncharacteristically effective performance in the Union victory in the Battle of Pea Ridge in Arkansas. Commanding I Corps in Pope's Army of Virginia, Sigel fought at Second Manassas, a big Union defeat, at the end of August. The following winter he was given command of the XI Corps, which was made up primarily of new, German-speaking immigrants.

Franz Sigel, like Butler, owed his position primarily to political factors and was not exactly a Union military luminary. "Sigel is merely a book soldier acquainted with the techniques of the art of war but having no capacity to fight with troops in the field," David Hunter Strother, one of his staff officers (and a cousin of Union general David Hunter), wrote during the war. He "has the air to me of a military pedagogue, given to technical shams and trifles of military art, but narrow minded and totally wanting in practical capacity." Strother said he once hoped that "Sigel was honest and patriotic, but I have since been led to believe that he was a mere adventurer."

Never a favorite of then general in chief Henry Halleck, who had a low opinion of all political generals, Sigel gave up his command in the spring of 1863 ostensibly for health reasons. In March 1864 Lincoln arranged to have Sigel appointed to command the Department of West Virginia. That put Sigel in charge of a huge geographic area starting at the western bank of the Monocacy River in Maryland and including all of the Shenandoah Valley.

Lincoln made the appointment primarily for political—rather than military—reasons. Sigel, it turned out, was skillful at one thing: recruiting much-needed German immigrants into his ranks at a time when recruiting was difficult in the North and the Union was forced, in July of 1863, to institute military conscription.

In May Grant ordered Sigel to move from his headquarters in Martinsburg up the Shenandoah Valley (that is, southward) to the crucial transportation hub of Staunton (pronounced "STAN-tin"). The German proved not to be up to the task.

Leading some 6,300 troops up the valley, Sigel on May 15 ran into a force of some 4,100 Confederate troops under Maj. Gen. John C. Breckinridge of Kentucky, the former American vice president under James Buchanan, at New Market, some forty-five miles north of Staunton. What ensued turned out to be one of the most embarrassing Union defeats of the war.

Sigel faced a Confederate force that Breckinridge—the commander of the Confederate Department of Western Virginia who would serve under Jubal Early during his move into Maryland in June and July—had hastily assembled just prior to the battle. The force included nearly the entire Virginia Military Institute (VMI) Corps of Cadets, 257 young men and boys (some as young as fifteen) who had marched some eighty miles from Lexington.

The cadets fought valiantly and were instrumental in routing Sigel. The story of the boy soldiers unhesitatingly answering the call for service and sacrifice at New Market—along with the importance of that effort in defeating the Yankees—is an important part of the fabric of VMI to this day.

After being routed at New Market, Sigel retreated ingloriously down the valley to Strasburg. The War Department, at Grant's request, demoted Sigel, assigning him to command the Department of West Virginia's reserve force. On July 7 he was removed from that command. Sigel's replacement as head of the Department of West Virginia was David Hunter—whose record and reputation were not much better than the departing German's.

The sixty-one-year-old Hunter, a West Point graduate, had served in the Mexican War and was known chiefly for his temper (he killed three men in duels), for his friendship with Abraham Lincoln, for his fierce abolitionist views, and for encouraging his men to pillage and burn the Shenandoah Valley. His mercurial temperament—or perhaps the fact that his hair and moustache at age sixty-one were jet black, or that he had a fairly dark complexion—earned Hunter the nickname "Black Dave."

When the Civil War broke out, Hunter was made brigadier general of troops under Gen. Irvin McDowell and was wounded at First Manassas. He subsequently served as commander of the Western Department of Missouri, and then, in March 1862, the Department of the South. Driven by an intense hatred of slavery, Hunter earned Lincoln's disfavor—and the hatred of millions of Southerners—for unilaterally abolishing slavery in Georgia, South Carolina, and Florida, and for recruiting a regiment made up of former slaves.

Lincoln rescinded Hunter's emancipation order and relieved him of his command. He wasn't given another until nearly two years later on May 21, 1864, when Grant named him as Sigel's replacement.

"I am ashamed to belong to such an army under such a tyrant," U. S. Army surgeon Alexander Neil said of his commanding officer in a letter home from the war. "He is tyrannical to his men. I have seen him [horsewhip] poor wounded soldiers, for some little misdemeanor with his own hand, until the spark of life had about fled."

With Black Dave Hunter in command, Grant's goal in the valley remained the same: to move Hunter's troops to Staunton and, if he didn't meet much opposition, to two other central Virginia cities that contained crucial Virginia Central Railroad connections, Gordonsville and Charlottesville, with the object of blocking Lee's supply route from the west.

On May 25 Grant turned his attention to the city of Lynchburg, which sits on the eastern edge of the Blue Ridge on the James River about seventy-five miles south of Staunton. Lynchburg was important to Grant because it served as the depot for Confederate supplies gathered from the valley, was a large manufacturing center and the site of a Confederate hospital complex.

"If Hunter can possibly get to Charlottesville and Lynchburg, he should do so, living on the country," Grant wrote to Halleck. "The railroads and canal should be destroyed beyond possibility of repairs for weeks."

Hunter and his army of some 8,500 men had initial success, mainly because nearly all of Breckinridge's troops had left the Shenandoah Valley after New Market to help with Lee's defense of Richmond. That left precious few Confederates to stand in Hunter's way.

Hunter rampaged up the valley, defeating 5,500 hastily assembled Confederate troops under Brig. Gen. William Edmonson "Grumble" Jones on June 5 at Piedmont, south of Harrisonburg. The CSA force at Piedmont included the Third Battalion Valley Reserves, which consisted mostly of boys and older men Jones had recruited just before the fight. In that engagement, Jones was shot off his horse and killed.

Hunter reached Staunton on June 8. In that city with a population of some four thousand he met up with Union brigadier generals George Crook and William W. Averell, who commanded some ten thousand men and two artillery batteries. In Staunton, his men "destroyed a large amount of public stores," Hunter wrote in his official report. These included mills, factories, and stables belonging to prominent civilians whose businesses supported the Confederacy.

"I also had the Virginia Central Railroad entirely destroyed for several miles east and west of the town, burning all the depot buildings, shops, and warehouses belonging to the road," Hunter added.

Two days later, on June 10, Hunter began the thirty-five-mile march to Lexington. He ordered his men to live as Grant ordered, "on the country." Hunter took that directive to mean seizing crops and livestock, burning houses and farms, and encouraging his men to take or destroy civilian food supplies and property. His army's performance in the valley—which may also have come in reaction to having seen on the way from New Market hogs and dogs eating the remains of dead Union soldiers—earned Black Dave Hunter even more enmity among the Southern population.

Army surgeon Alexander Neil described Hunter's men being given free rein to take part "in all kinds of vice, robbery and murder." Virtually every house along the way "was plundered of everything," Neil said.

"Women & children were driven to starvation, their persons violated; many were murdered after homes lain in ashes," Neil said. "I saw many inoffensive citizens murdered in their own yards. I saw many dangling from limbs of trees as I passed along. Villages were destroyed after being plundered, hundreds of private mansions were laid in ashes and great black smokes were arising at all times in the day in all directions."

The rampaging Union forces faced only scattered opposition as they marched to the city of Lexington. It came primarily in the form of hit-and-run attacks by a brigade of cavalry under Confederate general "Tiger" John McCausland, an 1857 VMI graduate who would go on to join Early's army and play a pivotal role in the Battle of Monocacy and the subsequent raid on Washington, D.C.

When Hunter's men reached Lexington on June 11, he exacted his form of revenge for the disgrace at New Market from VMI, as well as neighboring Washington College (today's Washington and Lee University).

Following a heavy artillery bombardment of the city, Hunter's men marched unopposed onto the VMI grounds—called the "post"—which also contained a Confederate arsenal. The Corps of Cadets and most of the town's citizens had fled. The next day Hunter, disregarding the protests of Crook and Averell, ordered his troops to burn the nation's first state military college, known as the West Point of the South, which had been founded in 1839.

The fires completely destroyed several buildings and badly damaged several others, including the cadet barracks. VMI's library, laboratory, and scientific equipment burned to the ground. Hunter even ordered his men to cart VMI's statue of George Washington to Wheeling, West Virginia. It was returned the year after the war ended, in 1866.

"Both the Institute and the College were well rummaged by the boys," Pvt. O. J. Humphreys of the Ohio Artillery's First Independent Battery wrote in his diary, "and the clothing of the cadets and the libraries of the two institutions received much attention."

The Union troops also burned other buildings in Lexington, including the home of "Honest" John Letcher (1813–84), whose four-year term as Virginia's governor had ended earlier that year. Letcher, who had fled the city just before Hunter's men arrived, described the scene in a letter to a friend in Richmond that the Staunton *Republican Vindicator* published in its July 22 edition.

"The threats made by the Yankees against me, for the past two years, satisfied me that they would destroy my house," the former governor wrote, "but I always supposed they would allow the furniture and my family's clothing to be removed." That proved not to be the case, at least according to Letcher.

At 8:00 on the morning of June 12, a Union captain and his guards rode up to the house and told Letcher's wife that they "were ordered by Hunter to fire the house." Mrs. Letcher, who had had assurances from Hunter the day before that the house would not be burned, protested and asked to be taken to the general.

"The order is peremptory," the Union captain replied, "and you have five minutes in which to leave the house."

Mrs. Letcher asked "to remove her mother's, sister's, her own, and her children's clothing," her husband said, but the captain "insolently refused." The Union troops "immediately thereafter poured camphene on the parlor floor and ignited it with a match."

Letcher's daughter took an "armful of clothing" out the door, but when the Union captain "discovered her, ran forward and fired the clothing in her arms. He then poured camphene in the wardrobes, bureau drawers, and ignited the clothing—taking out my clothing, which he said he intended to take North."

The troops then burned the stable on Letcher's seventy-eight-year-old mother's property next door, "with no other view," he said, "than to burn her out also." His mother's house caught fire twice, but a Union officer, a Captain Towns of New York, intervened and "made his men carry water and extinguish the flames."

The burning "was done by order of Gen. Hunter because of the finding of circulars calling on the people to poison and bushwhack Yankee invaders," William G. Watson, an Ohio Infantry soldier, wrote in his memoir. The burning was "protested against by Genl. Averill [sic] and Genl. Crooks [sic]."

One Staunton newspaper described Hunter's scorched-earth policy at Lexington as "one of the most wanton and barbaric acts of the war."

Hunter, said CSA general John Brown Gordon, "must have possessed some high qualities, or he would not have been entrusted with the grave responsibilities which attach to the commander of a department." But, Gordon said, "it is hard to trace any evidences of knighthood in the wreck and ravage which marked the lines of his marches."

If he had captured Hunter, Gordon said, "it would doubtless have been difficult to save him from the vengeance of the troops."

Nor did Hunter's modus operandi please Union officers and men. One officer who spoke out was the colonel commanding Crook's First Infantry Brigade, a forty-three-year-old Harvard-educated lawyer from Cincinnati who had joined the Twenty-third Ohio Volunteer Infantry Regiment when the war broke out.

"This does not suit many of us," future president Rutherford B. Hayes wrote in his diary. "Gen. C, I know, disapproves. It is surely bad."

Three days after entering Lexington on June 14, Hunter's troops left for Lynchburg, forty-five miles to the southeast.

"The troops," Union private Frank Reader wrote in his diary, "are in excellent condition and anxious to finish the grand work they have commenced."

Hunter's move to Lynchburg brought him very close to controlling the Shenandoah Valley—a state of affairs that would have proven disastrous to the South's ability to continue fighting the war. It precipitated a bold, risky move on the part of Robert E. Lee—a move that Lee hoped would slow up Grant's grand strategy to end the war.

THREE

Lee's "Bad Old Man"

I entered the military service of my State, willingly, cheerfully, and zealously.
—JUBAL EARLY ON JOINING THE CONFEDERATE ARMY
OF NORTHERN VIRGINIA IN 1861

On June 12, 1864, two days before Hunter set out for Lynchburg, Robert E. Lee, sitting outside Richmond waiting for Grant's next move, made a bold move of his own. It was a move so risky that if it failed, it would have left Lee extremely vulnerable in Richmond and easily could have given Grant an opening to make a successful final aggressive move against Petersburg and Richmond. If Lee's move succeeded, it could tip the scale 180 degrees in the other direction and force the Union to seek peace.

Unbeknownst to Lee, the success or failure of his audacious plan would hinge on an all-day battle at Monocacy Junction that would take place on July 9. What Lee did know on June 12 was that his plan's success hinged on the man he chose to carry it out, the newly minted lieutenant general Jubal Anderson Early, one of the Civil War's most controversial, enigmatic, and mercurial characters.

Jubal Early was born on November 3, 1816, in the small Franklin County, Virginia, town of Rocky Mount, in the south central part of the state about twenty miles south of Roanoke. He enjoyed a comfortable childhood, the third of ten children born to Joab and Ruth Hairston Early. His parents were Franklin County natives whose forebears from Ireland and Scotland had settled in the area in the 1760s.

The Early family was well connected and well-off. Joab Early, a gentleman farmer who had been a member of the Virginia legislature and a colonel in the county militia, had large landholdings. One of his sons was educated at the elite College of William and Mary.

Through connections, Joab Early arranged an appointment for his son Jubal at the U.S. Military Academy at West Point. Although he spent four years there and graduated in 1837, Jubal Early—who even as a young man liked to give orders, not take them—had no desire to be a professional military man.

"I was not a very exemplary soldier," Early admitted in his autobiography. "I had very little taste of scrubbing brass, and cared very little for the advancement to be obtained by the exercise of that must useful art."

After receiving his commission in the U.S. Army as a second lieutenant, Early completed his service obligation in the desultory, on-again-off-again war against the Seminole Indians. He served in and around Tampa Bay and the Everglades in Florida, in his chosen field, artillery. Early saw scant action in Florida. He mustered out of the army in the spring of 1838 when he was twenty-two years old.

Returning to his hometown in the fall, Early began studying the law. Early then began his own small-town law practice in 1840. He also started a political career. Early served two years, 1841–42, as a Whig Party member in the Virginia House of Delegates. At twenty-five, he was the body's youngest member.

Early lost his seat in the 1842 election to a Democratic opponent, then returned to his former job as the prosecuting attorney for Franklin and Floyd Counties. Early held those positions and continued to practice law until January 4, 1847, when he rejoined the U.S. Army to fight in the Mexican War.

He was commissioned a major in the Virginia Volunteer Regiment. Early, though, saw no combat in that war. His decidedly noncombat job was a two-month stint as acting governor of the city of Monterey.

Early gave himself high marks in that job. "It was generally conceded by officers of the Army and Mexicans that better order reigned in the city during the time I commanded there, than had ever before existed," he said without a trace of modesty, "and the good conduct of my men won for them universal praise."

His unit spent the balance of the war near Buena Vista, where Early saw no battle action. Early did experience something in Mexico, though, that affected him for the rest of his long life. He contracted a cold with a high fever, which led to a lifelong battle with what he called rheumatism but more likely was arthritis. Early became so ill that he was given a leave of absence and returned to his hometown in November 1847 to recuperate.

On his journey back to Mexico, Early suffered another physical mishap. At around one o'clock in the morning of January 8, 1848, the boiler on the steamboat *Blue Ridge* blew up on the Ohio River, killing fourteen passengers. Early escaped with only minor injuries.

"I experienced a decided improvement in my rheumatism," he noted wryly, "though I would not advise blowing up in a Western steamboat as an infallible remedy."

Early left the army for the second time in April 1848 and returned to practicing law in Rocky Mount. He took an active interest in politics, running (unsuccessfully) for a seat in the Virginia House of Delegates in 1853.

As for his personal life, Early had had a brief courtship with a woman from Philadelphia whom he had met at a resort in White Sulphur Springs in the summer of 1837 just after he had graduated from West Point. That relationship ended badly when Early received a letter from a friend while he was in Florida saying the woman had married someone else. Back home in Rocky Mount in 1848, Early met a young woman named Julia McNealey. They began an affair that lasted many years. They had four children between 1850 and 1864 but never married.

As the Civil War loomed, Jubal Early continued to take an interest in political matters. He participated in the Virginia Secession Convention in Richmond as a pro-Unionist delegate from Franklin County. The 152-delegate convention opened on February 13, 1861, at the behest of the Virginia General Assembly; the purpose: to determine whether or not the South's most populous and northernmost state would join South Carolina, Mississippi, Alabama, Florida, Georgia, Louisiana, and Texas in the breakaway Confederate States of America.

Early, like a significant number of other delegates, argued strongly against secession. "When the question of practical secession from the United States arose," he said, "I opposed secession with all the ability I possessed." His hope was that "the horrors of civil war might be averted," he said, and "that a returning sense of justice on the part of the masses of the Northern States would induce them to respect the rights of the people of the South."

The convention debated the issue, often tempestuously, until April 17, when the delegates, voting in secrecy, passed the Ordinance of Secession. "The adoption of that ordinance wrung from me bitter tears of grief," Early said. But those tears dried quickly, and Early wholeheartedly embraced the Confederate cause. He embraced it, in fact, as strongly as anyone south of the Mason-Dixon line.

"I at once recognized my duty to abide by the decision of my native State, and to defend her soil against invasion," Early said. He also recognized "the right of resistance and revolution as exercised by our fathers in 1776." Without "cavil as to the name by which it was called," he said, "I entered the military service of my State, willingly, cheerfully, and zealously."

Those who knew Jubal Early rarely, if ever, used the word "cheerful" to describe him. "Zealous" was a more apt description of the man Robert E. Lee, in 1864, called his "bad old man."

The fifty-seven-year-old Lee was speaking about a man who was nine years his junior. Early looked old, due to the fact that his arthritis caused him to stoop badly and because of his high forehead, often unkempt hair, piercing dark eyes, and long, bushy beard. He had a distinctive, rasping, high-pitched voice that his last chief of staff, Henry Kyd Douglas, characterized as a "falsetto drawl." His troops called him "Old Jube" and "Old Jubilee."

Early's "appearance was quite striking," Gen. G. Moxley Sorrel, James Longstreet's chief of staff, wrote in his war memoir, "having a dark, handsome face, regular features and deep piercing eyes. He was a victim of rheumatism, and though not old was bent almost double, like an aged man." Early never married, Sorrel noted, "but led the life of a recluse in Virginia, entirely apart from social and public affairs."

Early stood six feet tall and weighed about 170 pounds. He was "a person who would be singled out in a crowd," the Richmond Daily Whig newspaper said in 1864. "A large white felt hat, ornamented by a dark feather, and an immense white fully cloth overcoat, extending to the heels, give him a striking and unique appearance."

"I was quite erect and trim in stature," Early said of his pre-arthritis days. "When casual observers have seen me bent up, it has been very often the result of actual pain to which I have been very much subjected" since 1847.

Adding to the pain: two wounds Early received on May 5, 1862, while leading his troops at the Battle of Williamsburg in Virginia. The worst came

The cantankerous Confederate general Jubal Early left the defenses of Richmond on June 12, 1864, with a corps of troops on a daring and risky mission to invade the North and threaten Washington, D.C. *Credit: The Library of Virginia*

from a lead bullet (the ubiquitous Civil War minié ball) that tore into his shoulder and put him out of action for nearly two months.

Perhaps it was the physical pain from the arthritis and the serious shoulder wound, or maybe it was the psychic pain from his life-altering failed romance, but for whatever reason Jubal Early was a notoriously cantankerous, sarcastic, and bitter man. He gnawed on an ever-present chaw of tobacco, drank to excess, and cursed liberally and venomously.

Early was "of a snarling, rasping disposition," as Moxley put it. He had a "caustic, biting tongue," Maj. Robert Stiles, an artillery officer in Lee's Army of Northern Virginia, noted in his memoir. "He was a sort of privileged character in the army and was saucy to everybody, but many of his brightest utterances will not bear publication because of the sting in them."

Early had little but disdain for his superior officers (Lee excluded), for his fellow officers, and even for the men who served under him. He "hates his staff like blazes," one of his staff officers said late in 1864.

He "received with impatience and never acted upon, either advice or suggestion from his subordinates," Douglas added in his Civil War memoir. "Arbitrary, cynical, with strong prejudices, he was personally disagreeable; he made few admirers or friends either by his manners or his habits." If Early had "a tender feeling," Douglas said, "he endeavored to conceal it and acted as though he would be ashamed to be detected in doing a kindness."

Early's hatred also extended to Northerners. "Do you think if the Gates of Hell were opened wide open, that it would belch forth such another set of infernal scoundrels as the Yankees?" Early fumed in an 1866 letter.

He also was known for his misogyny, which probably stemmed from his overreaction to his broken engagement. "An old bachelor, he had during the war the reputation of being a woman hater," the journalist and author Edward Pollard wrote in 1871. "It is said that he never approved an application for furlough when the applicant wished it for the purpose of getting married, and he often declared that every officer who was married either became utterly worthless or straightway got himself killed."

And, although it was by no means an uncommon viewpoint in the South, Early nevertheless believed strongly in slavery, staunchly opposed emancipation, and viewed African Americans as an inferior species of human beings. African slaves, Early wrote in the preface to his 1866 Civil War memoir, were "ignorant and barbarous" and of "an inferior physical and mental organization" and "should be kept in a state of subordination."

Slavery, he said, "had not only resulted in a great improvement in the moral and physical condition of the negro race, but had furnished a class of labourers as happy and contented as any in the world, if not more so."

Despite this panoply of abhorrent personality traits, Early's military star rose quickly soon after he joined the Confederate army when the war broke out in April of 1861. Early served first as a colonel commanding the Twenty-fourth Virginia Infantry Regiment. In June Beauregard gave him command of his Army of the Potomac's Sixth Brigade. Early was promoted to brigadier general on July 21, 1861, at the Civil War's first large battle, First Manassas, where he fought courageously and well, personally leading his troops into the maelstrom of combat.

For the next three years Early physically led his men into battle at virtually all of the war's large—and many of the small—Eastern Theater engagements. That included Malvern Hill, Cedar Mountain, Second Manassas, Antietam (where he was promoted to division commander), Fredericksburg, Chancellorsville, Gettysburg, Wildnerness (where he became a corps commander), Spotsylvania Courthouse, and Cold Harbor. Early had been promoted to major general on April 23, 1863, and was given the CSA's highest rank, lieutenant general, on May 31, 1864, two weeks before Lee presented him with the secret order to go to the Shenandoah Valley and then to march to Washington.

Throughout the war Early displayed fearlessness under fire and aggressiveness in his battlefield tactics. In doing so, he achieved Lee's undying admiration.

It is more than a little ironic that Robert E. Lee would come to admire Jubal Early. The gentlemanly Lee and the coarse Early were about as far apart personally as it is possible for two human beings to be. Where Early was caustic and crusty, Lee was warm and friendly. Lee rarely lost his temper; Early seemed to live his life in a permanent state of high dudgeon. Early emitted a steady stream of foul language and drank to excess; Lee was quiet, modest, dignified, and pious.

Born in 1807 into one of Virginia's most notable families, Robert E. Lee, in 1831, married into another noted Virginia clan, the Custises. Lee's father, Henry "Light-Horse Harry" Lee (1756–1818), had fought in the Revolutionary War and was a three-term governor of Virginia, after which his fiscal fortunes waned. Robert E. Lee's wife, Mary Anne Randolph Custis, was the great-granddaughter of Martha Custis Washington, George Washington's wife. Lee and his wife lived at Arlington House, now the site of Arlington National Cemetery, until the start of the Civil War in 1861.

Robert E. Lee graduated second in his class from West Point in 1829. He served in the U.S. Army's Corps of Engineers until 1852 when he was appointed superintendent of West Point. He went on to perform brilliantly under Gen. Winfield Scott in the Mexican War, served in the U.S. Second

Robert E. Lee conceived of the audacious plan to send Early to the Shenandoah Valley and then into Maryland, a plan that he counted on to force Grant to part with significant numbers of troops surrounding Richmond and Petersburg. *Credit: The Library of Virginia*

Cavalry in West Texas, and led the ouster of John Brown at Harpers Ferry in October 1859.

Lee, like Early, opposed secession. Unlike Early, who espoused out-and-out racist views and strongly defended slavery, Lee, although he was a slave owner and strongly condemned abolitionists in the North, famously called slavery "a moral and political evil."

Scott offered Lee command of the Union army, but Lee resigned from the army after Fort Sumter fell and, primarily out of loyalty to the Commonwealth of Virginia, offered his military services to the Confederacy. Virginia governor Letcher immediately named Lee commander in chief of that state's army and naval forces. CSA president Jefferson Davis then called upon Lee to be his military adviser. Then, in May 1862, Lee took command of the famed Army of Northern Virginia.

For the next three years, Robert E. Lee led what most military analysts believe was a brilliant military campaign against overwhelming odds. He earned the respect of his fellow officers and men for his military abilities and proved to be as gracious in defeat as he was humble in his battlefield victories.

Lee had a high opinion of Jubal Early, which he expressed in word and deed. In a postwar 1865 letter, for example, Lee heaped praise on his "bad old man." "Being a graduate of the West Point Military Academy, he combines theoretical, with the practical knowledge of a soldier," Lee wrote. "He exhibited during his whole service, high intelligence, sagacity & bravery; & untiring devotion to the cause to which he had enlisted."

Lee was not alone in singing Early's battlefield praises. Henry Kyd Douglas, Early's chief of staff, who had no love for his commanding officer, nevertheless thought highly of his warrior traits. "Of all the generals who made for themselves a reputation in the Army of Northern Virginia, there were none of General Lee's subordinates, after the death of General [Stonewall] Jackson, who possessed the essential qualities of a military commander to a greater extent than Early," Douglas wrote. He went on to praise Early for his "clear, direct and comprehensive" mind, for his "boldness to attack" and his "tenacity in resisting."

On June 12, 1864, Robert E. Lee exhibited the strongest expression in his lifetime of his respect for Jubal Early's battlefield prowess when he ordered him to undertake a bold, risky mission: to oust Hunter from the Shenandoah Valley, then to move into Maryland and do what the Confederate army had never attempted: invade Washington, D.C.

FOUR

———◆———

A Plan of Great Boldness

Strike as quickly as you can, and, if circumstances authorize,
carry out the original plan.

—ROBERT E. LEE TO JUBAL EARLY, JUNE 18, 1864

The Shenandoah Valley had been on Lee's mind since early in 1864. He worried about Union troop movements there, and he worried about those troops cutting off his vital supply lines. "The maintenance of western Virginia," Lee told Jefferson Davis in January, is vitally important "to the successful conduct of war."

Lee's concerns reached an even higher level when Breckinridge took his troops back to Richmond after the May 15 Confederate victory at New Market. "Since I withdrew General Breckinridge from the Valley there is no general commander," Lee wrote to Secretary of War James A. Seddon on May 25. "A good commander should be at once sent to that brigade. The case is urgent. I shall return General Breckinridge as soon as I can."

Lee did send Breckinridge back to the valley, but he could only afford to give him about 2,100 men. It was not enough manpower to defeat Hunter, and the Kentuckian asked Lee for help. Lee hesitated to send more troops, he said, because he was afraid of the consequences of weakening his defense of Richmond.

Hemmed in by Union forces, Lee had serious doubts about sending a large number of troops west for fear that Grant would get wind of the plan and mount his final, potentially fatal, attack on Richmond. "If Grant cannot be successfully resisted here [in Richmond]," Lee said, "we cannot hold the Valley."

On June 1 Lee implored Gen. Grumble Jones to "beat back Seigel [*sic*] at all hazards."

Four days later Jones lost his life in the Union victory fighting against Hunter, who had replaced Sigel, at Piedmont. That news only increased Lee's anxiety. After learning of Jones's demise and the defeat at Piedmont, Lee wrote to Davis expressing his fears about Hunter's next move in the valley.

He "will do us great evil" there, Lee predicted.

On June 10 Gen. Braxton Bragg, the former commander of the Army of Tennessee serving as the quasi–Confederate army commander-in-chief advising Davis in Richmond, told the Confederate president that booting Hunter out of the valley could have an important fringe benefit. "It seems to me very important that this force of the enemy should be expelled from the Valley," Bragg said. "If it could be crushed, Washington would be open to the few we might then employ."

Davis forwarded that missive to Lee without any comment. The next day, June 11, Lee still had not decided what to do about the situation in the valley. He told Davis that he saw "the advantage of expelling the enemy from the Valley," but that it would take an "entire corps" of his army to do so. If, Lee said, "it is deemed prudent to hazard the defense of Richmond" by "diminishing the force here, I will do so." That was the case, he said, even though he would be playing into Grant's hands.

Lee, Davis, and Bragg also knew, through intelligence reports and from reading the Northern newspapers, that Washington was severely underdefended because Grant had nearly every able-bodied, experienced soldier with him outside Richmond and Petersburg. They also knew the potential political benefits that would come about if a corps of Confederate troops showed up on the doorstep of the nation's capital—not to mention what would happen if rebel soldiers penetrated the defenses of Washington.

Confederate troops running wild in the streets of the national capital, Lee, Davis, and Bragg knew, would have an enormous impact on Union morale and could easily influence the course of the 1864 presidential election.

Twenty-four hours after writing to Davis, Lee made up his mind. He came up with a risky strategy that one biographer called "a plan of great boldness."

Early in the evening the next day, June 12, Robert E. Lee summoned Jubal Early to his headquarters at Gaines's Mill near Cold Harbor. When Early arrived, Lee gave him the details of his bold plan.

How bold was it? Lee, surrounded by a far superior force, told Early to prepare the three infantry divisions of his Second Corps—about a fourth of Lee's infantry—along with two artillery battalions, to leave the scene. How risky was it? If Grant had heard of the plan, Lee knew, the aggressive Union commanding general very likely would have ordered an immediate attack on Lee's forces.

So the plan was kept as secret as possible. Lee and Jefferson Davis, for one thing, agreed not to broadcast the fact to the Southern newspapers. And Early wouldn't even divulge the details of the plan in a dispatch to Breckinridge.

"My first object is to destroy Hunter," Early cabled on June 16 from Charlottesville. His next objective, Early said, "is not prudent to trust to telegraph."

This is how Early described the then-secret mission in his autobiography: "I was directed to move," he said, "for the Valley." The object: "to strike Hunter's force in the rear, and if possible, destroy it, then to move down the Valley, cross the Potomac" and "threaten Washington City."

Lee took this bold gamble hoping that Early would, indeed, threaten Washington. If he did, Lee believed, Grant would be forced to send a significant number of his troops from outside Richmond and Petersburg to defend the Union capital.

"Success in the Valley," Lee wrote to Jefferson Davis on June 15, "would relieve our difficulties that at present press heavily upon us."

If Early did meet with success, Lee seriously considered ordering an attack of his own, an attack that could have driven what was left of Grant's Army of the Potomac out of Richmond's environs. At the very least, if Grant sent troops to Washington, the Union commander would not be able to launch his final invasion of the Southern capital.

At two o'clock in the morning of June 13, Jubal Early led his eight-thousand-man-strong veteran Second Corps out of their campsite. The men, some of whom had fought in the Shenandoah Valley in 1862 under Stonewall Jackson, were tough veterans who had seen more than their share of the worst that the Civil War had to offer. Most were infantrymen from Virginia. The rest hailed from North Carolina, Georgia, Louisiana, and Alabama. Of the Virginia contingent, nearly 30 percent were from the Shenandoah Valley.

They had been in the field for the previous forty days of nearly nonstop fighting. They'd survived the conflagration at Wilderness, the Bloody Angle at Spotsylvania Courthouse, and Grant's relentless charge at Cold Harbor, which had ended just the day before.

They were about to embark on a seventy-plus-mile forced march to Charlottesville, where they would board trains to Lynchburg. It was a daunting task for a corps of troops that had been severely tested by the enemy and by the elements.

"Constant exposure to the weather, a limited supply of provisions, and two weeks' service in the swamps north of the Chikahominy [River south of Cold Harbor] had told on the health of the men," Early said. "Divisions were not stronger than brigades ought to have been, nor brigades than regiments."

Fortunately for Early and his men, the major generals leading his three infantry divisions—Robert Emmet Rodes, Stephen Dodson Ramseur, and John Brown Gordon—were three of the most competent and courageous military men who fought on either side in the Civil War. And Early's brigadier generals were no slouches either.

Early characterized Rodes, who was thirty-five years old when the Civil War began, as "a most accomplished, skillful and gallant officer, upon whom I placed great reliance." A native of Lynchburg, Robert Emmet Rodes had graduated from VMI in 1848. He gave up a promising career as a railroad civil engineer in Alabama to take command of the Fifth Alabama Infantry Regiment in May of 1861, soon after the war started. Rodes fought extremely well at First Manassas and was rewarded with a promotion from colonel to brigadier general in October of 1861.

The blond-haired Rodes went on to serve under Lee at Antietam and under Stonewall Jackson at Chancellorsville. Jackson was so impressed with Rodes's courage under fire in the latter battle that, on his deathbed, he recommended that Rodes be promoted to major general. Rodes went on to fight brilliantly at Gettysburg and at all of the bloody battles of the Overland Campaign. He was one of the few division-level commanders in Lee's Army of Northern Virginia who did not go to West Point.

Maj. Gen. Robert Emmet Rodes, a VMI graduate who led a division of troops under Early, was one of the few division-level commanders in Lee's Army of Northern Virginia who did not go to West Point. *Credit: The Library of Virginia*

Ramseur—whom his biographer called "Lee's gallant general"—left Davidson College in his home state of North Carolina after one year to take an appointment at West Point, from which he graduated on July 1, 1860. When the Civil War began, Ramseur immediately resigned his U.S. Army commission and joined the Confederate army, becoming a captain in a North Carolina artillery battery.

Ramseur, who did not use his first name and whom his friends called "Dod," quickly rose in the ranks. He fought bravely and with distinction

Another division commander under Early, Maj. Gen. Stephen Dodson
Ramseur, known as "Dod," at twenty-five became the youngest general
in the Confederate Army in 1862. *Credit: The Library of Virginia*

under Robert E. Lee in the Seven Days' Battles near Richmond, including
the last one at Malvern Hill on July 1, 1862. Severely wounded in the right
arm, Ramseur refused to leave the field of battle until the fighting ended
(in a Union victory). Lee recommended his promotion to brigadier general in November of 1862. Ramseur, at twenty-five, thereby became the
youngest general in the Confederate army. In that position he commanded
a brigade of four North Carolina infantry regiments in Stonewall Jackson's
corps.

The young general fought at Chancellorsville (where he was wounded a second time), Gettysburg, Wilderness, Spotsylvania (where he led the charge at the Bloody Angle, and again was wounded, this time shot from his horse in the right arm, and again, refused to leave the battlefield), and Cold Harbor. On June 1, 1864, the day after his twenty-seventh birthday, Ramseur was promoted to major general.

John Brown Gordon, a native of Upson County, Georgia, attended Franklin College (later known as the University of Georgia), but left in his senior year to study law. He was the father of two young children and in business with his father developing coal mines in northwest Georgia when the Civil War began.

Gordon, at age twenty-nine, faced a difficult decision. He wanted to enlist in the Confederate army immediately, but he hesitated because he worried about the fate of his wife, Fanny, and their two children.

"The struggle between devotion to my family on the one hand and duty to my country on the other was most trying to my sensibilities," Gordon wrote in his memoir. "My spirit had been caught up by the flaming enthusiasm that swept like a prairie-fire through the land, and I hastened to unite with the brave men of the mountains in organizing a company of volunteers. But what was I to do with the girl-wife and the two little boys?"

Fanny Gordon, a spirited, capable woman who was seventeen years old when they married, came up with the solution. She "was no less taxed in her effort to settle this momentous question," Gordon said. "But finally yielding to the promptings of her own heart and to her unerring sense of duty, she" announced "that she intended to accompany me to the war, leaving her children with my mother and faithful 'Mammy Mary.' "

With the family problem out of the way, Gordon helped organize a company of volunteers from the mountainous regions of northwest Georgia, southeast Tennessee, and northeast Alabama. The men soon voted him captain of the ragtag unit, which he wanted to call the Mountain Rifles. That name didn't stick.

"Totally undisciplined and undrilled, no two of these men marched abreast; no two kept the same step; no two wore the same colored coats or trousers," Gordon said. "The only pretence at uniformity was the rough fur caps made of raccoon skins, with long, bushy, streaked raccoon tails hanging from behind them."

Because the only things they had in common were their rough-looking coonskin caps, Gordon's mountain men came to be known as the Raccoon Roughs. The Roughs marched from Georgia to Montgomery, Alabama, and joined the Sixth Alabama Regiment of Infantry.

Like Ramseur and Rodes, Gordon had a meteoric rise in the ranks. By November of 1862 he had become a brigadier general. In May of 1864 he rose to the rank of major general.

John Brown Gordon fought bravely and well in the thick of the action at many battles, big and small. These included Malvern Hill (where he was shot in the eye), Chancellorsville, and Antietam, where he survived an astounding five bullet wounds—any one of which easily could have felled a lesser man—at the infamous engagement known as the Sunken Road.

Gordon took his first bullet at Antietam through the calf of his right leg just as the battle began. Astoundingly, he shook that off and stayed with his men, leading them on into the battle. A second minié ball ripped into the same leg an hour later. Gordon remained on the field of battle. Then another ball tore through his left arm. Gordon did not leave his troops. In short order he took another round to his shoulder and then one in the face. The latter wound, which passed through his left cheek, finally took Gorton out of action, only because he passed out.

When his wife, Fanny, saw him right after the battle, she had to suppress a scream. For seven long months Fanny Gordon ministered to her critically ill husband. She dressed his wounds, fed him brandy and beef tea because his jaw was wired shut, and provided long hours of bedside care and devotion.

With his wife's constant care and his own strong will, John Brown Gordon miraculously recovered. He reported back to duty at the end of March of 1863 and went on to fight at Fredericksburg, Gettysburg, Wilderness, and Spotsylvania Courthouse, among other battles.

The irascible Early, who had a low opinion of women in general, had mixed feelings about Fanny Gordon's presence amid his army. "General Early, hearing of her constant presence, is said to have exclaimed, 'I wish the Yankees would capture Mrs. Gordon and hold her till the war is over,'" John Brown Gordon wrote in his memoir.

Later on in the war, though, sitting next to Fanny Gordon at a dinner, Early changed his tune. Fanny Gordon, her husband said, "good-naturedly" kidded Early regarding his feelings about wives accompanying their husbands in the war. Early "was momentarily embarrassed," John Brown Gordon remembered, "but rose to the occasion and replied: 'Mrs. Gordon, General Gordon is a better soldier when you are close by him than when

Maj. Gen. John Brown Gordon, who survived five bullet wounds—including one that passed through his cheek—at the Sunken Road during the Battle of Antietam, went on to command a division of Early's troops that took part in the bloodiest fighting at the Battle of Monocacy. *Credit: The Library of Virginia*

you are away, and so hereafter, when I issue orders that officers' wives must go to the rear, you may know that you are excepted.'"

Gordon, who had no military training, "had the natural instincts of a soldier and the persuasive power of an orator who knew his auditors perfectly," the noted Civil War historian Douglas Southall Freeman said. The men who served with him, enlisted and officers, also sung Gordon's praises.

"Gordon always had something pleasant to say to his men, and I will bear my testimony that he was the most gallant man I ever saw on a battle-field," said John W. Worsham, a foot soldier with the Twenty-first Virginia Infantry Regiment who also had served under Stonewall Jackson.

Gordon "had a way of putting things to the men that was irresistible; and he showed the men, at all times, that he shrank from nothing in battle on account of himself." The troops, Worsham said, "were devoted to him, and would generally do as he wished."

By the end of the war, Gordon "earned the reputation of being perhaps the most conspicuous and personally valiant officer surviving, and the one generally regarded as most promising and competent for increased rank and larger command," former CSA general Stephen Dill Lee wrote in 1908.

Gordon, Lee said, "had the God-given talent of getting in front of his troops and, in a few magnetic appeals, inspiring them almost to madness, and being able to lead them into the jaws of death."

Rodes, Ramseur, and Gordon set the bar high. So did the man who would become Early's second in command, John Cabell Breckinridge. Breckinridge was the scion of an old, distinguished Kentucky family. His grandfather, also named John Breckinridge (1760–1806), fought in the Revolutionary War, served in the U.S. Senate from 1801 to 1805, and was attorney general of the United States under Thomas Jefferson.

John C. Breckinridge graduated from Kentucky's Centre College and studied at Princeton and Transylvania Institute. He practiced law in Lexington, and served in the Third Kentucky Volunteers during the Mexican War.

Breckinridge returned to Kentucky after the war and began a political career. After a term in the Kentucky House of Representatives, he served two terms (1851–55) as a Democrat in the U.S. House of Representatives. Breckinridge became the youngest vice president in American history at age thirty-six when he was elected to that office with Pres. James Buchanan in 1856.

He unsuccessfully ran for president in the 1860 election, representing the Southern faction of the Democratic Party and finishing well behind the Northern Democratic nominee, Stephen A. Douglas, and the winning Republican, Abraham Lincoln. Breckinridge did win a seat in the U.S. Senate in that election, but his pro-Confederate views prompted the Kentucky legislature to order him to resign in October.

Breckinridge, who sported a distinctive, long, swooping moustache, quit the Senate and the following month became a brigadier general in the Confederate army. He took part in many engagements in the West, including

John Cabell Breckinridge of Kentucky, who at age thirty-six had been the youngest vice president in American history, joined the Confederate army when the war broke out and rose to become a major general and Early's second in command. *Credit: The Library of Virginia*

Shiloh on April 6–7, 1862, where he commanded the Reserve Corps. He was rewarded for his bravery at Shiloh with a promotion to major general and went on to fight in the Battles of Murfreesboro, Jackson, Chickamauga, and Missionary Ridge, before being named in 1863 to command the Department of Western Virginia, where he led the Confederate force that defeated Sigel at New Market.

The former vice president had a "striking and noble presence," an admiring

Southern writer said. "Perfect and well-proportioned in all his parts, dignified without a sign of stiffness, graceful as a woman, a veteran of society . . . he appears born both to command and please."

Breckinridge was "one of the finest looking men I ever saw," Alfred Seelye Roe, a young Union soldier who had been taken prisoner at the Battle of Monocacy, wrote in 1890. "His face was so classically cut, and his eye so piercing, at any distance, that now with an interval of nearly twenty-four years, I can see him as he sat his horse and directed his men."

A member of Breckinridge's staff painted a less flattering portrait of the general. Though "frequently petulant to others, he has always maintained the most courteous demeanor to me," William Barksdale Myers wrote to his father on July 23, 1864. "For the most part he is courteous, grandiose, not pompous, a sky rocket on the field and as thoroughly selfish a man as ever God created. That's my estimate of his character, which I consider strongly Napoleonic."

Early's Second Corps also had a group of hard-charging brigade-commanding brigadier generals, many of whom had fought long and hard and with distinction since the beginning of the war. These included Brig. Gen. Zebulon York, who commanded the consolidated Louisiana Brigade in Gordon's division.

Born in Maine, but educated in the South, York received his law degree from Tulane University, and practiced law in Vidalia, Louisiana, where he owned a large plantation with some 1,500 slaves. York, one of the few Northern-born Confederates to attain the rank of general in the CSA, formed the Concordia Rifles, Company F of the Fourteenth Louisiana Infantry. This was one of several Civil War Louisiana units known as "the Fighting Tigers" because of their penchant for aggressiveness on and off the field of battle. York was promoted to brigadier general on May 31, 1864.

Ramseur's division included four Virginia cavalry regiments that would come under the command of Maj. Gen. Robert Ransom and his second-in-command, Brig. Gen. John McCausland. A North Carolinian, Ransom graduated from West Point in 1850 and was one of the first officers in the First U.S. Cavalry in 1855. He resigned as a cavalry instructor at West Point on May 24, 1861, and accepted a commission in the CSA as a cavalry captain. The thirty-three-year-old was promoted to colonel in the First North Carolina Cavalry, to brigadier general in March of 1862, and to major general after the Battle of Fredericksburg in May 1863.

Tiger John McCausland, who had skirmished with Hunter's men in the Shenandoah valley following New Market, graduated from VMI first in his class in 1857. McCausland took a position at his alma mater as an assistant professor of mathematics, but when the Civil War broke out he was commissioned a colonel in the Thirty-sixth Virginia Regiment.

McCausland fought heroically at the losing battle at Fort Donelson in February 1862 in Tennessee, then spent the next two years fighting in southwestern and western Virginia. He was promoted to brigadier general on May 24, 1864.

Brig. Gen. John Echols, who commanded a brigade of Breckinridge's division, held degrees from VMI, Washington College, and Harvard. The six-feet-four Echols, a native of Lynchburg, Virginia, was thirty-eight years old and practicing law in Staunton when the war began. He commanded the Twenty-seventh Virginia Regiment at First Manassas and served under Stonewall Jackson in the Shenandoah Valley until he was severely wounded in March of 1862. Echols fought alongside Breckinridge at New Market before heading to Richmond with Breckinridge to reinforce Lee.

Brig. Gen. William Terry, another native son of Lynchburg, commanded Stonewall Jackson's old brigade in Gordon's division under Early. Terry, a lawyer who had graduated from the University of Virginia, served under Jackson at First Manassas and at Malvern Hill, Second Manassas (where he was wounded), Fredericksburg, Chancellorsville, Gettysburg, and in the battles of the Wilderness Campaign.

Early, riding at the head of the column, and his men arrived in Charlottesville at around 2:00 a.m. on June 16, having covered a distance of some seventy-five miles in three days. "My feet were so sore that I had to crawl around the fire and cook on my hands and knees," Pvt. John O. Casler of the Thirty-third Virginia wrote of his arrival at Charlottesville. "I got no sleep the whole night."

The day before Breckinridge's two infantry brigades had arrived in Lynchburg. They were joined there by a CSA cavalry brigade under Brig. Gen. John D. Imboden, who had fought under Stonewall Jackson in the valley in 1862. At around 2:00 a.m. on the following day, June 17, Early loaded a portion of his Second Corps into boxcars and passenger cars at the Keswick Depot just east of Charlottesville for the sixty-five-mile trip to Lynchburg. But a sizeable group of Early's men could not get on the same train. The first contingent arrived in Lynchburg at around 1:00 in the afternoon.

Brig. Gen. "Tiger" John McCausland, a former math professor at VMI, led John Brown Gordon's cavalry troops in the heaviest and bloodiest of the fighting at the Battle of Monocacy. *Credit: The Library of Virginia*

The next day Early received a telegram from Lee, who wrote that because Grant had crossed the James River and was now threatening Petersburg, he wanted Early's help there unless Early believed he could move north to threaten Washington.

"Strike as quick as you can," Lee said, "and, if circumstances authorize, carry out the original plan or move upon Petersburg without delay."

FIVE

Early's March to the Potomac

If you continue to threaten Grant, I hope to be able to do something for your relief and the success of our cause shortly. I shall lose no time.

—EARLY TO LEE, JUNE 30, 1864

It did not take long for Early to carry out Lee's order. Hunter, for no apparent good reason, had spent three days in Lexington before moving out for Lynchburg on June 14. His men faced a forty-five-mile march that included crossing the Blue Ridge Mountains between two of the three four-thousand-foot-high Peaks of Otter overlooking Bedford, about thirty miles west of Lynchburg. They arrived from the southwest and deployed on the southern and western roads and approaches into the city of Lynchburg just before noon on June 17, at almost the same time that Early and Ramseur's division reached the city by train.

"Much to the surprise of the men, we found the town in great excitement, because the enemy, under the command of General Hunter, had advanced to within two miles of the place," the young Virginia soldier John Worsham wrote in his memoir. "There was a small force in his front, and the citizens expected immediately to see the enemy march into the town."

The presence of the Confederate troops, Worsham said, "brought an immediate change. We were cheered to the echo, and the ladies waved their hands and gave us lunches and cool water as we marched through the city."

Early's troops were confident on the eve of the battle. "We laid down that night believing that the next day would bring a battle, in the result of which we had no doubt," Charles T. O'Ferrall, an officer in the Twenty-third Virginia Cavalry, wrote in his war memoir. "We had an abiding faith in the ability of 'Old Jube,' as General Early was called by his men, to thresh Hunter most soundly."

The men's "hearts were buoyant," O'Ferrall remembered, "and they wanted a chance to chastise the burner of the Virginia Military Institute—Virginia's pride—and the house of Governor Letcher, who was honored and beloved the State over."

Early fought what would be the anticlimactic Battle of Lynchburg with few casualties and without the help of Breckinridge. The Kentuckian was in bed and out of action, recuperating from injuries he had received after the horse he was riding fell on top of him during the Battle of Cold Harbor. Early temporarily replaced Breckinridge with Maj. Gen. Daniel Harvey Hill, the South Carolinian West Point graduate who had been without a command since the September 18–20, 1863, Battle of Chickamauga.

The fight began at noon on June 18 when elements of the opposing forces went at each other in sporadic engagements along the Salem Turnpike just south of Lynchburg. Early ordered a halt to the fighting two hours later. Hunter, although he outnumbered Early by about two thousand men, then ordered a full retreat.

"It was then and still is incomprehensible to me that the small force under Early seemed to have filled Hunter with sudden panic," John Brown Gordon wrote in his memoir. "His hurried exit from Lynchburg was in marked contrast with his confident advance upon it."

Hunter, Gordon said, "ran away without any fight at all—at least, without any demonstration that could be called a fight. He not only fled without a test of relative strength, but fled precipitately, and did not stop until he had found a safe retreat beyond the mountains toward the Ohio."

Hunter fled on June 19, heading southwest. Early at first decided not to pursue him. "It was not known where he was retreating, or moving so as to attack Lynchburg on the south where it was vulnerable, or to attempt to join Grant on the south side of the James River," Early said, by way of explanation in 1866.

At first light on the following day, June 20, Early figured out that Hunter was retreating, and sent infantry and cavalry after the fleeing Union troops. Early's men, O'Ferrall said, "were like blood-hounds on their tracks," on a day that "was scorching hot and the trail was dusty." Ramseur's division caught up with the rear elements of Hunter's men twenty-five miles from Lynchburg at Liberty. There was a brief skirmish that night.

The next day McCausland's cavalry overtook another part of Hunter's retreating troops at Hanging Rock, near Salem. The cavalrymen captured or destroyed fifteen to eighteen of Hunter's guns and confiscated or burned many Union army wagons. Later that day, though, Early called off the pursuit after Hunter had crossed the Blue Ridge and Early realized Hunter was heading for West Virginia. Early knew that going after Hunter in that extremely rugged terrain would be difficult, at best, for his exhausted men.

"My command had marched sixty miles" over "very rough roads," Early later wrote. The troops "had had no rest since leaving Gaines's Mill." Early decided, he said, to give his men a day of rest on June 22. Another factor: the weather; summer had come to central Virginia with a vengeance.

It was extremely hot and dry and dusty. Early also needed the rest to wait for the balance of his supply wagons and artillery to reach Lynchburg. And his men were hungry. Many of them had "had nothing to eat for the last few days, except a little bacon," Early explained, and they were not in shape to chase Hunter through rough mountainous terrain.

"I knew," Early said, "that the country through which Hunter's route led for forty or fifty miles was, for the most part, a desolate mountain region." Early also knew the limits of his men. "I had seen our soldiers endure a great deal, but there was a limit to the endurance even of Confederate soldiers," Early said.

Hunter and his men, low on ammunition and food, fled for ten days, finally stopping at Charleston, West Virginia. Hunter's plan was to put his men on steamships and head down the Kanawha River to the Ohio River, and eventually board B&O railroad cars to Martinsburg, his supply base in the northern Shenandoah Valley. If everything had gone according to plan, Hunter would have been able to cut off Early and his men before they reached Martinsburg.

All did not go according to plan, however. Hunter hadn't planned on the rivers being too low to carry troop transports because of a summer-long drought. He was therefore forced to march his exhausted men to the Ohio River, where the water was barely high enough to support the ships. The long delays—at times the ships had to be pulled over shoals on the Ohio— took time, and, as we shall see, prevented Hunter from catching up to Early until well after the Confederate general had won the Battle of Monocacy and reached the gates of Washington on July 11.

Hunter's ignominious retreat paved the way for Early to move virtually unimpeded through the Shenandoah Valley into Maryland and on to Washington. "All the gateways of the Shenandoah Valley—its roads, passes, gaps—were standing wide open, with Washington exposed, its very nakedness inviting attack," Lew Wallace—who would lead the Union troops at Monocacy—later wrote. "What an opportunity for General Lee!"

Hunter and his men went through many "hardships and privations" on the way to Charleston, as Col. Rutherford B. Hayes put it.

The surgeon Alexander Neil gave a more detailed, agonizing portrait of the hardships. Hunter's army marched day and night for seven days, Neil said, "getting no sleep during that time except what I got in the saddle, the enemy fighting us in the rear as far as Salem." The men "were on the verge of starvation coming over the mountains, the greater part of us getting not a bite to eat for four or five days. Our suffering was almost unendurable, thousands fell by the way to the mercy of the enemy and many starved to death, of these I saw many instances."

Neil himself resorted to picking through leftover horse feed to survive. "I often got off my horse and picked up grains of corn out of the dirt where the cavalry horses had eaten the day before, and I would eat it to keep alive," he said. "I saw many an officer offer ten dollars for an ear of corn or half pint of grain to keep starvation away."

That long, horrendous retreat took Hunter and his men out of the war for more than a month. More importantly, Hunter's ignominious retreat left the Shenandoah Valley virtually undefended all the way to the Potomac River.

After the day of rest, Early's corps, which he called the Confederate Army of the Valley District (the combination of Early's Second Corps and Breckinridge's valley men), marched northward on June 23. Early, riding at the head of his troops as usual, reached Staunton on June 26. The strain of the almost constant marching from Richmond began to show on Early's men.

"Day intensely hot and dusty," Lt. Thomas Feamster of the Fourteenth Virginia Cavalry wrote in his diary that day. "Our Brigade is very much broken down and worn out. Our troops are dirty and dusty."

The men looked "very much fatigued," Feamster noted, but they were "of good cheer." They had "been in a tramp, in the saddle, day and night for 26 days with the exception of 2 days' rest. Now we remain to rest all day, which will help us much."

The day before Early's men had passed through Natural Bridge, stopping at that formidable natural rock formation for a couple of hours at the request of the men so they could take in the famed site and rest.

The men, a good number of whom had served under Stonewall Jackson, then marched fifteen miles to Lexington, where they paid homage to Jackson, who had died May 10, 1863, following the Battle of Chancellorsville. As they filed past the Confederate army hero's grave, "not a man spoke, not a sound was uttered," Kyd Douglas, who was among them, said. "Only the tramp, tramp of passing feet told that his surviving veterans were passing in review, while the drooping and tattered flags saluted his sacred dust."

Every soldier "pulled off his ragged cap and wiped a tear from his eyes when we remembered [Jackson's] splendid leadership and his untimely death," said Pvt. I. G. Bradwell of the Sixty-first Georgia Infantry in Gordon's division. The men also took in the charred ruins of VMI and Washington College, a site that "reminded us of General Hunter," Bradwell pointed out.

A battalion of Maryland cavalry under Col. Bradley Tyler Johnson joined Early's Army of the Valley at Staunton. Johnson, a native of Frederick, Maryland, had graduated from Princeton in 1829 when he was twenty years old, and had gone on to study law. He was practicing law in his hometown when the war broke out.

Johnson threw his lot in with the Confederacy, helping organize the CSA's First Maryland Regiment. He fought in many battles, including First Manassas and the 1862 Shenandoah Valley Campaign under Stonewall Jackson. Two days after he reported to Early at Staunton, Johnson was promoted to brigadier general, replacing the recently departed Grumble Jones as a cavalry commander.

Early's army now numbered about sixteen thousand men, the vast majority of whom were experienced, savvy fighters.

Early took the time in Staunton, too, to reorganize his new army. He placed Gordon's division under Breckinridge, who had recovered from his wounds and was back in the saddle. Early did so likely to honor Breckinridge's stature; the battle-hardened and experienced Gordon wound up making the division's tactical decisions, most likely with advice from Breckinridge. Early also brought in Robert Ransom, as we noted, from Richmond to command his cavalry and artillery. Early stripped down the number of artillery pieces, getting rid of the broken-down ones, and also cut down the number of supply wagons.

Early received a cable in Staunton on June 26 from Lee in which his commanding general, reacting to Grant's movement across the James to the gates of Petersburg, gave Early the choice of moving north or coming back to Richmond. The cable, Early later explained, stated "that the circumstances under which my original orders were given had changed, and again submitting it to my judgment, in the altered state of things, whether the movement down the Valley and across the Potomac should be made."

Early, ever aggressive, "determined to carry out the original design at all hazards," he said, "and telegraphed General Lee my purpose to continue the movement." In the telegram, dated June 28, Early told Lee that he had decided "to turn down the valley and proceed according to your instructions to threaten Washington and if I find an opportunity—to take it."

There "is nothing at Washington," Early told Lee, "but the same kind of [inexperienced hundred days'] men and not in larger force."

Lee wrote to Davis on June 29 after receiving Early's letter, telling the Confederate president that Early's "general plan of action" was "in conformity to my original instructions & conversations with him before his departure."

Three days earlier Lee had written to Davis recommending that Early continue his march north and cross the Potomac. "At this time, as far as I can learn," Lee said, "all the troops in the control of the United States are being sent to Grant, and little or no opposition could be made by those at Washington."

Lee, moreover, was convinced, nearly two weeks after Early had left Richmond, that the Union high command had no clue that Lee's force had shrunk by an entire corps. "I think I can maintain our lines here against Genl Grant," Lee told Davis. "He does not seem disposed to attack, and has thrown himself strictly on the defensive."

Lee was correct; the Union war brain trust did not know that Lee's bold plan had been set in motion. Union intelligence reported that only a relative handful of Confederate troops were in the Shenandoah Valley. Grant, in fact, did not discover that Early's Second Corps had detached itself from Richmond until July 5.

Union misinformation, miscommunication, and just plain intelligence failures had begun on June 17 when U.S. Army chief of staff Halleck wired Grant from Washington to report that "Pickett's division, about 6,000 infantry, and Breckinridge's division, about 7,000 infantry, passed through Gordonsville [Virginia, north of Charlottesville] (in cars) on the 6th and 7th, against Hunter." There was a grain of truth in that report; Lee had indeed sent Breckinridge's division back to the valley. But Halleck was completely wrong about Pickett's division and about his statement that Lee's army was "well supplied with provisions." In fact, one of Lee's biggest worries at the time was procuring supplies for his army.

That same day Grant misinformed Halleck that, according to Gen. Benjamin Butler, who was ingloriously pinned down at the Bermuda Hundred, "Lee has sent Doles' and Kershaw's brigades and Gordon's division to Lynchburg." Gordon had been sent to Lynchburg, but Brig. Gen. George Doles had been killed at Cold Harbor on June 2. His brigade in Rodes's division had been taken over by Gen. William R. Cox. Joseph Kershaw had been promoted to major general that same day and been given the command of a division in Lt. Gen. James Longstreet's corps, which was not part of Early's army.

Grant, moreover, showed little concern about the wrong brigades' impact on his plans for Hunter. "The only apprehension I have for Hunter," he said, "is that he may get out of ammunition."

Grant's apprehension level no doubt would have increased greatly if he had known that Lee, in his June 26 missive to Davis, had made a decision—based on a plan concocted by Jefferson Davis and his naval aide, navy commander John Taylor Wood—that Early should head north with a new wrinkle in his bold plan: the release of Confederate prisoners of war held at Point Lookout south of Washington.

The Union army had begun sending Confederate prisoners to Point Lookout, located in Saint Mary's County, Maryland, on the southern tip of the southern Maryland peninsula where the Potomac meets the Chesapeake Bay, in August 1863 after the Battle of Gettysburg. A total of some fifty thousand

CSA prisoners were held there during the two years the camp was in opera-tion. In June of 1864 Point Lookout housed about twelve thousand prisoners.

"Great benefit might be drawn from the release of our prisoners at Point Lookout if it could be accomplished," Lee said. He recommended using Bradley Johnson and his Maryland cavalry troops for the job. "He is bold & intelligent, ardent and true," Lee said of Johnson. But Lee also wondered out loud if Johnson possessed "all the requisite qualities" for such a daring, im-portant mission.

Still, the thought of rescuing what would amount to an entire corps of troops tantalized Lee. "By throwing [a Confederate raiding party] on the beach with some concert of action among the prisoners," Lee told Davis, "I think the guard might be overpowered, the prisoners liberated & organized, and marched immediately on the route to Washington." The federal capital was just eighty miles away.

"The sooner it is put in execution the better," Lee said. "At this time, as far as I can learn, all the troops in the control of the United States are being sent to Grant, and little or no opposition could be made by those at Wash-ington."

It also was true that Early faced little or no opposition as he and his men continued their way down the Shenandoah Valley on the Valley Turnpike on June 28. Early's problem was not Union forces; it was supplies. He reck-oned that his force, which now numbered about sixteen thousand men, had only about five days' rations in their wagons and two days' worth in their small knapsacks (called haversacks).

The biggest supply problem, though, involved shoes and uniforms. Many of his men were wearing torn and tattered uniforms, and many were shoeless, some of them resorting to tying blood-soaked rags on the bot-toms of their feet. Early had hoped that boxcars of new boots, which he had requisitioned before leaving Gaines's Mill, would arrive in Staunton. They didn't, but with a promise from the CSA quartermaster general that the footware would come before he reached the Potomac, the march con-tinued.

In his official dispatches, though, Early emphasized the positive. On June 30 at New Market, Early cabled Lee to report that his troops "are in fine condition and spirits, their health greatly improved. We will have no diffi-culty about supplies."

He went on to reassure Lee on strategic matters, as well.

"If you continue to threaten Grant, I hope to be able to do something for your relief and the success of our cause shortly," Early said. "I shall lose no time."

Early did not lose much time marching his men north. The men may have been poorly clothed and roughly shod, but many of them "felt perfectly at home" on the march north of Staunton, John Worsham said. The reason: "nearly all the valley from Staunton to the Potomac river was familiar to us, and many of its inhabitants [were] old acquaintances. We stopped regularly at night and continued the march each day."

The army reached Winchester, Virginia, on July 2, the one-year anniversary of the start of the Battle of Gettysburg. Early's army had covered about a hundred miles in four days. That night and the following day Early divided his army, sending out his three cavalry brigades commanded by McCausland, Bradley Johnson, and Imboden north on a railroad-bridge-burning mission.

Franz Sigel, the pompous, incompetent German-born general who was disgraced at New Market, was in command of some five thousand troops of the Reserve Division of Hunter's army in Martinsburg, about twenty miles north of Winchester in present-day West Virginia's Eastern Panhandle. When Sigel got wind that the Confederates were heading in his direction, he decided to move as many supplies as he could to Harpers Ferry and then abandoned the city, where he had been charged with guarding a large amount of Union stores and protecting the B&O Railroad.

Sigel labored under the misapprehension that three divisions—not Early's cavalry augmented by Breckinridge's corps—were heading his way. The general—whom the Southerners nicknamed "the Flying Dutchman" because of his propensity to move quickly out of harm's way—moved on July 3 into a strong defensive position on the Maryland Heights across the Potomac River from Harpers Ferry.

The Flying Dutchman's "stampede" from Martinsburg, Union lieutenant colonel Charles G. Halpine wrote nine days later, "is beyond any doubt the most disgraceful affair of the war." Sigel's retreat, Halpine said, "was commenced before a rebel cavalry force of sixty men, who took possession of one end of [Martinsburg] as he quitted it at the other!"

Four days later Sigel's commanding general, U. S. Grant, expressed his contempt for the Flying Dutchman in a telegram to Henry Halleck. "All of Sigel's operations from the beginning of the war have been so unsuccessful

During their march down the Shenandoah Valley, Early's troops, many wearing torn and tattered uniforms, suffered more from scarce rations and a severe shortage of footwear than from Union attacks. *Credit: The Library of Virginia*

that I think it advisable to relieve him from all duty, at least until the present troubles are over," Grant wrote. "I do not feel certain at any time that he will not, after abandoning stores, artillery & trains, make a successful retreat to some safe place."

Early described Sigel evacuating Martinsburg "after very light skirmishing." The Union general left behind "considerable stores, which fell into our hands," Early wrote. Early brought Rodes's and Ramseur's divisions up from Winchester, but the troops were too tired to chase Sigel into Maryland.

"It was too late," Early said, "and these divisions were too much exhausted to go after the enemy."

The next day, July 4, 1864, Ransom's cavalry troops occupied Shepherdstown, nine miles east of Martinsburg just south of the Potomac River. Rodes's and Ramseur's division that day moved into Harpers Ferry, about twelve miles south of Shepherdstown, just after Union forces fled to join Sigel across the river at Maryland Heights.

Early let his men celebrate the Fourth of July by delaying their usual early morning march and distributing some of the booty they had confiscated at Martinsburg. That included a good amount of food sent to the Union troops from home. The food was "divided among the men as fairly as possible, F Company getting a few oranges, lemons, cakes and candy, and a keg of lager beer," Worsham remembered. "We certainly enjoyed the treat, and celebrated the day as well as we could for our hosts, and regretted they did not stay to preside for us." It "was the biggest Fourth of July picnic celebration we enjoyed during the war."

The U.S. Congress in Washington adjourned for its Independence Day recess that day as well. One after-the-fact rumor had it that the congressmen fled Washington in order to get out of town before a Confederate attack. In its July 11 editions, for example, the *Richmond Dispatch*, quoting "some" Washington correspondents, noted: "The United States Congress adjourned on the 4th of July, and the members hurried out of the city of Washington as fast as possible . . . for fear of capture by the Confederates."

If that rumor were true, which is unlikely, those congressmen knew more about what Early was up to than the Union high command did. Even with Early on the banks of the Potomac on July 4, Grant, Halleck, and company still did not have a clear picture of what was happening. "Some say that Breckinridge and Pickett are following the cavalry, which has just made a raid on the Baltimore and Ohio Railroad," Halleck cabled Grant on July 1, "while others say they are not in the Valley at all."

Grant wrote back that evening: "Ewell's corps has returned" to Richmond, "but I have no evidence of Breckinridge having returned."

"The enemy that attacked Harper's Ferry was of Ewell's corps," Sigel reported in a telegram sent from Maryland Heights at 6:00 a.m on July 5. The strength of the attacking force, he said, "was not developed." The next day Sigel reported that the Confederate "main force" was "variously reported from 20,000 to 30,000."

Nor did the local newspapers have a clear idea of the extent of Early's force. In an article headlined "The Rebel Invasion," the *Valley Spirit* newspaper in Chambersburg, Pennsylvania, for example, reported on July 13 that the "enemy" force was "commanded by Early, Ewell, or somebody else and is variously estimated at from 5,000 to 40,000." Said enemy force, the paper said, "may be possibly the latter number, if as we believe, his design is to advance on Baltimore and Washington, he would scarcely attempt so hazardous a movement with a less number."

One influential Northerner, though, did know what was going on: John

W. Garrett, the forty-three-year-old president of the Baltimore and Ohio Railroad. Garrett had a strong interest in Civil War developments in western Maryland and the Shenandoah Valley, where the B&O tracks connected Washington, D.C., and Baltimore with the surrounding area. His goal was to keep his trains running, and Garrett used his workforce of railroad agents and engineers to keep tabs on Southern troop movements and to forward that information on to the Union high command.

Garrett, in fact, provided Washington with the earliest accurate intelligence about Early's move down the Shenandoah Valley. "I find from various quarters statements of large [Confederate] forces in the Valley," Garrett reported in a June 29 telegram from his headquarters at Camden Station in Baltimore to Halleck in Washington. "Breckinridge and Ewell are reported moving up. I am satisfied the operations and designs of the enemy demand the greatest vigilance and attention."

Other than confusing Ewell (the former commander of the Second Corps) with Early, as Sigel and Grant did, Garrett's intelligence and analysis were completely correct.

Breckinridge's troops crossed the Potomac on July 5, 1864, at Boteler's Ford just outside Shepherdstown. The rest of Early's corps followed on July 6. Many of the men had made the crossing at this shallow point in the Potomac more than once. Earlier in the war Southern sympathizers had turned out to wave Confederate flags and serenade the troops with "Maryland, My Maryland," the anti-Union song written in April 1861 that begins with the line "The despot's heel is on thy shore."

On July 5 and 6, though, the CSA troops had to provide their own musical accompaniment. "We crossed the Potomac at Shepherdstown, wading it," Sgt. Maj. John G. Young of the Fourth North Carolina wrote in his diary. "It was about waist deep. . . . Our bands struck up 'Dixie' and 'Maryland My Maryland.'"

The Confederate soldiers, many still without shoes, crossed the river very carefully.

"I took off my clothing, made a bundle, secured it around my neck with my belt. I walked into the water and commenced to ford," John Worsham remembered. "I got along very well until I reached the level granite bottom, which was covered with minute shells, adhering to the granite, so very sharp that they stuck into my feet at every step. . . . Tears actually came into my eyes. I was never in as much torture for the same length of time in my life. Finally I got over, with the resolve never to ford there again without shoes."

When Worsham and Early's men crossed into Maryland it marked the third time that a Confederate army had invaded the North. It "was a desperate thing to do," Kyd Douglas wrote in his war memoir. "It was so reckless that historians are still examining figures to see if it can be possible. [Stonewall] Jackson being dead, it is safe to say no other General in either army would have attempted it against such odds."

On July 6, with Early bivouacked near Antietam, a young Confederate officer came galloping into his camp. Twenty-one-year-old CSA captain Robert Edward Lee Jr., the son of the Confederate army commander, was on a mission at the behest of his father. He'd ridden a relay of horses nonstop all the way from Richmond, a distance of about 175 miles. Young Lee carried with him a top-secret order—an order so secret that Lee senior did not trust sending it by telegraph.

"My father gave me verbally the contents of his letter, and told me that if I saw any chance of my capture to destroy it," Lee Jr., known as Rob, said in his postwar memoir. "Then, if I did reach the General, I should be able to tell him what he had written." His father cautioned him, Rob Lee said, "to keep my own counsel, and to say nothing to any one as to my destination."

The letter that Rob Lee carried in his head while racing north gave Early the details for the first time of the plan to liberate Point Lookout. The secret letter, Early said, informed him "that, on the 12th, an effort would be made to release the prisoners at Point Lookout, and [directed him] to take steps to unite them with my command, if the attempt was successful."

Early took the step of sending Bradley Johnson and his 1,500 cavalrymen north on July 9 to cut telegraph wires, destroy railroad bridges and tracks between Washington and Baltimore, and to stand by to make the move down to Point Lookout.

Early's adored commanding general, Robert E. Lee, had issued orders calling on Confederate troops not to harm "unarmed and defenseless" civilians in the North and to refrain from the "wanton destruction of private property." Early himself on July 5, in reaction to what he called "deplorable accounts of plundering and confusion at Martinsburg," forcefully reminded his division commanders of Lee's order.

And Early went further, telling his generals that it was "absolutely necessary" that "the most rigid discipline be enforced, else disgrace and disaster will overtake us." Confederate officers, he said, "for the good of the service and the success of the cause, must forego the propensity to provide for their personal comfort and convenience."

Early reminded his commanders that they were engaged "in no marauding expedition, and are not making war upon the defenseless and unresisting." The "strictest discipline," he said, "must be preserved, and all straggling, marauding, and appropriation of property by unauthorized parties must be prevented."

A thin line, though, existed between what Early and his commanders considered legitimate targets of military opportunity and non-war-related civilian personal property. The former, they certainly believed, included lines of communication and transportation, along with food, clothing, and other basic necessities—as well as money taken from Northern cities to be used for purchasing those goods.

In addition to destroying telegraph lines, burning bridges, and tearing up railroad tracks in Maryland, Early's men also wrecked parts of the Chesapeake & Ohio (C&O) canal alongside the Potomac River, destroying locks, burning canal boats, and stealing the mules that pulled the boats.

When Union loyalists in Maryland heard that Early's army had crossed into their state, some hid in their cellars and others fled west into mountain hideaways, or north to Carlisle, Harrisburg, and other Pennsylvania cities, taking with them their most precious portable possessions, including horses. What they couldn't take with them on short notice—china, silver, and the like—they buried on their farms and in their backyards. Free blacks also fled the oncoming Confederate forces for obvious reasons.

On July 6 Early dispatched McCausland and his men to Hagerstown, Maryland, about twenty miles northwest of Frederick, where they easily occupied the city. Early told McCausland to demand the huge sum of $200,000 from the city's fathers. McCausland either misread the order or the order was missing a digit because he asked for—and received—$20,000 from the city's officials.

He also demanded clothing and other supplies from the citizens and threatened to burn the city if they did not come up with the merchandise in a matter of hours. By day's end the city's businesses handed over hundreds of coats, pants, underwear, socks, boots, shoes, hats, and shirts. Then McCaus-land's men moved on to Middletown, Maryland, halfway to Frederick, where they demanded at first $5,000, but settled for $1,500 as the price for not burn-ing down the small village.

For the next three days McCausland's and other Confederate troops, un-mindful of Lee's and Early's orders—and with revenge on their minds for what Hunter did in the valley—forced themselves into retail stores and pri-vate homes and farms, where they took food, livestock, and other items. They "would go into the people's houses in the country," one local man wrote in his diary, "and if they did not give them what they wanted, they would threaten to set fire to the house, and in some places they carried coles [sic] on a shovel in the rooms before the people would give up their money." Confed-erate troops, another local man wrote in his diary, stole "from the Farmers money, meat, chickens, cattle, sheep, & anything that came their way."

The Confederate troops didn't discriminate in their looting. "Neither foe nor friend escaped," Chaplain Edwin M. Haynes of the Tenth Vermont later wrote. "If in sympathy with the rebellion, they paid tribute with what they had, and if enemies, all was taken and deemed a just reprisal."

The Confederate footwear finally showed up on July 7, the day that Early sent most of his cavalry east toward Frederick. "That night," Early said in his autobiography, "the expected shoes having arrived and been distributed, or-ders were given for a general move next morning."

Early had decided to do an end run around Sigel's heavily entrenched forces with their heavy artillery in Maryland Heights overlooking Harpers Ferry after Gordon's men couldn't dislodge them. The idea was to move east and on to Washington less than fifty miles away.

SIX

Wallace at the Bottom

Soon will be heard the thunder of captains, the sound of the trumpet and the shout, and I not there.

—LEW WALLACE TO HIS WIFE, SUSAN, APRIL 24, 1864

Sometime between July 2 and July 5, John Garrett, the prescient, self-preserving president of the B&O Railroad, paid a visit to Union major general Lew Wallace, the commander of the Middle Atlantic Department, at his headquarters in Baltimore. Garrett told Wallace, according to the latter's creatively written early-twentieth century autobiography, that he had had reports from his agents that Confederate troops were engaging in "serious operations" in the Shenandoah Valley.

Garrett expressed serious concerns that the rebel force would attack Washington, which both men knew was lightly defended. He suggested that Wallace, whose jurisdiction extended to the Monocacy River, send troops there to stop the CSA advance.

"That is not badly thought, Mr. Garrett," Wallace told Garrett, "but there are two things that make it impossible for me to be voluntarily a party to the scheme." First, Wallace said, he had no cavalry. Second, "the Monocacy is the western limit of my department. All beyond it belongs to General Hunter, and I wouldn't like to provoke the monster of military jealousy." Hunter, unbeknownst to Wallace, was hundreds of miles west at the time.

Seeing the urgency in Garrett's demeanor, though, Wallace promised that he would "assume guardianship" of the Union blockhouse on the eastern bank of the Monocacy near the B&O's iron bridge, and that he would keep a close eye on the situation.

"You may take with you my promise," Wallace told Garrett, that "the bridge shall not be disturbed without a fight." That fight turned out to be the July 9 Battle of Monocacy, which was "the most trying, and in point of service rendered, the most important of my life," Wallace later wrote.

Lewis Wallace—known universally as Lew—had a long, eventful life. He was born into a prominent Indiana political family on April 10, 1827, in Brookville, twelve miles from the Ohio border. He grew up in Crawfordsville, about forty-five miles west of Indianapolis. His father, David Wallace (West Point Class of 1821), served as lieutenant governor (1831–37) and as governor of Indiana (1838–40), and as a one-term U.S. congressman from the Hoosier State (1841–43). His maternal grandfather, John Test (1771–1849), had served two terms as a U.S. congressman from Indiana and later was presiding judge of the Indiana Circuit Court.

A voracious reader but an indifferent student, Lew Wallace worked briefly as a reporter for the *Indianapolis Daily Journal*. He was studying law in his father's office when the Mexican War broke out in 1846. The nineteen-year-old promptly formed the First Regiment of Indiana Volunteers. Army lieutenant Wallace's Mexican War experience, like Jubal Early's, consisted almost exclusively of garrison duty.

In 1847 Wallace came home from Mexico and went back to studying the law in Indianapolis. He briefly edited a small newspaper, was admitted to the bar in 1849, and began practicing law in Indianapolis. In 1850 Wallace won a two-year term as the First Congressional District's prosecuting attorney in Covington, Indiana.

He returned to Crawfordsville in 1852. On May 6 he married Susan Elston, the daughter of a prominent Crawfordsville merchant and banker. Three years later Lew Wallace was elected to the Indiana State Senate as a moderate (antislavery, but antiabolitionist) Democrat.

Wallace, feeling the pull of military life, in 1856 formed sixty-five young men from Crawfordsville into a local military company called the Montgomery

Union army major general Lew Wallace, best known as the author of *Ben-Hur*, undertook the unenviable job of trying to stop Jubal Early's army at Monocacy Junction on July 9, 1864.
Credit: The Library of Congress

Guards. Before long, he shaped them into a Zouave unit, specializing in close-order drills. Like other Zouave companies in Illinois, New York, and elsewhere in the Northern states, the Montgomery Guards wore flamboyant uniforms with fezzes, balloon pants, and red and blue Greek tunics. They performed their sharp drills regularly in front of large, adoring crowds.

Lew Wallace quit the Democratic Party when fellow Indiana Democrats urged him to support the Southern cause following Abraham Lincoln's election in 1860. "This is my native state," Wallace later quoted himself as saying when pressed to throw his allegiance to the South. "I will not leave it to serve the South. Down the street yonder is the old cemetery, and my father lies there going to dust. If I fight, I tell you, it shall be for his bones."

Within days after Fort Sumter fell on April 14, 1861, Indiana governor Oliver P. Morton, a childhood friend, appointed Wallace state adjutant general in charge of the effort to raise six Indiana regiments for the Union army. Wallace immediately devised an aggressive statewide recruiting campaign that in less than two weeks induced more than a dozen regiments' worth of men to sign up.

On April 26, 1861, he resigned as adjutant general, and Morton gave him a commission as a colonel in the Eleventh (Zouave) Regiment of Indiana Volunteers. Several dozen of the enlistees in the regiment were members of the recently disbanded Montgomery Guards.

Wallace, who sported an extralong and bushy moustache and goatee that stretched down to his chest, presented a striking figure leading his Zouave-clad men. "His deep, flashing eye, straight, shining black hair and erect figure," a contemporary observer wrote, "would be no discredit to the haughtiest Aboriginal."

Wallace's Civil War career started out well. After an all-night, twenty-three-mile march over mountainous terrain on June 11, 1861, he led his men to victory the next day over a larger Confederate force at the Battle of Romney, Virginia (in present-day West Virginia about forty miles west of Winchester). The spoils of that battle included "seven officers' marquees, a quantity of uniforms, and large quantities of clothing, a secession flag, four horses (one of which was the rebel colonel's riding-horse), four large chests of ammunition, camp equipage, and a great variety of articles," one of Wallace's men wrote after his Indiana regiment routed a Confederate force of some one thousand.

Coming as it did so early in the war, the modest victory at Romney went over well in Washington and gave a boost to Union morale. Northern newspapers and magazines magnified the accomplishment, heaping praise on Wallace and his men. Later that summer Lew Wallace met in Washington with newly named Union commander in chief George McClellan. Wallace claimed in his autobiography that McClellan asked Wallace to serve under him and that Wallace declined the offer. No other source confirms that contention, however. In September Lew Wallace was promoted to brigadier general.

The men of the Eleventh Indiana Zouaves went home after their three-month enlistment ended. Wallace promptly recruited another regiment of men back in Indiana, and the unit joined the Union Army of Tennessee (then known as the Army of the District of West Tennessee) under one of its commanders, Maj. Gen. Ulysses S. Grant. Wallace and his men fought under Grant at the winning February 1862 battles in Tennessee at Forts Henry, Heiman, and Donelson. On March 21, Wallace reaped another reward: a promotion to major general. At thirty-four, he became one of the youngest Union officers to hold that rank.

Lew Wallace's rising military star plummeted precipitously, though, less than three weeks later as a result of his actions at the bloody April 6–7 Battle of Shiloh in southwestern Tennessee. When Confederate general Albert Sidney Johnston's Army of the Mississippi attacked the Army of the Tennessee on April 6, Grant ordered Wallace to wait in reserve. What followed was a day-long fog-of-war cascade of unclear, inaccurate, and contradictory orders.

The result was that when Wallace arrived at his destination (Pittsburg Landing) at nightfall, the fighting—which nearly pushed Grant into the Tennessee River—had all but ended for the day. On April 7, Wallace's regiment joined in Grant's winning offensive in a vicious battle that resulted in some twenty-four thousand dead and wounded on both sides. The dead included Johnston himself. As Wallace noted in his autobiography, the number of casualties at Shiloh exceeded the total number of American dead and wounded in the American Revolution, the War of 1812, and the Mexican War combined.

The carnage and the near defeat at Shiloh almost cost Grant his job after scathing accounts of his performance at Shiloh ran in the Northern press. When one partisan Republican correspondent lobbied Lincoln to fire Grant, the president reportedly replied: "I can't spare this man. He fights."

Grant's commanding officer, Maj. Gen. Henry Wager Halleck, did blame Grant for the near loss. Halleck, no friend of Grant's to begin with, arrived at Grant's headquarters on April 11 and personally took over command of all Union forces there, relegating Grant for several months to a non-decision-making subordinate role. When Halleck went to Washington in July to become President Lincoln's military adviser and the Union army's general in chief, he reluctantly gave Grant back his job as the commander of the Army of Tennessee.

Lew Wallace did not fare so well. Both Grant and Halleck blamed him for malfeasance at Shiloh. Wallace asked for leave on June 23. "Somebody in the dark gave me a push," Wallace wrote in his autobiography, "and I fell, and fell so far that I could almost see bottom."

Wallace went home to Crawfordsville, and spent the summer on leave, with the thought of returning to Grant's army in October. Wallace asked for another command, but in November Halleck instead assigned him to preside over the military commission that investigated, and eventually blamed, Union major general Don Carlos Buell for his lack of leadership in a series of defeats in Kentucky in the summer and fall of 1862.

After the commission's work ended in May of 1863, Wallace lobbied heavily to get back into action. He helped his cause by chasing invading Confederate brigadier general John Hunt Morgan out of Indiana and Ohio in the summer of 1863. But when no orders came from Halleck, Wallace again went home to Crawfordsville and sat out the war until March 12, 1864, when he was given a new job: commander of the Eighth Army Corps and of the Middle Department based in Baltimore. Wallace succeeded Brig. Gen. Henry H. Lockwood, who had taken over temporary command from Maj. Gen. Robert Schenck. The command included all of Delaware and Maryland from Baltimore West to the Monocacy River.

It may have been a good political move for Wallace, with Washington so close by, but it was not exactly a plum military assignment. Wallace spent most of his time dealing with local secessionists. The war seemed far away.

Maryland was under martial law, meaning that Wallace was, in effect, the military governor of the city of Baltimore (with nearly 250,000 people, the nation's third largest) and the state. He took his governing orders directly from Secretary of War Edwin Stanton, whom he met in Washington before taking command. That meeting followed a tête-à-tête with Abraham Lincoln at the White House.

Wallace, who had met Lincoln two years earlier, found the president physically altered by the strains of war. "Time and care had told upon him," Wallace said in his autobiography. "His face was thinner and more worn, and I thought the stoop he had brought with him from his home in Illinois more decided."

Lincoln's secretary of war Edwin McMasters Stanton, who was fifty years old, was a native of Steubenville, Ohio. His father, a physician, died when Stanton was thirteen and the young man had to drop out of Kenyon College because of his family's strained financial circumstances. Stanton read the law on his own, passed the bar exam in 1835, and practiced law in

Overlooking their political differences, Lincoln chose a Democrat, Edwin M. Stanton of Ohio, to be his secretary of war in 1862. Lincoln bowed to Stanton's judgment on war tactics and strategy. *Credit: The Library of Congress*

Cadiz, Ohio, and Steubenville. He rose quickly in legal circles, taking top jobs in Pittsburgh in 1847 and Washington, D.C., in 1856. In the nation's capital he argued cases before the U.S. Supreme Court. Abraham Lincoln served as one of his coattorneys in a big 1856 case. A pro-Union, antislavery Democrat, Edwin Stanton was appointed attorney general of the United States by Pres. James Buchanan late in his term, in December 1860.

When Lincoln took over in March of 1861, Stanton returned to private life. He became a close adviser to Gen. George McClellan—and a critic of the Lincoln administration. Stanton, among other things, advocated arming slaves. It came as something of a surprise, then, that Stanton became the legal adviser of Lincoln's first secretary of war, Simon Cameron. And it was more of a shock that when Cameron resigned in January 1862, Lincoln appointed Stanton as his successor.

Lincoln, it turned out, overlooked their political differences because he trusted Stanton's judgment on military matters and war tactics and strategy. "So great is my confidence in Stanton's judgment and patriotism that I never wish to take an important step without first consulting him," Lincoln once said.

Stanton turned out to be an honest, able, and active war secretary. He also was short-tempered, humorless, impatient with subordinates, and single-minded in action and deed. Lew Wallace described Stanton at their first meeting as "cold, sharp, blunt, decisive," with "a massive head crowned plentifully with dark hair, clear eyes nearly black, a ruddy face whiskered long and iron gray."

Lew Wallace came to have a begrudging respect for Stanton; he never made peace with Halleck. Henry Wager Halleck of Westernville, New York, was educated well at the Hudson Academy, Union College, and West Point, receiving his commission as a lieutenant of engineers in the U.S. Army in 1839. Halleck went to Europe to study military defenses in 1844 and wrote two treatises on the subject after he came home. Those and other scholarly works earned Halleck the derisively used nickname "Old Brains."

Halleck served ably in the Mexican War in an administrative capacity, as the military government of California's secretary of state. Among other things, he helped write the California state constitution.

Halleck resigned his commission in 1854, headed a top law firm in California, and made a small fortune in mining and railroads. He married Elizabeth Hamilton, a granddaughter of Alexander Hamilton, in 1855. Halleck, with friends in high places, received a commission as major general in the Union army in August of 1861, and was put in charge of the Department of Missouri and then named commander of the entire Western Theater. The only times in his military career that Halleck physically took the field of battle were when he relieved Grant after Shiloh, and when he took command of three western Union armies that united in the campaign against Corinth, Mississippi, which began in April of 1862.

Union army commander in chief Henry W. Halleck, nicknamed "Old Brains," was taken by surprise when Early crossed the Potomac on July 5, 1864, and all but panicked at the prospect of a Confederate attack on Washington. *Credit: The Library of Congress*

Halleck's military reputation went downhill rapidly after that, despite the fact that Lincoln brought him to Washington in July of 1862 to be his military adviser and army commander in chief. Halleck—whom one Union officer called "the marplot [someone who ruins a plan by meddling] of the war"—alienated nearly everyone he dealt with in Washington with his brusque, haughty personality and with his penchant for indecision and timidity.

Halleck "is in a perfect maze," navy secretary Gideon Welles wrote on July 8, the day before the Battle of Monocacy, "bewildered, without intelligent decision or self-reliance." Halleck, Welles also wrote, "originates nothing, anticipates nothing . . . takes no responsibility, plans nothing, suggests nothing, is good for nothing."

On March 12, 1864, the day Lew Wallace took the job commanding the Middle Department, Lincoln demoted Halleck, putting the Union military effort in the hands of newly minted lieutenant general Ulysses S. Grant. That still placed Halleck, the brusque, impersonal office general, above Lew Wallace in the military chain of command—a situation that Wallace chafed under.

Halleck has the "habit of looking at people with eyes wide open, staring, dull, fishy even, more than owlish," Wallace commented. "The effect was of talking to somebody over my shoulder."

Lew Wallace assumed command in Baltimore on March 22. "The department, as I am painfully aware, is crowded with perplexities," Wallace said in his official announcement upon taking over, "and for that reason I pray all good men residing in it to unite and give me their earnest support." Providing that support, Wallace warned, would be "more for their own welfare than for mine."

Wallace ruled strictly. "Rebels and traitors," he announced, "have no political rights whatever." Wallace used his troops to continue the virtual martial law that had been put into effect on Baltimore's streets, giving them unlimited powers of search and seizure, and drafted local men into a Union militia. His methods worked; he had little trouble with the Maryland secessionists.

Wallace found time, also, to enjoy life in Baltimore, especially after his wife and eleven-year-old son joined him. The Wallaces enthusiastically took part in the social life of the city; he made it a point to go riding every day with his son. And his work cracking down on Confederate sympathizers in Maryland pleased Lincoln and Stanton, if not the standoffish Halleck.

The thirty-seven-year-old Wallace, though, felt that the war was passing him by.

"Great battles are to be scented far off," he wrote to his wife in late April. "Soon will be heard the thunder of captains, the sound of the trumpet and the shout, and *I not there*."

SEVEN

An Invasion of a Pretty Formidable Character

I wondered why we were ordered to Baltimore. I see now.
—COL. WILLIAM W. HENRY, TENTH VERMONT INFANTRY, JULY 8, 1864

Wallace's wish came true on July 5. At around midnight he and his aide, Lt. Col. James R. Ross (a lifelong friend from Indiana), boarded a B&O locomotive that Garrett provided for him at Baltimore's Camden Street Station. A few hours later, Wallace and Ross alit at Monocacy Junction. It was Wallace's second visit to the banks of the Monocacy. He had made a brief trip there shortly after he had taken command of the Middle Atlantic Department.

Wallace made the July 5 trip on his own and without the benefit of orders or the permission of any of his superiors. He did so, moreover, knowing that he risked invoking Halleck's severe displeasure.

"The truth is I did not care to have my absence reported in Washington," Wallace said in his autobiography. "That the Junction to which I was going was in my department, and that I was gone to the front, might not save me." There "was no telling in advance how small a thing, under the able management of General Halleck, might be turned to my serious disadvantage."

When Wallace left Baltimore, in fact, Halleck and nearly all of Wallace's other superiors had no clear idea of where Early and his men were, where they were heading, or their ultimate military objectives.

"The enemy (Jubal Early) appeared at Harper's Ferry last Saturday," Union major general Ethan Allen Hitchcock wrote in his diary on July 6, "and even yet we do not know in precisely what force. Sigel has been surprised at Martinsburg. We have only 15,000 men for the defence of Washington, and they are largely raw recruits. Any enterprising general could take the city."

The sixty-six-year-old Hitchcock (West Point Class of 1817), the grandson of Revolutionary War hero Ethan Allen, had come out of retirement to serve as a special adviser to the War Department in Washington. He went to Halleck a few days earlier expressing his concerns about what Early was up to. He came away upset and disappointed.

"I broached this danger last week to General Halleck," Hitchcock wrote. "I asked him if he was satisfied with the security of the Shenandoah Valley. His answer was, substantially, that General Grant and not himself was responsible. This did not at all satisfy me."

A few days later, Hitchcock went to see Halleck again. He "not only received no satisfaction," the old general wrote in his diary, but Halleck told him that "if he were in the President's place, he would not order General Grant to send reinforcements" to Washington. Halleck's answer again did not sit well with Hitchcock, so he went to see Secretary of War Stanton, the man who convinced him to come to Washington. Stanton, though, "was not able to give me any information and said little."

So Hitchcock went to the next man in the chain of command, President Lincoln.

"I found him in his usual seat, surrounded with papers and many members of Congress in attendance," Hitchcock said. The following conversation ensued, according to Hitchcock's diary entry:

"I have just seen General Halleck," Hitchcock told the president. "Is it possible that he can be under the influence of any painful feeling on account of the appointment over him of General Grant?"

Hitchcock added, he said, "that although Early was on the Potomac near this city, General Halleck seemed very apathetic."

"That's his way," Lincoln said. "He is always apathetic."

With Lincoln unwilling to intervene, Hitchcock looked the president "in his eye, leaning forward on the table," and said, "If Stonewall Jackson were living, and in command of Early's troops, in my opinion, sir, he would be in Washington in three days."

Lincoln replied, "I'll speak to the secretary of war about it."

Navy secretary Gideon Welles also was unhappy about Halleck and Stanton's apathy in the face of what he saw as a potentially catastrophic Confederate invasion of Washington. On July 8 Welles railed in his diary about the "profound ignorance" at the War Department "concerning the rebel raid in the Shenandoah Valley." Halleck, Stanton, et al., he said, "absolutely know nothing of it—its numbers, where it is, or its destination."

Welles, like Hitchcock and everyone else in Washington, knew that the city was lightly defended, and he pondered the city's—and the Union's—fate if the Confederates invaded. "I think we are in no way prepared for it," Welles said, "and a fierce onset could not well be resisted."

The navy secretary doubted that the Confederates would invade the capital, but he continued to fret. "Stanton seems stupid, Halleck always does," Welles complained in his diary the next day, July 9.

"I am not, I believe, an alarmist," and "I do not deem this raid formidable if rightly and promptly met, but it may, from inattention and neglect, become so. It is a scheme of Lee's strategy, but where is Grant's?"

Grant knew more than Welles gave him credit for—but not that much more. His first official dispatch that even mentioned Jubal Early in conjunction with the Confederate movement down the Shenandoah Valley hadn't come until July 3 at 4:00 in the afternoon. That happened to be three full weeks after Early had left Lee outside Richmond.

It was in the form of a cable that Grant had sent from his headquarters at City Point, Virginia, just northeast of Petersburg (the present-day city of Hopewell) to Halleck in Washington reporting on what he'd heard from the retreating Franz Sigel. The Flying Dutchman, Grant said, "reports that Early, Breckinridge, and Jackson with Mosby's guerrillas, are said to be moving from Staunton down the Shenandoah Valley."

That report—in keeping with so much of the Union intelligence about Early's move—was not completely accurate. CSA colonel John Singleton Mosby (more on him later) and his guerrillalike Rangers were not attached to Early's corps.

It wasn't until late in the afternoon of the following day, July 4, that Grant cabled Halleck with the first official Union suggestion that Jubal Early might be headed to the nation's capital. Grant told Halleck that a Confederate deserter had reported that "Ewell's corps" was "off in the Valley with the intention of going into Maryland and Washington City."

Grant advised the army chief of staff to "hold all the forces you can" in Washington, Baltimore, Cumberland, and Harpers Ferry, even while giving little or no credence to the reliability of the deserter's report. Aside from "dispatches forwarded from Washington," Grant said, he saw no other evidence "which indicated an intention on the part of the rebels to attempt any northern movement."

Grant continued to place his faith in Black Dave Hunter galloping to Washington's rescue from the west. "If Genl Hunter is in striking distance, there ought to be veteran force enough to meet anything the enemy have," Grant said. Once the Confederate troops were "put to flight," Grant added, they "ought to be followed as long as possible."

Assistant Secretary of War Charles A. Dana, whom Lincoln and Stanton had sent to Grant's City Point headquarters, was equally clueless. Dana did not know where Early or his troops were as late as July 5. Grant's headquarters, Dana reported to Stanton on the very day that Early crossed the Potomac from Virginia into Maryland, "seemed to have pretty good evidence that Early was with Lee defending Petersburg."

An "intelligent deserter," Dana's dispatch said, "says General Early is here in person, but does not know where his troops are." So much for that deserter's intelligence.

Halleck continued the Union stream of confusion that day, cabling Grant at 1:00 in the afternoon that he had no reliable estimates of Early's strength. "Some accounts, probably exaggerated, state it to be between 20,000 and 30,000." In this case Old Brains was right; those accounts were exaggerated. Early had, at most, 16,000 troops.

Halleck went on to remind Grant that Baltimore and Washington were poorly defended. We "have almost nothing in Baltimore or Washington, except militia, and considerable alarm has been created by sending troops from these places to reenforce Harper's Ferry."

Old Brains was referring to the relative handful of Union soldiers under Gen. Albion Howe—the 170th Ohio National Guard, some dismounted cavalry, and some light artillery—that he had sent on July 4 by train from Washington to join Sigel as he was fleeing to safety at Maryland Heights overlooking Harpers Ferry.

Halleck on July 5 advised Grant to send "a large dismounted cavalry force" to Washington immediately.

The first completely accurate Union information about Early's whereabouts and intentions came, coincidentally, also at 1:00 in the afternoon of July 5: a cable from George Meade at his Army of the Potomac headquarters outside Richmond to Grant. Two CSA deserters had walked into Meade's camp that morning, he said, with the following information: "Early, in command of two divisions of Ewell's corps, with Breckinridge's command and other forces, was making an invasion of Maryland with a view of capturing Washington, supposed to be defenseless."

At 10:30 that night Halleck had second thoughts about his advice to Grant to send troops north. If "Washington and Baltimore should be so seriously threatened as to require your aid," Halleck said, "I will inform you in time."

Halleck then once more mentioned the inadequacy of the "invalids and militia" defending Washington. But, he said, "I have no apprehensions at present about the safety of Washington, Baltimore, Harper's Ferry [which the day before had fallen to the Confederates], or Cumberland."

At ten minutes before midnight on July 5, not long after Grant had received that late-night telegram from Halleck, Grant decided to act. Worried by Meade's report, Grant decided to send a division of infantry troops north. He wouldn't send more than a division, Grant said, because he believed that Hunter would be coming to Washington's rescue from West Virginia. Hunter, although he fully realized he would not make it in time to head off Early, never conveyed that news to Grant or Halleck.

"We want now to crush out and destroy any force the enemy have sent north," Grant told Halleck, although the commanding officer of the Union forces still thought he was dealing with Early's predecessor Ewell.

"I think," Grant said, "there is no doubt but Ewell's corps is away from here."

Unlike Grant, Halleck, Dana, and Stanton, Lew Wallace had little doubt about where Early and his corps were when he arrived at Monocacy early in the morning on July 6. Wallace, writing in an after-action report a month later, said that he had received information on July 5 that "a column of rebel cavalry" was "in the Middletown Valley, moving eastwardly."

Wallace believed the intelligence. "Taking this report as true," he said, "the enemy had turned his back" on Pennsylvania and "reduced his probable objectives to Washington, Baltimore, or the Maryland Heights."

That's why Wallace chose the east bank of the Monocacy River to make his stand against Early. "I felt it my duty to concentrate that portion of my scanty command available for field operations at some point on the Monocacy River," Wallace said. "There in the space of two miles, converge the pikes to Washington and Baltimore, and the Baltimore and Ohio Railroad; there also is the iron bridge. . . ."

Wallace, who had no formal military training, chose an excellent defensive position. He had the river in front of him, a river with few easily crossed fords. He had a small mountain, what Wallace called "commanding heights," on which to set up his headquarters overlooking the Monocacy's eastern bank, and nearly all of the ground between him and the enemy was, as he put it, "level farmland with few obstructions."

With so many experienced Union soldiers hunkered down under Grant around Richmond and Petersburg, though, Wallace had only about 2,300 Middle Atlantic Department troops that he could spare. Many of them were untested in battle; all were widely scattered throughout his large department. Putting together a force to make a stand at Monocacy, Wallace said, "was like gleaning a field for a second and third time."

On July 3 Wallace had sent his First Separate Brigade under forty-two-year-old Brig. Gen. Erastus B. Tyler, a successful Ohio fur merchant who had been fighting since the outbreak of the war, to Monocacy Junction. By the end of the day on July 6, the rest of Wallace's troops had arrived: five companies of the First Potomac Home Brigade under Capt. Charles J. Brown; part of the Third Potomac Home Brigade under Col. Charles Gilpin; Col. William T. Landstreet's Twelfth Maryland Infantry Regiment; and three companies of the 144th Ohio Infantry Regiment and seven of the 149th Ohio under Col. A. L. Brown.

The force also included Capt. Frederick W. Alexander's six-gun Baltimore Battery of Light Artillery, which had been stationed in Northwest Baltimore since February. The unit's commander, Wallace said, looked "like a college professor," and "a man of . . . evident good breeding."

Alexander's battery received orders from Wallace on July 3 to be ready to march at a moment's notice. "Here ended the good time we had so near home," Frederick W. Wild, one of Alexander's men, wrote in his war memoir, "where we could go three or four times a week, and get a square meal, have a good bath and change clothes, go to the theatre and other amusements."

Alexander's battery broke camp in Baltimore at 9:30 p.m. on the Fourth of July. The men marched to the train depot and left town at 1:00 in the morning of July 6. They arrived at Monocacy Junction a few hours later.

"We were on the alert all day," Wild wrote, "our cavalry was moving hither and thither, skirmishers were thrown out beyond our sight [and] our battery was kept in harness ready to take any position which might be assigned to us."

The cavalry at Wallace's disposal consisted of about 250 men of the Eighth Illinois Cavalry Regiment under Lt. Col. David R. Clendenin; some 100 men of the 159th Ohio National Guard serving as a mounted infantry regiment under Capt. Edward H. Leib of the Fifth U.S. Cavalry; and a detachment of 250 horsemen from several units, including the First New York Veteran Cavalry under Maj. Charles H. Wells.

Wallace's force also included a small contingent of Loudoun Rangers, two companies of loosely organized Virginia cavalrymen from the Northwestern Loudoun County towns of Lovettesville and Waterford near the Maryland border. Made up primarily of Quakers of German and Scotch/Irish descent, these antislavery Virginians had rebelled against the Confederacy and served primarily as scouts for the Union army in their home territory.

Nearly all of the Maryland and Ohio troops in Wallace's force were what were known as hundred days' men. That is, they had joined the Union cause under a program introduced earlier in 1864 by Ohio governor John Brough to serve as temporary garrison troops in Northern states, performing rear-echelon duties to free experienced troops to fight in the South. The nickname came from the fact that the objective of the new temporary recruitment program was to end the war in a hundred days.

Wallace and the Union command, at this point, believed that he would be facing a force of from twenty thousand to thirty thousand veteran CSA troops. Halleck for the first time on July 6 spoke of Early's move as an "invasion" and one "of a pretty formidable character."

This realization of the invasion's formidable nature finally spurred Halleck and Grant to—as Lee had hoped—send significant numbers of troops northward. At around 5:00 a.m. on July 6, two brigades of the Union army's Sixth Corps' Third Division, some five thousand men, under the command of Brig. Gen. James Brewerton Ricketts, left their encampment outside Petersburg. They marched about fifteen miles to City Point, where they boarded four fast-moving, steam-powered transport ships (the *Columbia, Thomas Powell, Jersey Blue,* and *Sylvan Shore*) on the James River that would take them to Baltimore.

The night before, a messenger had appeared in the tent of Gen. George Meade, waking him up, bearing the order from Grant to send troops to Maryland. "Presently the General said: 'Very well, tell General [Horatio] Wright to send a good division. I suppose it will be Ricketts's,'" Meade's volunteer aide-de-camp, Col. Theodore Lyman, wrote in a letter the next day.

Meade, Lyman said, then "turned over and went asleep again." But "not so Ricketts, who was speedily waked up and told to march to City Point, then to take steamers for . . . Baltimore." Lyman expressed his awe "that a division of several thousand men may be suddenly waked at midnight and, within an hour or so, be on the march, each man with his arms and ammunition ready, and his rations in his haversack."

Meade, Lyman said, "says, 'Send Ricketts,' and turns over and goes to sleep. General Ricketts says, "Wake the Staff and saddle the horses. By the time this is done, he has written some little slips of paper, and away gallop the officers to the brigade commanders, who wake the regimental, who wake the company, who wake the non-commissioned, who wake the privates."

Each private, Lyman said, "uttering his particular oath, rises with a groan, rolls up his shelter-tent, if he has one, straps on his blanket, if he has not long since thrown it away, and is ready for the word 'Fall in!' When General Ricketts is informed that all are ready, he says: 'Very well, let the column move'—or something of that sort.

"There is a great shouting of 'By the right flank, forward!'; and off goes Ricketts, at the head of his troops, bound for City Point; and also bound, I much regret to say, for the Monocacy, where I fancy his poor men [would do] all the fighting."

It was not an altogether unpleasant sea journey as the troop ships steamed past Hampton Roads into the Chesapeake Bay and headed north, passing, as fate would have it, Point Lookout. "We are on the Steamship *Columbia* which has been one day a splendid boat," Sgt. Maj. William Burroughs Ross of the Fourteenth New Jersey Volunteer Infantry Regiment wrote aboard the ship en route to Baltimore on July 7. "Nice berths and state rooms and mattresses, all in the berths. Something we have not been used to."

The Fourteenth New Jersey—which the eminent Civil War historian James McPherson called "one of the best regiments in one of the best fighting corps in the Union army"—even had its brigade band on board to entertain the troops. "Some of the boys are dancing a cotillion on the upper deck," Ross said. "Yesterday we passed an excursion boat full of ladies, when such a time as we had cheering and waving handkerchiefs you never saw."

The ships reached Baltimore (not Washington, because Grant expected them to unite with Hunter in the valley) in the late afternoon on July 7. Not surprisingly, Wallace at Monocacy did not learn that the veteran troops had arrived from his superiors in Washington. The first word came to him in a telegram that John Garrett sent from Camden Station in Baltimore at around 4:00 in the afternoon on July 7, soon after the troop ships had docked.

"A large force of veterans has arrived by water," Garrett said, "and will be sent immediately. Our arrangements are to forward them with the greatest possible dispatch."

Garrett reminded Wallace—who didn't need reminding—of "the great importance of preserving" the iron B&O bridge on the Monocacy.

"If it be damaged or destroyed," Garrett said, "great delay will result in getting forward re-enforcements to General Sigel" at Maryland Heights. "I trust you will be able to maintain your position, and protect fully this most important structure."

"I will hold the bridge at all hazards," Wallace cabled back immediately. "Send on the troops as rapidly as possible."

The rapidity of the troop movement hit a snag, though, because Ricketts had ordered that no one leave the ships until he had arrived. When Garrett found out, he interceded with Stanton, new orders were cut, and the troops made their way to the railway station at Camden Street and boarded B&O trains heading west.

The Union troops were happy to see friendly faces along the route. "Every house along the road displayed the national flag and waving handkerchiefs," Osceola Lewis of the 138th Pennsylvania later wrote, "as old men and matrons, fair ladies and wondering children, farm-laborers and blacks watched, cheered, and wished the troop trains 'god-speed.'"

The first train arrived at Frederick Junction just before dawn on Friday morning, July 8. When Wallace's men heard the sound of the trains heading into Monocacy Junction, they were taken by surprise—and they were overjoyed. Wallace, who was sleeping in a jerry-rigged, wooden pallet bed, got the word from one of his orderlies.

"I hear a train in the direction of Baltimore," the orderly said as he woke the general.

Wallace listened to the sound. "Sure enough," Wallace wrote in his autobiography, "they were coming! Thunder in a drought-stricken land was never more welcome than the increasing roar of the cars."

Wallace had no idea, though, which troops were in the trains. Here is how he described his thoughts at that pivotal moment in his creatively written autobiography:

"A flock of questions arose. Who were they? Who was in command? Were they for me? Or would they go by? Whoever they were, I knew they must stop, for at the iron bridge there was a strong guard with orders to allow nobody to pass."

Wallace had Ross flag down the first train and bring the commanding officer to his makeshift headquarters. "In a little while, the colonel came bringing a stranger," Wallace remembered. "Behind them the locomotive followed slowly, like a huge animal in leash, and back of it many door-spaces were filled with human heads. The train stopped."

Ross then introduced him to Col. William W. Henry, the commander of the Tenth Vermont Infantry Regiment.

"He was tall, broad-shouldered, with a campaign complexion," Wallace said of Henry. "His uniform had seen hard service. I noticed one of his hands minus a finger—probably shot off. His manner, accent, and general appearance were suggestive of Ethan Allen and the Green Mountains. I set him down for a shrewd, brave, conscientious soldier."

Wallace was in for a shock, though, when Henry informed him of the Sixth Corps' destination. "I shook Colonel Henry's hand, telling him I was glad to see him; and heaven knows how very sincerely I spoke," Wallace said. "The colonel's face, however, did not reflect the gladness that must have shown in mine. He was evidently vexed."

Henry was vexed because his orders were not to stop at Monocacy Junction, but to go to Maryland Heights to help Sigel. Wallace quickly informed Henry that thousands of Jubal Early's men stood between Monocacy and the Heights.

"We left Early, as I thought, somewhere in our front at Petersburg," Henry told Wallace. "I wondered why we were ordered to Baltimore. I see now."

Wallace convinced Henry to stay put, and within minutes the Tenth Vermont and many of the rest of the Sixth Corps' Third Division's First Brigade set up camp amid Wallace's forces. "A few minutes then and there were a hundred little fires started, each with a black pot in the blaze or hanging from a cross-stick," Wallace remembered, "and each the center of an expectant group of rugged soldiers, whose handiness with fire, skillet, and coffee-pot bespoke the veteran."

Ricketts himself did not arrive until around 1:00 in the morning on Saturday, July 9. James Brewerton Ricketts, a career military man from New York City, had graduated from West Point in 1835 and served as an artillery officer in many assignments, including combat assignments in the Mexican War and the Seminole War.

Ricketts commanded a battery in Brig. Gen. Irvin McDowell's army at First Manassas, was wounded, taken prisoner, and later exchanged for a CSA officer. He went on to fight at Cedar Mountain, Second Manassas, and Antietam, where he was wounded a second time. After recovering, Ricketts took command of the Sixth Army Corps' Third Division and fought in all the bloody battles of the Wilderness Campaign.

Ricketts "was slightly above the average height of a man, a little inclined to corpulency, quick and bluff in manner and speech, Celtic in feature and complexion," Wallace said of the forty-six-year-old fighting general in his autobiography, as he described their first meeting at Monocacy. "Beyond the usual handshake, there was no ceremony between us, no asking after health or news, no gossip, no apologies."

Wallace told Ricketts that he was determined to put up a fight to stop Early from moving on Washington, and that—aside from Halleck sending the Eighth Illinois Cavalry—he had had no encouragement in that regard from his superiors. In fact, Howe, with Halleck's blessing, had suggested that Wallace head west and come to his aid at Maryland Heights, where Howe and Sigel perched out of harm's way.

Union brigadier general James B. Ricketts arrived at
Monocacy Junction with about five thousand battle-
hardened Sixth Corps troops a matter of hours before
the fighting began. *Credit: The Library of Congress*

"Instead of strengthening me here," Wallace said of Halleck, "he has
sent batteries and thousands of men to [Harpers Ferry], and they are on
Maryland Heights now, of no more account in the defence of Washington
than so many stones. I have been here three days and he has not so much as
wired me a word of intelligence respecting the enemy, or in the way of encouragement."

———◦·◦———

EIGHT

The Best Little Battle
of the War

*Here, as the situation appeared to me, the fate of Washington
was to be determined.*

—LEW WALLACE, JULY 8, 1864

Back on July 4, Old Brains Halleck had made an uncharacteristically decisive move. He didn't know it at the time or intend it to happen, but that move would provide Lew Wallace with desperately needed information about Early's troop movements. It also would provide Wallace with desperately needed experienced troops for the upcoming Battle of Monocacy.

On the Fourth, Halleck ordered the 230 officers and men of the Eighth Illinois Cavalry Regiment in Washington to go west. Their mission: to drive off an incursion at Point of Rocks, Maryland, by the famed Confederate guerrilla leader Lt. Col. John Singleton Mosby.

Known as "the Gray Ghost" because he and his men seemed to appear and disappear without warning, Mosby had conducted hit-and-run operations in an area centered on western Loudoun County, Virginia, about fifty miles west of Washington, D.C., since early in 1863. That section of the northern Virginia Piedmont, stretching from western Prince William County to West Virginia, came to be known as "Mosby's Confederacy."

Mosby—contrary to Franz Sigel's July 3 missive to Halleck—never was part of Early's corps. He had operated on his own since January 2, 1863, when CSA general J. E. B. Stuart acceded to Mosby's wish and granted him the authority to form his own independent ranger operation in and around Loudoun.

Mosby's Rangers, which officially became Company A, Forty-third Battalion, Partisan Rangers, on June 10, 1863, lived in their own or sympathetic families' houses—known even back then as "safe houses"—and scattered after each engagement. They furnished their own horses, food, weapons, and uniforms. Mosby himself favored a feathered hat and carried two pistols at his sides.

John Singleton Mosby grew up on a farm in Albemarle County outside of Charlottesville. Mosby attended the University of Virginia (leaving after he shot and wounded a fellow student), read the law, married, and set up a law practice in the extreme southwestern Virginia city of Bristol.

Like Jubal Early, Mosby opposed Virginia's secession from the Union. But once the Civil War started, the twenty-seven-year-old Mosby pledged his allegiance to the Southern cause. Standing five feet, eight inches tall, and weighing about 125 pounds, Mosby had enlisted as a private in a militia company, the Washington Mounted Rifles, before the war began. After Fort Sumter, the rifles became Company D of Grumble Jones's First Virginia Cavalry, under Col. J. E. B. Stuart.

Mosby went on to serve with distinction as a scout under Stuart. He fought at First and Second Manassas and at Antietam. While traveling on horseback in July 1862, Mosby ran into a band of Union soldiers and was captured. He spent about a month as a prisoner of war in the Old Capitol Prison in Washington before being sent south in a POW exchange for a Union army lieutenant.

In July of 1864 Mosby and his men were doing what they did most effectively to help Early and his march northward. "On July 4," Mosby wrote in his memoirs, "hearing of General Early's movement down the Valley, I moved with my command east of the Blue Ridge for the purpose of cooperating with him."

That Independence Day Mosby and about 250 of his men routed a federal force of some 350 men that included the Loudoun Rangers at Point of Rocks, a small village that sits where U.S. Route 15 today crosses the Potomac from Loudoun County into Maryland. Mosby's men took over the little town, blocked the B&O Railroad tracks with logs, cut the telegraph lines, burned the Union army camp, and looted the five stores in Point of Rocks.

"Most of the men went into the dry-goods business, and soon four regular shops and one sutler's establishment were emptied of their contents," Mosby ranger Maj. John Scott wrote in his war memoir.

Some called it "the Calico Raid" because when Mosby's men rode back into Virginia that night some of them wore bonnets on their heads and had dresses slung over their shoulders. They were "bedecked in a very grotesque and original manner with their captured goods," Major Scott said. "As they passed along the road, some arrayed in crinoline, some wearing bonnets, and all disguised with some incongruous and fantastic article of apparel, they looked like a company of masqueraders."

Mosby, who was not shy about describing his feats, called the raid an "invasion." Its "magnitude," he said, "was greatly exaggerated by the fears of the enemy, and panic and alarm spread through their territory."

That panic and alarm induced Halleck to send the Eighth Illinois Cavalry west under its thirty-three-year-old commander, Lt. Col. David Ramsay Clendenin, a Pennsylvanian and one of the Union army's ablest cavalrymen. When the war broke out, he joined the Union army as a private with the Washington Clay Guards in the nation's capital soon after graduating from Knox College. Clendenin earned a commission as a captain with the Eighth Illinois when it formed in September of 1861, eventually taking over as its commander.

Clendenin led his regiment out of Washington at 7:00 in the evening on July 4. The men rode twenty miles that night, stopped to rest at 1:00 a.m., and set out again at 6:00 the next morning. They reached Point of Rocks at about 12:00 noon on July 5.

"I found Mosby with two pieces of artillery and about 200 men posted on the south back of the Potomac," Clendenin said in his official after-action report.

Half of Clendenin's men dismounted. They then exchanged fire with Mosby's guerrillas across the river. The fighting went on for a good ninety minutes. Clendenin claimed he killed one of Mosby Rangers, wounded two others, and had no casualties of his own.

Mosby, as was his wont, slipped away while the guns were still blazing, heading to Leesburg to the southeast. He sent two of his men, Fount Beattie and Harry Heaton, to find Early at his camp near Antietam to deliver a message of support.

"I will obey any order you will send me," Mosby pledged to Early.

That was the last cordial communication between the two. The prickly Early soon thereafter accused Mosby of not supporting his invasion into Maryland. The prideful Mosby strongly resented the blatantly untrue accusation, and the two feuded for decades after the end of the war.

At 11:30 a.m. on the morning of July 5, Clendenin received a telegram from Howe at Maryland Heights ordering him to go to Frederick eleven miles up the road to see what Early's cavalrymen were up to. Clendenin's horsemen didn't get to Frederick until 8:00 that night. There he received orders from Wallace to report to him at Monocacy Junction.

Lew Wallace, once again, was operating on his own. Clendenin's force was not under his command. When he had learned that Clendenin was at Point of Rocks, Wallace telegraphed Halleck asking for the use of the Eighth Illinois Cavalry. When he did not get a reply, Wallace went ahead and used them anyway.

Why? Because, he said, "I had work of the utmost importance for him."

Clendenin, Wallace wrote in his autobiography, "did not disappoint me. He came in during the latter part of the night and waited upon me immediately. He appeared a very earnest man, fine-looking, tall, and quick, and acceded to my suggestions without argument—orders I was not authorized to give him, General Halleck not having replied to my request."

The orders: take two of Alexander's artillery pieces, move out to the foothills of South Mountain near Middletown west of Frederick, and find the enemy.

Clendenin "accepted the proposal much as if it were an every-day order, asking merely when the guns would report to him," Wallace said. "I saw I was dealing with a soldier and was greatly pleased."

Wallace asked Clendenin when he could move out. As soon as his horses were fed, the cavalryman said. Wallace took the opportunity to impress upon Clendenin how important his mission would be.

"You see, colonel," he said, "as yet nobody seems to know how strong the enemy is, or what he has in aim. Suppose it Washington, and it should turn out that he is in force to take it. How can we here in his front hope ever to be excused if he pockets the great prize through our failure to unmask him?

"We all look to General Grant to save the city," Wallace continued. "Is it probable he will detach a corps, or even a division, from his work in hand upon nothing better than a rumor or a conjecture?"

At daybreak on July 7, Clendenin moved out. When he crossed the Catoctin Mountains west of Frederick on the road to Middletown at around 10:00, Clendenin ran into some 250 Confederate cavalrymen under Gen. Bradley Johnson, who happened to have been born and raised in Frederick. A two-hour fight ensued.

"The heat was very oppressive," the Eighth Illinois unit history notes. "The rebels charged twice on our men, but were each time handsomely repulsed."

But Clendenin was outnumbered and soon had to fall back to Frederick. Wallace quickly sent in reinforcements, mounted infantrymen of Col. Charles Gilpin's Third Potomac Home Brigade, along with one artillery piece. Wallace hoped that move would stave off a Confederate assault on Frederick.

"Though out of my department, it had become my duty to save the town," Wallace wrote in his after-action report, "and as it was but three miles distant, I thought that could be done without jeopardizing the position at the railroad bridge."

Fierce fighting broke out at about 4:00 that afternoon on Frederick's western outskirts. It lasted for five hours, well into the night. Although the Confederates under Johnson and the Union forces under Gilpin were about equal in number, Johnson "had the advantage," as Wallace put it. His "men were veterans, while Gilpin's, with the exception of Clendenin's squadron, had not before been under fire."

At 5:00 Gilpin, feeling the heat, asked his commanding officer, Gen. Erastus B. Tyler, for help. "The enemy are pressing us, and the Eighth Illinois Cavalry have expended nearly all their ammunition," Gilpin said. "The telegraph operator has run away. What shall we do in the emergency?"

In the emergency, Gilpin's inexperienced men held off the Confederate cavalry until dark, when both forces withdrew for the night. Tyler could not praise Gilpin and his men enough. "The conduct of both officers and men was brave, gallant, and creditable," Tyler wrote in his after-action report.

Gilpin and Clendenin "conducted themselves in the most gallant manner, deserving great credit for their skill and efficiency from first to last. These officers speak in very high terms of the officers and men under them and they deserve it all."

Alexander's guns, Tyler said, also performed magnificently. They "were

served splendidly," he said. "I do but simple justice when I say that the officers and men are entitled to high esteem and admiration for their skill and
bravery exhibited in this action."

The performance also impressed Wallace. That night he sent a cable to
his aide, Lt. Col. Samuel B. Lawrence, who was back in Baltimore, calling
the action in Frederick "the best little battle of the war." Our men, he said,
"did not retreat, but held their own. The enemy were repulsed three times."

That skirmishing, reports from "citizen scouts" in the area, and Clendenin's reconnaissance convinced Wallace that he soon would be engaged
in a significant battle at Monocacy Junction. "The enemy was coming,"
he later wrote, and "I was directly in his road, and holding my ground *must*
result in collision." The "very probable," he said, "had become the inevitable."

Wallace later said that he agonized over whether or not to subject his vastly
outnumbered men to what surely would be at best a difficult fight. "It was
questionable whether the enemy had Washington for his objective, or Baltimore," Wallace said. "Enough that I believed it Washington. Then when I
ran over all the consequences of the capture of that city, they grouped themselves into a kind of horrible schedule."

Union ships at the navy yard "would be given over to flames," he specu-
lated. He worried about Early seizing "millions of bonds" in the Treasury Department. He pondered the "storehouses in the city filled with property of
all kinds, medical, ordnance, commissary, quartermaster." They amounted
to "the accumulation of years, without which the war must halt, if not stop
for good and all."

He worried about Washington's buildings, including the Library of Congress, "all under menace—of prestige lost, of the faith that had so sublimely
sustained the loyal people through years crowded with sacrifices unexampled
in history. . . ." He choked on the thought of France and England recogniz-
ing the Confederacy.

What upset Wallace the most, though, he said, was contemplating the
image of President Lincoln, "cloaked and hooded, stealing like a malefactor
from the back door of the White House just as some gray-garbed Confederate brigadier burst in the front door."

All of those thoughts cemented in Lew Wallace, he said, "the determination to stay and fight."

The next morning, July 8, Wallace sent more troops to Frederick: 96 mounted infantrymen under Capt. Edward H. Leib, 256 assorted cavalrymen under Maj. Charles H. Wells, hundred days' men from the Eleventh Maryland Infantry Regiment, several artillery pieces, and a group of Loudoun Rangers. General Tyler himself arrived at daybreak to take stock of the situation.

Among the Eleventh Maryland were three young men in civilian clothes carrying muskets. The three unlikely looking soldiers, Julius H. Anderson, Hugh M. Gatchell, and Samuel S. Thomas of Baltimore, had been dragooned into the unit three days earlier. They had taken the train from Baltimore to celebrate the Fourth of July holiday at Araby, the stately farmhouse near Monocacy Junction owned by Samuel Thomas's father, Col. C. Keefer Thomas. Anderson was engaged to young Alice Thomas. Gatchell was the fiancé of Alice Thomas's friend Mamie Tyler.

A squad of Union soldiers showed up at the Thomas Farm, which is less than a half mile from Monocacy Junction on the Georgetown Road, on July 5, asked for the three young men by name, and arrested them, saying they had orders to do so from General Wallace. The men marched under guard to the Eleventh Maryland's encampment, were issued weapons, and assigned bunks. The three unlikely soldiers spent the next two days drilling with the Union troops.

When a Union officer noticed them in civilian clothes with the Eleventh Maryland outside Frederick on July 8, he ordered them back to Monocacy Junction. The next day Anderson, Gatchell, and Thomas were with Wallace's troops when the Battle of Monocacy began. With Confederate bullets flying, another Union officer spotted them in harm's way.

"Young men if you should be captured fighting in civilian clothes, you are likely to be shot," he said. "General Wallace is now at some distance and I advise you to get away from here as fast as you can."

The men did not hesitate. They threw their muskets down and fled to the home of a neighbor, James H. Gambrill. As the battle roared around them the rest of the day, the three young men hunkered down inside Gambrill's Mill.

As for the two young women, they frantically searched for the men for two days, including at least part of the day of July 9, in the Union camp as the battle raged. "Two extremely attractive young women are very much in evidence as they flit from place to place, obviously in deep distress over something," one Union soldier said. "The last we saw of them was their rapid crossing of the railroad bridge to the westward."

Back on the morning of July 8, Wallace, along with the men of Henry's Tenth Vermont, also took the short train ride from Monocacy Junction to Frederick. Henry's troops immediately went to the front. Wallace met up with Tyler and together they "rode from flank to flank," he wrote, "and with hearty congratulations, I shook hands with Gilpin, Alexander, and Clendenin."

Later that morning Tyler spotted Confederate cavalrymen riding down South Mountain. "Their movements indicate a disposition to fight at no very distant hour," Tyler reported at the scene. CSA skirmishers, Tyler said, "are opening upon my advance this moment."

The "rebels," he said, "are jubilant this morning and anxious to get to the front."

The jubilant rebels commenced to attack the Yankees, and sporadic fighting went on for most of the day. But, as Wallace rightly guessed, Early held back his main force and "did not design attacking in earnest."

The future novelist described the scene: It "was rattle, rattle, and for a wide space the air, low-lying upon the ground, was speckled with whiffs of pale-blue smoke that dissolved before they could rise."

The fighting then lagged. Occasionally, Wallace wrote, "a man came back limping or helped by a comrade. But for such occurrences one could not have realized that what was going on did not belong to a Fourth-of-July programme."

There were more brutal exchanges that day, including one inside the city. "Our [command] had quite a severe little fight in the streets of Frederick City," Confederate cavalryman Henry Trueheart said in a letter home. During the fight the men got "terribly mixed up in the dense clouds of dust produced by the air. Really, you could not see more than a horse's length, & that indistinctly."

In the vicious hand-to-hand combat that ensued, he wrote, one "of our Lts was struck across the nose with a saber but instantly killed the Yank. He killed another just in the act of cutting at one of our men with his saber and then another."

Initial reports of the battle of Frederick were glowing. "Since the arrival of Gen. Lew Wallace, with his reinforcements, the appearance of the city is entirely changed," *The New York Times* reported in a front page article date-lined "Frederick, Md., Friday, July 8—2 P.M." Business, the article said, "has been resumed, and the people seem confident that the danger has passed."

"Everything," the dispatch said, "looks well. Frederick is in no danger. . . . The Eleventh Maryland one hundred day men have arrived here, and been enthusiastically received."

That afternoon at 1:00 Franz Sigel, from his perch out of the action at Maryland Heights, reported to Washington that Early's main force was on the move. Early's men were "advancing in strong force, said to be a whole corps, in the Middletown Valley," Sigel said. According to "all information which has been received, it seems certain that the enemy with his whole force is marching for Frederick."

Early, as Wallace surmised, was not interested in an all-out attack on Frederick. He kept just enough pressure on the city to force the Union troops out.

At about the time that Sigel sent his telegram, Albion Howe cabled Wallace, "suggesting," as Wallace put it, that Wallace come to Howe and Sigel's aid in the Maryland Heights.

"Who was Howe?" Wallace said he asked himself. The last he had heard from Maryland Heights, Sigel was in command; and the last thing he had heard from Sigel was the information that a large Confederate force was heading toward Frederick.

"Instead of my joining Howe, whoever he might be," Wallace later wrote, "why did he not come to me? Early was here, not there, and here was fighting."

Wallace dashed off a telegram to "Major-General Sigel or Brigadier-General Howe" at 12:45 that afternoon, saying he thought it would be "injudicious" for him to move from Frederick to Maryland Heights.

Wallace himself confirmed what Early was up to at around 4:00 as he peered westward through his binoculars at the "purpling face" of the South Mountain west of Middletown. He caught sight, he said, "of three long, continuous yellow cloud-lines . . . crawling serpent-like slowly down towards the valley." The cloud lines, he soon realized, "were columns of infantry, with trains of artillery—good strong columns they were too, of thousands and thousands."

What he saw were three divisions of Early's troops under Gordon, Rodes, and Ramseur. What he saw also convinced him to pull his troops back to Monocacy Junction and make a stand there.

Wallace put out the order and made his way through Frederick on horseback with his orderlies and a few of his officers. It was "the twilight hour, not yet dusk," he said. Citizens of Frederick "put themselves in my way," and asked where he was going.

"I could but observe their anxiety; their voices conveyed it," he said.

It was "extremely difficult abandoning" the Union loyalists in Frederick, Wallace said. "I remember few circumstances in my life more trying."

Wallace's last act before pulling out was to send a cable to Halleck in Washington. "Breckenridge, with a strong column," he said, is "moving down the Washington pike towards Urbana" and "is within six miles of that place. I shall withdraw immediately from Frederick City, and put myself in position on the road to cover Washington, if necessary."

Aside from giving Halleck the true picture of what was happening in Frederick, Wallace's telegram for the first time brought home to the Union army chief the startling and disturbing fact that Jubal Early's goal very likely was an attack on the nation's capital.

Wallace's warning finally convinced Old Brains Halleck of the gravity of the situation in the Monocacy Valley. At 10:30 on July 8 he sent a telegram to Grant informing the Union commander that "a heavy column of the enemy" had crossed the Monocacy and was moving on Urbana, a town just south of the junction.

Halleck told Grant that his intelligence—which he described as information from "scouts, prisoners and country people" gathered by Sigel and by Maj. Gen. Darius Couch, who commanded the Pennsylvania Department—"confirm" previous reports that the rebel force numbered "some 20,000 or 30,000." Early, as we have seen, had about 16,000 men under his command.

Aside from overestimating Early's force by some 4,000 to 14,000, Halleck also misjudged how much of Lee's army Early's force represented. "It is the impression," he told Grant, "that one-third of Lee's entire force is with Early and Breckinridge."

That force could do serious damage to Washington, Halleck worried. "We have nothing to meet that number in the field," he said, "and the militia is not reliable even to hold the fortifications of Washington and Baltimore."

Halleck begged Grant to come to the city's rescue. "None of the cavalry sent up by you has arrived nor do we get anything from Hunter," Halleck said. "Troops sent from the James River should come here, not Baltimore." We "must have more forces here. Indeed, if the enemy's strength is as great as represented, it is doubtful if the militia can hold all of our defenses. I do not think that we can expect much from Hunter. He is too far off & moves too slowly.

"Very considerable re-enforcements," Halleck concluded, "should be sent directly to this place."

NINE

The Whiz of Flying Iron

Not a living thing could be discovered in the field.

—Lew Wallace, 11:30 a.m., after McCausland's first attack

The first shots of the Battle of Monocacy rang out at around 6:00 a.m. on Saturday, July 9. "It was a beautiful day in this beautiful country," CSA foot soldier John Worsham wrote in his war memoir.

"The sun was bright and hot, a nice breeze was blowing which kept us from being too warm, the air was laden with the perfume of flowers, the birds were singing in bush and tree, all the fields were green with growing crops."

A "few floating clouds," he remembered, added "effect to the landscape."

The morning of July 9 "dawned with a halo on sunshine and beauty," W. T. McDougle of the 126th Ohio Volunteer Infantry later wrote. "The birds (which we had been so unaccustomed to hear during our late journey from the Rapidan to Petersburg), never appeared to be so joyful.

"The large [Worthington] farmhouse on the hill to our left seemed almost a paradise, with its surroundings of horses, hogs, cattle, fowls, etc. I remember the gather of the wheat from the field." The Union soldiers, McDougle said, "could hardly believe it possible that before the setting of the sun this beautiful place would be the scene of such deadly strife."

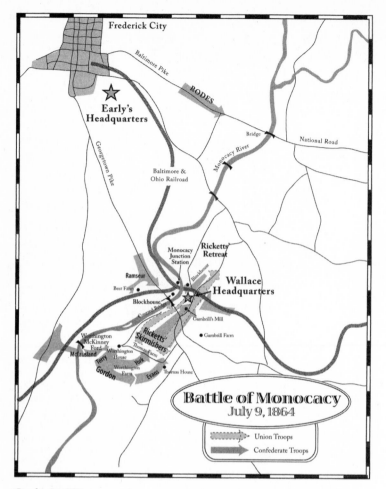

Credit: Liz Weaver

When Wallace arose that morning—after having "slept never more soundly"—he surveyed the scene while his orderly prepared his "slender" breakfast.

"Everywhere I read the promise of a beautiful summer day," he said. "There was not a spec in the sky, and the departing night had left a coolness in the air delicious and most refreshing."

The delicious air, however, soon became filled with smoke from both sides' cooking fires.

"Behind me little columns of smoke were slowly rising; the same indications across the river told me where our pickets were in post and wide awake; beyond them, in the direction of Frederick, a denser smoke lay along the earth in the form of a pallid cloud hanging not higher than a tree top and it spoke of the enemy," Wallace wrote.

"Everywhere friends and foes alike were at coffee or making it. The smell of new mown hay from the yellowing stubble-fields was lost in the sooty perfume of the many fires."

The battle's opening salvo came when advance skirmishers of Confederate brigadier general Robert D. Lilley's brigade of five Virginia infantry regiments in Ramseur's division met up with skirmishers from Col. Allison L. Brown's 149th Ohio National Guard Regiment. The fighting took place at the Baltimore Pike (also known as the National Road) just west of the stone bridge (known as Jug Bridge) over the Monocacy River. The skirmishing there, on the northernmost edge of the three-mile-long Union line, went on for about two hours. Ricketts's and Ramseur's skirmishers also started exchanging gunfire at about the same time on the Georgetown Pike.

Jubal Early was not on the scene. In fact, he would sit out the first few hours of the fighting because he had business to attend to in the city of Frederick. Early and his entourage, including four supply officers, entered the city sometime around 8:00 on the morning of the battle. He made his temporary headquarters in the house of Dr. Richard Hammond, a Southern sympathizer, and asked to borrow writing materials.

Early then wrote out an order to Frederick's mayor, William G. Cole, and the city's Board of Alderman and Common Council. To wit: "By order of Lieut.-Gen. Comdg: We require of the mayor and town authorities $200,000 in current money for the use of this army." His quartermaster also asked for twenty thousand pounds of bacon, six thousand pounds of sugar, three thousand pounds of coffee and salt, and five hundred barrels of sugar.

The demand for money and materials, Early told Mayor Cole and Frederick city officials, was in retaliation for Hunter's wanton destruction in the Shenandoah Valley. At first the town fathers refused, protesting that Early was asking too much from a city of just eight thousand citizens. Early threatened to torch the city if they did not come up with the money. The negotiations went on for hours.

It appeared that Frederick's leaders were stalling for time, waiting for the outcome of the fighting that had begun at Monocacy Junction. If the Union troops succeeded, they would refuse Early's demands. However, when word came that the Confederates were prevailing at Monocacy, the city officials caved in. Four banks came up with the $200,000 in greenbacks. Nothing came of the demand for the foodstuffs.

Early and his staff proceeded to spread some of the money around town. We "bought what we wanted & paid for it in their own money," Maj. Jedediah Hotchkiss, Early's topographical engineer and mapmaker, wrote in a letter home.

After that morale-building fiscal victory in Frederick, Early and his entourage rode toward Monocacy Junction. A procession of refugees from Frederick preceded him earlier in the day, before the battle had begun. They "were coming in in great numbers," McDougle said, "men, women and children, old and young, black and white, appearing to be moving with them all of their household effects."

Among the refugees were two Tenth Regiment of Vermont Volunteers surgeons and the Reverend Edwin M. Haynes, the unit's chaplain. The three men had spent the night before in a hotel in Frederick and had unwittingly ran into a force of Confederate cavalry on the way back to Monocacy Junction.

We "had approached within one hundred and fifty yards of a squad of rebel cavalry, thinking they were our own," Haynes wrote in his 1870 history of the regiment. "We were soon undeceived, however, as the rebels gave us a volley from their carbines, at an uncomfortably short range." This "was not what we had bargained for," Haynes said, "and we ran."

When Early arrived on the scene, he set up his headquarters at the Best farm, about a mile to the west of Monocacy Junction—at roughly the same place where Robert E. Lee had camped two years earlier prior to Antietam and had written the famous "lost order."

From there Early saw that Wallace had been reinforced during the night when the last of the Union troops to arrive, regiments of the Sixth Corps' Third Division, completed their journey by train from Baltimore. The Third Division included the Ninth New York Heavy Artillery under the command of twenty-five-year-old colonel William Henry Seward Jr. of Auburn, New York, the son of Lincoln's secretary of state. With the last of the troops of the Sixth Corps in place, Wallace's forces now totaled some 5,800.

That number did not include what some observers mockingly called the "missing brigade," about a thousand Third Division soldiers from the Second Brigade who never made it to Monocacy Junction. The railroad cars from Baltimore carrying the Sixty-seventh Regiment of Pennsylvania Volunteers, part of the 122nd Ohio Infantry Regiment, and the Sixth Maryland Infantry Regiment stopped at the small town of Monrovia, eight miles east of Monocacy Junction. The troops, under the command of Col. John F. Staunton of Philadelphia, the Second Brigade commander who had organized the Sixty-seventh in 1861, spent the day in Monrovia and the nearby town of New Market. They missed the entire battle.

A history of Pennsylvania's Civil War volunteer forces written for the Pennsylvania legislature following the war puts a favorable light on the "missing brigade" situation. The troops of the Sixty-seventh, according to this account, were on "slow boats" from City Point and did not arrive in Baltimore "until after some time after the balance [of Ricketts's men] had gone forward."

Staunton stayed in Baltimore until the last of the troops had arrived and accompanied them on the train. "On arriving at New Market," the report says, "Colonel Staunton drew up his force in line of battle across the road on which Ricketts was retiring, so as to protect the rear of the retreating column and when it had passed brought up the rear."

The official Union war records note that the Sixth Maryland, Sixty-seventh Pennsylvania, and part of the 122nd Ohio "had been delayed by the slowness of the transports." But Wallace and Ricketts justifiably blamed Staunton for purposely avoiding taking part in the battle and relieved him of his command on July 10, replacing him with Capt. Samuel Barry. Staunton was subsequently court-martialed and dismissed from the Union army.

Jubal Early did not want to fight the Battle of Monocacy. His goal was to threaten Washington. His troops had been marching for three weeks. He was within forty miles of the nation's capital. The last thing he wanted was an all-out field battle against a significant enemy force bolstered by hardened, veteran Sixth Corps troops holding high ground on the other side of a river.

But Lew Wallace forced Early's hand.

Early didn't particularly like what he saw when he arrived at the Best

Farm. "The enemy, in considerable force under Gen. Lew Wallace, was found strongly posted on the eastern bank of the Monocacy near the Junction," Early said in his war memoir, "with an earthwork and two block-houses commanding both the railroad bridge and the bridge on the Georgetown pike."

Early had arrived at Monocacy as McCausland's cavalry found a ford in the river and moved forward to attack Ricketts's men from the Union's left flank. McCausland's men ran into a hail of gunfire and were forced to retreat, and Early eventually would have to send Gordon across the river to attack Ricketts. Early also ordered Rodes's division to his left to relieve Lilley's brigade and threaten the troops at the Jug Bridge, where the Baltimore Pike crossed the Monocacy. And he kept Ramseur's men in the center along the Georgetown Pike just on the other side of Monocacy Junction facing the pike's covered wooden bridge and the iron railroad bridge just to the north.

The covered bridge, Glenn Worthington wrote, "was an old, wooden affair, but strong and substantial, weatherboarded and covered with a shingle roof." The bridge was about 250 feet long, 50 feet wide, and 16 feet high. It had, Worthington said, "heavy arched timbers on each side and in the middle a line of heavy supporting timbers running through" its center, "thus dividing the bridge into two driveways, one for eastbound and one for westbound traffic."

Earlier, at about the time that skirmishing began along the National Road, Ramseur's pickets and Union troops exchanged fire along the Georgetown Pike close to the river. But Early never gave Ramseur or Rodes orders to launch full-fledged attacks. Early had his ultimate objective, Washington, D.C., in mind. His goal was to dislodge the Union troops as economically as possible.

Wallace had arrayed Ricketts's brigades on high ground to his left across the Georgetown Pike and along the river right up to the corn and wheat fields of the Worthington and Thomas Farms, so that they were, in effect, facing Ramseur. Erastus Tyler's brigade was positioned on the Union right along the river up to the National Road to the north. These were Wallace's least experienced troops, mainly hundred days' men of the ten companies of the 144th and 149th Ohio National Guard, along with six companies of the First and Third Potomac Home Brigades of the Maryland Volunteers and the Eleventh Maryland Infantry Regiment.

Wallace also sent skirmishers from the Ninth and 106th New York into the fields of the Best Farm on the other side of the Monocacy. Finally, he positioned a small force from the First Maryland Potomac Home Brigade and the Tenth Vermont in the area around Monocacy Junction itself, between he railroad and the river.

The Union troops took cover behind their two blockhouses and the rifle pits that they had built into the east side of the Monocacy River. Alexander's artillery—six three-inch rifle guns and a twenty-four-pound howitzer— backed up the Union troops.

The Union guns began blazing at around 10:00, soon after Wallace and Ricketts spotted Ramseur's men heading their way and three Confederate shots flew over their heads. Alexander's howitzer "took up its cry," Wallace said, "a very loud note it was, an immense pounding sound singularly laden with encouragement to us."

The big howitzer "lost not a minute, so fair was the target. Then shortly the skirmishers joined in with their practice, ours firing from cover, and sending theirs vis-à-vis to the ground crawling like snakes."

The Confederate artillery, consisting of nine batteries with at least thirty-six big guns, including twenty twelve-pound Napoleon howitzers, was arrayed in the fields behind the Best and Worthington Farms. The Confederate guns immediately answered Alexander's artillery.

"We could not see their guns, as they were masked behind some bushes," Frederick Wild of Alexander's battery said, "and for every shot fired, we received two in return; we were having it hot and heavy, while the other [Union] guns in the center and left were waiting for further developments."

The noise overhead, Wallace said, "became deafening, and the whiz of flying iron incessant. Up all around us sprang little gushes of gravel and yellow dust. There was not an instant I did not look to see a horse, possibly a horse and rider, go down."

A cannon ball, McDougle said, "struck the tree by which we were posted; another dropped a few feet to our rear and went bounding across the valley like a schoolboy's rubber ball; another struck and buried itself in the earth a few feet to our front. All was now commotion."

At about the same time that the outgunned Union artillery tried to match the Confederate cannons, at around 10:30 that morning, Tiger John McCausland, arriving from Jefferson, Maryland, to the southwest, led his four Virginia cavalry regiments made up of perhaps as many as one thousand men across the Monocacy at a spot known as the Worthington-McKinney Ford on the Worthington Farm, about a mile south of Monocacy Junction.

The Worthington House stood amid the fiercest fighting at the Battle of Monocacy. The National Park Service has restored the house's exterior to its 1864 condition. *Credit: Michael Keating*

The rest of Breckinridge's corps, under John Brown Gordon, stood in abeyance well to the rear.

After crossing the Monocacy, McCausland ordered his men to dismount. Led by officers on horseback, they moved out past the Worthington farmhouse and through a field of waist-high corn toward a fence line on the Thomas Farm. McCausland did not know that Ricketts had deployed a skirmish line of men from several of his five regiments (the Tenth Vermont, Eighty-seventh Pennsylvania, Fourteenth New Jersey, and the 106th and 151st New York) of Col. William Truex's First Brigade behind that post-and-rail fence.

Ricketts had his men hold their fire until the Confederates were within rifle range, about 125 yards from their position. Here's how Wallace, in his novelist's inspired prose, described what would be the Union's high point of the day-long battle:

McCausland's dismounted cavalrymen "started forward slowly at first; suddenly after the passage of a space, arms were shifted, and, taking to the double-quick, the men raised their battle-cry." The famed rebel yell to

Wallace's ears sounded "sharper, shriller, and more like the composite yelping of wolves than I had ever heard it."

He saw "a tempestuous tossing of guidons, waving of banners and a furious trampling of the young corn that flew before them like splashed billows." The charge, he said, "was really fearful."

Ricketts, meanwhile, sat on his horse behind the Union line, "like a block of wood, calm, indifferent." On his command, "up rose the figures behind him, up as one man." Wallace saw "the gleaming of the burnished gun-barrels as they were laid upon the upper rails" of the fence. Then came "a ragged eruption of fire."

"My God," one of Wallace's aides cried. "They are all killed."

The Confederate line, Wallace said, "had disappeared. Not a man of it was to be seen, only the green of the trodden corn, some horses galloping about riderless and a few mounted officers bravely facing the unexpected storm."

The Union troops let out a cheer, then began "firing at will." More "saddles emptied, other horses rushing madly about." Within minutes, "not a living thing could be discovered in the field. Even the masterless horses were gone; while the wounded, crouching close to avoid the pitiless rain of bullets in the air above them, lay under the corn hidden as by a mantel."

"We received a murderous volley from the Yankee line," Randolph Jones Barton, an officer with Gen. William R. Terry's brigade of Virginia Consolidated Infantry Regiments, wrote in his war memoir. Barton escaped the fighting unscathed, although barely. "In a little while, I felt a blow upon my sword belt," he said, "a blow which as I now recall it was severe, but not painful, evidently made by a glancing ball."

Barton's horse did not fare as well. The "thud of a ball and the wincing of my horse, who was behaving splendidly, assured me that he was wounded," he said of his mount, a "large, strong sorrel" farm horse he had taken just before the fight from the Worthington Farm. "After galloping a short distance, I felt him reeling, and, jumping off, the poor animal fell, rolling over on its side and lay mortally wounded."

Members of the Worthington family, including six-year-old Glenn Worthington, watched the action from the basement windows of the farmhouse. In his history of the battle written in the early 1930s, Glenn Worthington described McCausland's troops as "brave and experienced" men, who "were panic stricken by the deadly ambush into which they were unwittingly led."

When the panic set in, Worthington said, the CSA officers "tried in vain to rally the men. They swore at them and threatened them with sword and pistol, but for a while they would give no heed." The officers' curses and threats to kill the retreating cavalrymen unless they turned around, he said, "could be plainly heard by the occupants of the cellar, as the retreating force passed the house. Mrs. Worthington was moved to exclaim, 'Poor creatures, it means death to them either way.'"

The Worthingtons next saw "the blue pants of the pursuing Yankees" through the window. "The noise of the clamour and straining of these men in mortal combat could be distinctly heard as they passed," he said.

The Confederate troops then rallied and chased the Union men back to the fence line. Their retreat "was like that of men fleeing from a deadly peril," Worthington said, "panting aloud mingled with exclamations of pain and terror. More than one received his death wound close to the house and fell there to die, in the Worthington yard. Others were wounded thereabout and their moans could be heard by the family in the cellar of whom the writer was one."

Early later portrayed McCausland's disastrous actions in a positive light, sprinkled with postbattle untruths. As soon as McCausland crossed the Monocacy, Early wrote, "he dismounted his men, and advanced rapidly against the enemy's left flank, which he threw into confusion, and he came very near capturing a battery of artillery." If anything, the Union troops threw McCausland's men into confusion, and there was no artillery battery to be captured.

The Union troops, Early went on, "concentrated on him, and he was gradually forced back obstinately contesting the ground." That was true. Early's next statement—that "McCausland's movement" was "very brilliantly executed"—was not true. McCausland's first attack was the biggest tactical mistake made by a Confederate commander during the entire, day-long Battle of Monocacy.

His second attack, after rallying his troops, was well executed. McCausland moved out for a second time against Ricketts's men at around 2:30. This was preceded by artillery fire that Wallace described as "terrible." The Confederate guns "swept [Ricketts's] whole formation from flank to flank," Wallace said. Shells "seemed to be in flight from every direction, and the horrible hissing and screeching they made in going were more dreadful to the imagination than were their explosions in fact."

This time McCausland moved a few hundred yards to his right, surprising Ricketts and pushing his men back past Araby, the stately house on the Thomas Farm. The rebel troops "indulged in no foolishness," Glenn Worthington said. "They were firing as they went forward, and they were in a mood to avenge the loss of their many comrades who had fallen in the first charge."

Soldiers on both sides "were loading and firing," Worthington said. "It was load and fire, load and fire: Kill, kill, kill. . . ." The sun, he said, "was very hot. The shocks of wheat in the Thomas field are overthrown, and the sheaves scattered."

McCausland's men reached the Thomas House, and took possession of it. About twenty minutes later Wallace ordered Ricketts to send in the men of the Eighty-seventh Pennsylvania and the Fourteenth New Jersey. "The two regiments went forward in gallant style," Worthington said, "driving the rebels before them, occupying the Thomas house and establishing their lines. . . ."

McCausland's men were driven back to the Worthington Farm for a second time and then the skirmishing ended. About a hundred rebel troops were killed or wounded in the two engagements.

At 2:30, just about the time when McCausland made his second attack, Lew Wallace sent a telegram to the commanding officer of the Sixth Corps. It said: "Hurry up your troops; I am greatly in need of them. Fighting going on. The enemy outnumber us."

Skirmishing and artillery barrages continued intermittently all morning and into the afternoon across the river from Wallace's vantage point at Monocacy Junction. Wallace—writing decades later and with the benefit of hindsight—reported that during the heat of battle he would pause periodically to give thanks that his men held their positions because he realized that each passing hour was pivotal in the race to bring Grant's troops to Richmond to defend Washington.

At eleven in the morning, for example, Wallace said he "felt a thrill of gratification." He had gained four hours, he marveled. "Four hours, and Early still in Frederick, not one step nearer his great prize than when the dawn delivered the steeples of the town from the envelope of night!"

At noon, he said, the fighting had gone on for "five hours [against] my very able antagonist, General Early." Wallace counted the hours, he said, "beginning at seven o'clock, not once but many times, much as I fancy a miser counts his gold pieces."

At 2:45, he said, he placed the hours that had gone by "in the column of time against General Early, much as one hungry for a smoke puts pinches of tobacco in his pipe. Nearly eight hours now!" At 4:00, he said, "in my account of time against General Early [it made] the ninth hour—and how I turned the finding over and over in my mind!"

Earlier in the day, at around noontime, Ramseur had told Early that in the face of the steady fire coming from the area along the Georgetown Pike he did not want to risk a frontal assault. While Early pondered that, Wallace decided his best course of action would be to burn the covered wooden bridge spanning the Monocacy—at least, that is the way the novelist remembered it.

"My object," he said, "was to release the guard taking care of it, that they might join their regiments, then never in such need of every available man, and I could see but one way of relieving them."

Wallace said he had a captain set the bridge on fire, that he ordered his men to run off, and that he "lingered awhile to see that the flames did their work reliably." A "great smoke began to fill the sky and blot out the sun," he said. "Soon the floor timber fell into the water. The structure was then beyond salvation; whereupon we left it, and set out in return to our lookout above the block-house."

That's not exactly how another witness to the burning, nineteen-year-old Alfred Seelye Roe, a private in Company A of William Henry Seward Jr.'s Ninth New York Heavy Artillery, described what happened. At around 12:30, Roe said in his war memoir, Lt. L. B. Fish, the commander of Company B, which had been detached at 9:00 that morning by Seward to "hold the bridge at all hazards," received new orders to torch the structure.

"Members of the company procured sheaves of wheat from a nearby field, and placed them under the southeast corner of the roof of the structure," Roe said. "Pvt.s Alven N. Sova, Samuel R. Mack, and Sgt. Albert L. Smith participated in setting the fire, which wrapped the roof in flames like magic."

The bridge burning left about 275 Union troops—75 from the Tenth Vermont under the command of Lt. George Davis and about 200 mostly hundred days' men with Capt. Charles Brown of the First Potomac (Maryland) Home Brigade—stuck on the west side of the Monocacy River directly next to the railroad junction. They had been sent to that spot that morning to protect the bridge and the junction. Their main protection was a blockhouse that stood adjacent to the railroad tracks.

If the Union soldiers needed to escape the overwhelming Confederate force in front of them, Davis, Brown, and their men would have to wade back across the river or try to cross the forty-foot-high iron railroad bridge just to the north. That bridge's bed of railroad ties was made for trains, not human foot traffic.

Not long after the wooden bridge burned, Ramseur's men made their first charge. The Vermonters and Maryland men, against all odds, held off that attack until about 3:30 in the afternoon, after which Brown ceded command to Davis and led his men across the railroad bridge. Davis and his 75 Vermonters were left to fend off the Confederates for an additional hour, during which Ramseur's men kept coming at them in overwhelming numbers.

One of the units that charged was the Twenty-third North Carolina Infantry Regiment, commanded by Col. Charles C. Blacknall. The men of the Twenty-third "made a dash for the blockhouse," Capt. V. E. Turner later wrote, only to be "met by a hot enfilading fire from a line of battle in the railroad cut" and artillery support from across the river that "swept them with a raking fire."

Several North Carolinians were shot, including Colonel Blacknall. He "was stunned for the moment by an impact of a bullet on the head," Turner said, "which fortunately did not penetrate, and the regiment was driven back."

The attacks continued until the Confederate forces' overwhelming numbers won the day.

Near the end, Union private Daniel B. Freeman found himself alone facing yet another rebel charge. "Every time I raised my head above a certain rail, a bullet would hit the rail, embankment of dirt, or go whistling past," he wrote in 1897. "On and on I saw them come, and our troops were being withdrawn." Freeman looked for a break in the action and then made a dash for the railroad bridge.

"I heard Lieut. Wilke calling to me to come in quickly," he said. "As I crossed the pike I saw our reserve on the railroad bridge, and a little to the rear was Lieut. Wilke urging me on. As I neared the depot and looked back along the railroad, I saw one of my comrades under the [burned] Pike Bridge fighting a dozen Johnnies charging down the railroad toward him. He was riddled with lead."

Freeman "sped on," he said, "paying no heed to the orders to halt. I reached the bridge and, stepping from tie to tie, crossed over in safety under a crossfire from others of the enemy at the bend of the river a few rods below."

Davis "ordered us to fall in behind the railroad," Freeman said. "After getting across, I fired one or two shots more, and heard the order, 'Every man for himself!'"

George Davis and Alexander Scott of the Tenth Vermont later received the Medal of Honor, the nation's highest award for courage under fire, for their actions that day. Davis's citation reads: "While in command of a small force, held the approaches to two bridges against repeated assaults of superior numbers, thereby materially delaying Early's advance on Washington."

TEN

Short, Decisive, and Bloody

When the struggle was ended a crimsoned current ran toward the river.
—CSA MAJOR GENERAL JOHN BROWN GORDON

The third, final, and decisive attack by the Confederates on the left of the Union line began at around 3:30 that hot afternoon. This time McCausland took a backseat to one of the South's most experienced, capable, and bold fighting generals, John Brown Gordon.

The fearless Georgian led three brigades of Georgia, Louisiana, and Virginia infantry regiments under Gens. William Terry, Zebulon York, and Clement Evans back across the Worthington and Thomas Farms. The Southern troops marched right into the teeth of Col. William S. Truex's and Col. Mathew McClennan's brigades of Ricketts's division of battle-hardened troops from New York, Pennsylvania, Vermont, and New Jersey in the wheat fields of the Thomas Farm.

What ensued was a vicious, full-bore field battle that, before it was over, would turn the tide of the Battle of Monocacy in the Confederacy's favor.

Gordon's men had set out that morning from Frederick, marching along the Buckeystown Pike. When they arrived at the periphery of the skirmishing at Monocacy, the men took a break. "We were told to stack arms and rest, as we would not go into the fight," Pvt. John Worsham of the Twenty-first Virginia in Terry's brigade wrote in his memoir. "The men took off blankets, oilcloths, etc., and stretched them in fence corners, on muskets and rails, to make a shelter from the sun."

The troops encamped on a slight hill. They had a good view of Ramseur's men periodically skirmishing with Union troops along the Georgetown Pike in front of them and McCausland's cavalrymen's charges on the Worthington and Thomas Farms to their right.

"We made ourselves comfortable and lay down under the shelter provided," Worsham said, "to *look* at a battle, something we had never done."

After taking in the skirmishing and the artillery displays, the men saw a Confederate soldier gallop up to Gordon bearing an order from Breckinridge, his division commander. Within minutes the word came down the ranks to move out.

"We were called to attention," Worsham said, "the men taking down their blankets and oilcloths, and rolling them up to take with them. The order was given, 'Take arms!—no time now for blankets, but get into your places at once.' 'Right face! forward march!' was the command all down the line, and away we went."

The men, Worsham said, "thought we were to be spectators," and were not happy about the order to move out. Just as things "began to get interesting," he said, the troops were forced to "leave our blankets and oilcloths, articles we had captured in some former battle. The men seemed to dislike to lose those articles more than miss seeing the battle."

Gordon marched his men diagonally off to their right. They crossed the small Ballenger Creek, made a sharp left turn, crossed the railroad tracks, and then stood at the west bank of the Monocacy River behind the Worthington House close to the ford.

Gordon's men "stopped to remove their shoes before wading in the water," Glenn Worthington said, "but the order was given to jump in and not stop to remove shoes." General "Gordon sat on his horse at the ford and as we came up he said, 'Plunge right in, boys; no time for pulling off clothes,'" remembered I. G. Bradwell of the Sixty-first Georgia in Evans's regiment. When the men reached the other side of the river, Bradwell said, "we saw a number of dead horses lying scattered about the small field," a meadow on the Worthington Farm.

"Their feet were sodden," Glenn Worthington said of the Confederate soldiers, "but that made little matter considering the serious nature of the work before them."

Gordon had about 3,600 men. He sent Evans's seven Georgia regiments to the far right flank; Zebulon York's five Louisiana regiments (each of which had dwindled down to no larger than company-sized units) to the center; and Terry's decimated Virginia regiments to the left.

Gordon and his aides rode ahead of the men so they could see what faced them. Worsham painted an indelible picture of the Georgian on the field of battle: "There was Gordon—I shall recollect him to my dying day—not a man in sight—he was sitting on his horse as quietly as if nothing was going on, wearing his old red shirt, the sleeves pulled up a little, the only indication that he was ready for the fight."

Gordon wrote in his memoir that he found himself "separated from all other Confederate infantry, with the bristling front of Wallace's army before me." He saw that the fields of the Worthington and Thomas Farms were crisscrossed with "strong farm fences," which his men would be forced to climb in the heat of battle.

"Worse still," he said, "those fields were thickly studded with huge grain-stacks, which the harvesters had recently piled. They were so broad and high and close together that no line of battle could possibly be maintained while advancing through them."

Gordon said that he quickly realized—as did "every intelligent private in my command"—before the battle began that when the lead started flying "the battle line would be tangled and confused in the attempt to charge through these obstructions."

From the Union side, Ricketts's men—the Fourteenth New Jersey, Eighty-seventh and 138th Pennsylvania, the 151st and 106th New York, William Seward Jr.'s Ninth New York, the 110th, 122nd, and 126th Ohio Infantry, and elements of the Tenth Vermont—spotted the initial movement of Evans's Georgians "advancing on us, in two lines of battle, mostly on our left flank, at least a half a mile away, without a tree or obstruction to hide them," Cpl. Roderick A. Clark of the Fourteenth New Jersey's Company F recalled years later.

"It was certainly a grand sight as they advanced, in good order, with their numerous battle flags waving in the breeze."

Col. William Henry of the Tenth Vermont told his men to be patient and not let loose until the Confederate troops were close by. "Wait boys," he said, "don't fire until you see the C.S.A. on their waist belts and then give it to 'em."

As Evans's troops reached the first line of fences and began climbing over them, "they were met by a tempest of bullets," Gordon wrote, "and many of the brave fellows fell at the first volley."

"We could not see a Yankee on our part of the line during the whole advance," Pvt. George W. Nichols of the Sixty-first Georgia later wrote. "All that we could shoot at was the smoke of their guns, they were so well posted."

That first volley, J. G. Bradwell said, "wounded General Evans and Capt. [Eugene C.] Gordon, his aide-de-camp [and General Gordon's younger brother], and killed Col. [John H.] Lamar and Lt. Col. [James D.] Van Valkenburg, of the Sixty-first Georgia Regiment, and nearly every officer in the brigade and many of our best soldiers."

Lt. James Mincy of the regiment's Company D, who carried his unit's battle flag, took a bullet to the chest. "He had picked [the battle flag] up after the fifth man had been shot down while carrying it in this battle," Private Nichols remembered. "He had already been wounded at Manassas and was *severely* wounded at Gettysburg. Here he was shot through the left lung, the ball just missing his back bone. Bloody froth from his lungs would come out of his mouth and nose, and in the front and back where the ball passed through." Mincy, amazingly, survived.

Thomas Nichols, a foot soldier with the Sixty-first Georgia, was not so lucky. George W. Nichols (who was not related) came upon his fellow solider in the Thomas Farm wheat field "with his brains shot out."

When "I saw him, he was sitting up and wiping his brains from his temple with his hand," George Nichols said. "I went to try to render him some assistance and did so by giving him some water. He seemed to have some mind, for he said he wanted to go back to Virginia and get a horse and try to get home and never to cross the Potomac again. He lived twelve hours before death came to his relief."

Jubal Early, who generally had volumes to say about his military exploits, was uncharacteristically brief in his description of the fighting at Monocacy. Gordon's attack, he said in his autobiography, was made "in gallant style, and, with the aid" of Confederate artillery, "he threw the enemy into great confusion and forced him from his position."

Gordon's depiction of the battle is far more detailed and replete with the horrors of war. After Evans's brigade was cut to ribbons, Gordon sent in York and Terry's men. After climbing the fences and tearing many of them down so that their officers on horseback could ride through, the men then faced another big obstacle: the huge stacks of wheat.

"The whole field was in wheat," Glenn Worthington remembered, "and the ripened grain had been reaped and bound in sheaves, and was then standing in rows of shocks all over the field." In fact it was not all wheat. The battle also raged over fields planted in corn and at least one pasture.

"Around them and between them they pressed on, with no possibility of maintaining orderly alignment or of returning any effective fire," Gordon said. "Deadly missiles from Wallace's ranks were cutting down the line and company officers with their words of cheer to the men but half spoken."

Another factor that worked against the Confederate troops: the rude realization that they were not facing hundred days' men, as they had been told, but experienced Union veterans. "We did not know of the presence on the field of any portion of the Sixth Corps," Gordon told Wallace when the two met many years later. "They told us in Frederick you had only hundred-day men, a class of soldiers we had often met and cleaned out without firing a shot."

Gordon said that the battle became "one of those fights where success depends largely upon the prowess of the individual soldier." Nothing, he said, could "deter" his men.

"Neither the obstructions nor the leaden blast in their front could check them. The supreme test of their marvelous nerve and self-control now came." His troops made it through the "forest of malign wheat stacks" and had climbed a second row of fences. They now faced the first line of Union troops, "which stood firmly and was little hurt."

Gordon gave the command. "I ordered 'Forward!' and forward they went," he said. "I recall no charge of the war, except that of the 12th of May against Hancock [at Spotsylvania Courthouse], in which my brave fellows seemed so swayed by an enthusiasm which amounted almost to a martial delirium."

The "swell of the Southern yell rose high above the din of battle," he said, as his men "rushed upon the resolute Federals and hurled them back upon the second line." The Union line held. But the Confederates kept coming, and Gordon's men finally pushed Truex's brigade back to the Georgetown Pike on the Thomas Farm.

"Over the fence we went, the enemy running in all directions," Worsham wrote. "Up went our old yell all along the line of our division, and it was answered by our comrades on the other side of the river."

At the Georgetown Pike "Porter Wren of F Company received his fatal wound. He turned and managed to walk back to the fence, tried to get over it, but fell back—dead! Immediately on the brow of the hill I passed a Yankee colonel, laying on the ground dead."

The fighting, Gordon said, "was desperate and at close quarters. To and fro the battle swayed across [a] little stream, the dead and wounded of both sides mingling their blood in its waters." When the fighting ended, he said, "a crimsoned current ran toward the river. Nearly one half of my men and large numbers of the Federals fell there."

Maj. Peter Vredenburgh of the Fourteenth New Jersey said the din of battle was as severe "as I have ever heard from such a small force (say 400) of ours actually engaged and 7 or 8000 of the rebels advancing."

The Confederate batteries, Vredenburgh wrote in a July 12 letter, "enfiladed us and did excellent execution but our boys fought as if they were fighting for their own homes [and] literally mowed down the first two lines of the rebels who thought they only had to fight 100 day men."

When Vredenburgh reached the Thomas House, he said, the Confederate artillery "commenced shelling it and in less time than I write, it had sent a half a dozen shells into it." The New Jerseyan rushed into the house, where he had been a visitor two years earlier, to check on the Thomas family. He found them "in the cellar frightened to death."

The group included Mamie Tyler, the friend of the young Thomas woman who had been frantically searching for her fiancé at the Union camp. Tyler and the Thomas family members spent six long hours in the cellar, she told an interviewer in 1914. They were "hours of suspense, anxiety, and at times terror," Tyler said. "You can imagine how strange the sounds outside those walls, 'minie' balls slashing the shrubbery, while the larger missiles of the war's fearful instruments twisted huge limbs from the trees, leveled chimneys and tore out an angle of the house."

At about that time Frederick W. Wild, who served with Alexander's battery, came upon a scene behind the Union line that stayed with him for years. "I met a horrible sight," he said in his war memoir, "in passing by the improvised field hospital."

Wild saw wounded Union troops "all begrimed with blood, and black with dust and powder smoke." He saw "an assistant surgeon raise a piece of canvas to add one more to the bloody pile of amputated hands, feet, legs and arms." He saw, as Gordon did, "a small stream which we crossed [that] was red with human blood."

James B. Sheeran, the Catholic chaplain of the Fourteenth Louisiana, walked the Thomas Farm field after the battle. He came upon a line of dead

Union soldiers, he wrote in his journal, "lying in every direction and position, some on their sides, some on their faces, some on their backs with their eyes and mouths open, the burning sun beating up on them and their faces swarmed with flies."

In the heat of the battle, Gordon had his horse shot out from under him—a turn of events, he said, that easily could have been very costly. "In that vortex of fire my favorite battle-horse . . . , which had never hitherto been wounded, was struck by a Minié ball, and plunged and fell in the midst of my men, carrying me down with him," Gordon remembered.

"Ordinarily the killing of a horse in battle, though ridden by the commander, would scarcely be worth noting," he said, "but in this case it was serious. By his death I had been unhorsed in the very crisis of the battle. Many of my leading officers were killed or disabled. The chances for victory or defeat were at the moment so evenly balanced that a temporary halt or slight blunder might turn the scales."

The moment was saved, he said, when an unidentified "thoughtful officer" brought him another horse, he climbed on it, and led the troops to victory.

The Battle of Monocacy ended when Gordon's men, aided immeasurably by the overpowering, massed Confederate artillery, managed to flank the last of Ricketts's line of Union troops on the Georgetown Pike. When Lew Wallace saw through his binoculars that Gordon's troops had pushed Ricketts's men back to the Thomas farmhouse, he knew that the Confederates had won the day. "My hope, already faint, began shriveling up like a child's rubber balloon while the air goes whistling out through an unlucky rent," Wallace later wrote.

The Confederate big guns came alive again at that point, Wallace said, "reminding me of sleeping dogs responding to a kennel cry." The artillery, he said, drowned out the "crackle of the more distant skirmishers." Shells "searched the low places and the high everywhere behind, over, and in front of Ricketts."

Then the cannonballs homed in on Wallace's position on the hill above Monocacy Junction. "With a mighty *swishing*, comparable to nothing else I know of, though nearest the ragged tear of rushing locomotives, the missiles rent the air over our heads seemingly not more than an arm's length too high," Wallace wrote in his superheated, if accurate, prose.

Wallace looked back at Ricketts's line and saw Confederate battle flags "in display clear to the Thomas mansion, and they were so steady in their uprightness, so motionless, I knew their sharp steel shoes had been driven into the earth to *stay*."

Union major Peter Vredenburgh wrote three days later that he had "never seen such accurate [Confederate artillery] firing—every one of our captains was killed or wounded except one and he did not stay up [on his horse] or he would have been too." The wounded also included Lt. Col. Caldwell K. Hall, the Fourteenth New Jersey's commanding officer, who had been shot in the arm.

"It is queer," Vredenburgh said, "that I was not hit, for I was right up to the front most all the time and though several shells exploded so close that many men said they saw me killed, yet I did not get a scratch. Our Adjutant General [Lemuel F. Buckalew] who was mounted also, came up by me and was shot almost instantly in the leg and arm."

Turning back to the iron railroad bridge in front of him, Wallace took in the sight of the last of the Tenth Vermont men making their dash across the structure, with Ramseur's men at their heels. Wallace and his officers "were astonished, I never more so," he wrote, at witnessing the valor and abilities of the Vermonters.

"To judge this feat, and what courage was involved in it," Wallace reminded his readers, "the great steel structure was of goodly length, sixty or sixty-five yards at least, and unfloored, leaving passage over it afoot along cross-ties and girders." He also pointed out that the bridge was forty feet above water that was running "swiftly enough to make your head swim, and only too ready to catch a sufferer falling, and hide him in its remorseless, dark-brown current."

Not to mention the fact that Ramseur's men were in hot pursuit the entire time. Or, as Wallace put it: "Every step taken was under fire of antagonists pressing forward furious at sight of the possible escape."

More than a few Tenth Vermont men were killed on their mad dash across the iron bridge. "Now and then," Wallace wrote, "we could see one stop short, let go his musket, throw up his hands convulsively, and with a splash disappear in the stream beneath."

The man of many, many words said he "had not words to express" his admiration for the men of the Tenth Vermont. "Enough that I cannot now recall an incident of occurrence under my eyes more desperate in the undertaking, yet more successful in outcome," he wrote. "From every point of view it was heroism."

Looking back to his left at the Thomas Farm, Wallace saw that his position was hopeless. "The call was for prompt action," he wrote. "It was no longer mine to say when Ricketts and his stubborn regiments should be brought off. They must go now."

Wallace looked at his pocket watch. It was 4:20 in the afternoon.

"The shadows of the sun were stretching out, telling of evening and night, of the day almost gone," he wrote. "A sense of relief came to me: if the day was lost to me, General Early might not profit by it."

Wallace ordered his men to retreat, believing, he said to his dying day, that by holding up Early for nearly an entire day, he had reached his goal of giving Grant time to get experienced troops up from Petersburg to defend Washington and letting Halleck know, with no degree of uncertainty, that Early and his men would be moving on a beeline toward Washington.

"Measured by his designs, and the importance of time to my cause, my loss was scare worth a pinch of good old Scotch snuff," Wallace wrote, "and so thinking, I betook myself to action."

Those were the last words Lew Wallace wrote in his autobiography.

ELEVEN

---·◆·---

Aftermath

They overwhelmed me with numbers.
—LEW WALLACE

The way to Washington was opened for General Early's march.
—JOHN BROWN GORDON

At 5:15 that afternoon, about fifteen minutes after Wallace ordered his men to retreat, Pres. Abraham Lincoln sent a two-sentence telegram to John Garrett.

"What have you heard about battle at Monocacy to-day?" the president asked the railroad man. "We have nothing about it here except what you say."

Garrett's reply came at 7:15 that evening. He had just that minute received word from his telegraph operator in Monrovia, Garrett told the president, "that an aide of General Wallace has arrived there, who reports that 'our troops at Monocacy have given way, and that General Wallace has been badly defeated,' the bridge having been abandoned."

Grant learned the bad news from Halleck in a telegram sent by Old Brains at 9:00 p.m. "A dispatch, not signed by Lew Wallace, but approved by him to the newspaper press," Halleck said, "states that they had a severe battle to-day near Monocacy bridge, and that our troops were defeated and are now retreating on the Baltimore road."

Aside from delivering distressing news, Halleck couldn't resist also getting in a jibe at Wallace, telling Grant: "Knowing the character of the source, you can judge of its reliability."

A few hours later Wallace officially informed Halleck about the day's events. "I fought the enemy at Frederick Junction from 9 a.m till 5 p.m., when they overwhelmed me with numbers," Wallace wrote at 11:40 that night. "I am retreating with a foot-sore, battered, and half-demoralized column. Forces of the enemy at least 20,000. They do not seem to be pursuing."

As Garrett's telegram indicated, Wallace had indeed abandoned the bridge that the railroad man cared most about—the iron B&O railroad bridge. Wallace also abandoned the two other bridges (the mostly burned covered bridge and the Jug Bridge) over the Monocacy when he ordered his men to retreat. Ricketts's division, along with Wallace himself and his forces at Monocacy Junction, moved north on the east side of the river along narrow country lanes through heavily wooded and hilly terrain, heading for the Baltimore Pike. His aim was to return to Baltimore, his base of operations as head of the Union's Middle Atlantic Department. Ramseur's men came after them initially, pounding them with artillery.

The Union retreat, Wallace wrote in his first official after-action report the next day, "was accomplished with an extraordinary steadiness." The "men of the Third Division," he said, "were not whipped, but retired reluctantly, under my orders." The hundred days' men, he said, "straggled badly," but the veterans of the Sixth Corps marched "in perfect order, and covered the retreat."

It was during the initial retreat of Ricketts's Sixth corps men that Cpl. Alexander Scott of the Tenth Vermont performed the act that earned him the Medal of Honor. As the men fled through the woods behind Gambrill's Mill, the Tenth Vermont's two color bearers abandoned their flags. Scott picked both of them up off the ground and carried them to safety. Scott's Medal of Honor citation, dated September 28, 1897, reads: "Under a very heavy fire of the enemy saved the national flag of his regiment from capture."

Ramseur's men "were endeavoring to surround us, cut off our retreat," Frederick Wild of Alexander's artillery, which was forced to leave behind its only big gun, wrote in his memoir. The rebel soldiers, he said, "had to cross the river, and the bridge was burned during the fight, but they got there and were shelling us with twelve pounders."

The Union troops fled along "a narrow road with a small stream on one side and woods on the other," Wild wrote. The Confederate shells "burst with terrific noises into the woods, cutting off limbs and branches and the fragments humming at a fearful rate."

Despite the firing, the order came down for the men to walk, not run, toward the Baltimore Pike. "There was every incentive to get out of that hell," Wild said, "but the order was passed along the line to walk." Walking, he said, "was trying on the nerves, but we had to do it." The Union artillerymen "marched along just as sullenly as they had a few hours before, when we were firing at them."

They "crept along," as Wild put it, for "a mile or two." When the men reached the Baltimore Pike, they broke into a trot and headed east until they believed they were out of danger. By that time it was well past dark. The artillerymen then marched all night in the sticky July heat, arriving at Ellicott's Mills (the present-day Ellicott City, about forty miles from Monocacy and fifteen miles west of Baltimore) at 4:00 a.m. At noon on the following day, July 10, they marched home to Baltimore, which, Wild pointed out, "we had left but four days before."

Ramseur's men, led by the Twentieth North Carolina, had crossed the railroad bridge at around 4:30, and fanned out around Wallace's former headquarters. They captured the makeshift Union hospital at Gambrill's Mill and took the wounded prisoners. The rebels also rounded up several hundred ablebodied Union troops who had been trying to escape but were captured after they fell far behind Wallace's main force of troops heading east.

The Union troops under Gen. Erastus Tyler held the Jug Bridge at the northernmost point of the battle until about 6:00, when Rodes's men attacked in force. Wallace had ridden to the bridge shortly after giving his retreat order at 4:00 to impress upon Tyler the importance of his mission of covering the Union withdrawal.

Wallace said in his after-action report that he ordered "the bridge to be held at all hazards by the force then there until the enemy should be found in its rear, at least until the last regiment had cleared the country road by which the retreat was being effected."

At 6:00 Confederate infantrymen did get to Tyler's rear after fording the river. Then they started firing on Tyler's men from the woods on the east side of the Monocacy as well as from their positions on the other side of the river.

"I attempted to rally my men," Col. Allison Brown of the 149th Ohio wrote in his after-action report, "when the enemy brought his artillery to bear on the bridge and threw several shells, one of which struck it while my men were crossing it."

Brown managed to rally his inexperienced troops, who had been skirmishing on and off with Rodes's men all day, for a time. They exchanged fire with the Confederate forces, allowing most of Tyler's men to escape east.

The remaining Union troops kept up the fight until they "learned from citizens," as Brown put it, that most of Wallace's forces had quit fighting about two hours earlier. That state of affairs, along with renewed enemy fire, finally broke the Union troops' fighting will. Panic set in.

In the "considerable confusion," Brown said, "the men broke and threw away their guns and accouterments and attempted to save themselves" and "to break their guns to prevent them from falling into the enemy's hands."

The Ohio men ran for their lives, most of them heading east to join Wallace, Ricketts, and the rest of the Union forces on their way to Baltimore. "I joined the main body," Brown said, "at New Market about 8 p.m."

General Tyler, though, along with his staff, became separated from his men. They hid from Ramseur's troops in a heavily wooded area not far from the Jug Bridge for several hours, then spent the night in a nearby Union-friendly house. Word reached Wallace that Tyler was captured, but the general from Ohio had made his way safely into Frederick and eventually returned to Baltimore.

Wallace and his superiors in Washington also received a report—which also turned out to be false—that twenty-five-year-old Col. William Henry Seward was captured. Seward was wounded at the very end of the battle when his horse was hit by an artillery shell and fell on him. After that artillery blast, Seward managed to escape Early's men, but just barely.

"When the final order was given to retire, Colonel Seward had little more than a color guard left," his brother, Frederick William Seward, later wrote. "Crippled, and surrounded by the enemy, [he] escaped with great difficulty. With the help of one of his men, he reached a piece of woods, where mounting a mule, and using his pocket-handkerchief for a bridle, he succeeded, after a painful ride of many miles during the night, in rejoining the forces, which had then made a stand at Ellicott's Mills."

While nearly all of Wallace's small army fled east, three companies of Clendenin's Eighth Illinois Cavalry galloped south of Monocacy Junction to the village of Urbana a few miles away. Before long the Seventeenth Virginia Cavalry rode into Urbana, trying to find a route to the east so they could harass Wallace's retreating troops. Clendenin saw them coming, formed a line, and charged. During the fighting that ensued, Clendenin's men killed Maj. Frederick F. Smith of Company F, and Clendenin himself captured the Seventeenth Virginia's unit flag.

After prevailing in that skirmish, Clendenin and his men rode north and east, where late that night they met up with the rest of Wallace's retreating forces at New Market. Two of Clendenin's companies, though, split off and rode south toward Washington. In the next two days they would harass McCausland's cavalry during the Confederate march to Washington along the Georgetown Pike.

Clendenin's main force served as the rear guard for Wallace's final retreat to Baltimore by day and as pickets in front of the troops by night. "To say that the men and horses were exhausted when they reached Baltimore, after their week's campaign," the Eighth Illinois's unit historian later said, "would be superfluous."

Gordon's troops were as exhausted as Clendenin's men were. Most of the men in Ramseur's and Rodes's divisions, which never fully engaged Wallace at Monocacy, were close to exhaustion because they had fought on and off all day. That included Robert Johnston's brigade of North Carolina infantrymen, who did battle with the Tenth Vermont men in the triangular field at Monocacy Junction. Early did not order them to pursue Wallace. The reason he gave: chasing Wallace would have resulted in taking too many prisoners. As Early put it in his autobiography: "The pursuit was soon discontinued, as Wallace's entire force had taken the road towards Baltimore, and I did not desire prisoners."

But Early's men did wind up taking a significant number of Union prisoners, from six hundred to seven hundred of them, many from the Sixth Corps' Third Division and from the ranks of the Ohio hundred days' men. One of the first Union prisoners was W. G. Duckett, a hospital steward serving with the Ninth New York Heavy Artillery's Second Battalion. Duckett, heading back from Frederick to Monocacy Junction, happened upon a Confederate soldier wearing a Union uniform sometime between

7:00 and 8:00 in the morning. The rebel soldier promptly identified himself, took Duckett prisoner, and hauled him behind the Confederate lines for an audience with Brig. Gen. John Echols, who commanded a brigade under Breckinridge.

Echols "asked me to what command I belonged," Duckett later wrote.

When Duckett told Echols he was with the Sixth Corps, he replied: "Damn that Sixth Corps. We meet them wherever we go."

At which the bold Union hospital steward told the battle-hardened Echols, at least according to Duckett, "The whole corps will be here to welcome you with bloody hands to hospital graves."

Another Union prisoner, Alfred Roe, also of the Ninth New York Heavy Artillery, was captured near the end of the battle. As the young former schoolteacher fled the final Confederate charge, "shot of assorted sizes was falling about us," Roe wrote in his memoir. "The rebel artillery was giving us canister as fast as possible, and every few seconds some poor fellow would throw up his hands and go down. . . ."

As he made his way, Roe stopped to pick up an abandoned Union soldier's knapsack. "I helped myself to an excellent pair of stockings and to the tobacco," Roe wrote, "already wondering with what one of the boys I would trade that and for what," when he was "rudely interrupted."

"Look here, Yank," someone shouted.

"Looking upward, I found myself gazing into the mouth of a six-shooter held in the hand of a stalwart cavalryman," Roe remembered.

"Resistance was out of the question," Roe said. "I was too much surprised for anything else than unconditional surrender."

"Let's have your money—damned quick, too," the rebel cavalryman said.

Roe could come up with only thirty-five cents.

"Is that all you've got?"

"Every cent," Roe replied.

"Well, keep it, then. It isn't worth taking."

After that exchange, Roe was herded with the other Union prisoners to makeshift POW camps in Frederick and its environs, including some places near where the battle had raged. Duckett and a group of other prisoners, for example, spent the night in a cow pen near Gambrill's Mill at Monocacy Junction.

The next day the Union prisoners joined Early's men on the march to Washington. "We crossed over a part of the battlefield and saw many of our dead on the field and generally stripped of their clothing," Duckett remembered. Fellow prisoner Alfred Roe described seeing "the burning stubble of the battlefield—dotted here and there with the naked bodies of our comrades slain." Images of the smoldering battlefield would remain etched in Roe's mind for decades.

We "repeatedly [turned] to look at the scene," Roe remembered years later. "The river; the railroad, with its iron bridge; the turnpike bridge, now smoking in ruins; the big stone mill, near whose base I heard the last order, 'Elevate your pieces, men'; Colonel Thomas's house, around which the tide of battle had surged the day before, and lastly, the wheat field, whence on that 9th of July, we had seen two harvests gathered: the one in the early morn of wheat, the staff of life, and the other at eve of men, and the reaper thereof was Death."

Many of the captured Union men ended up weeks later in the brutal Confederate prison in Danville, Virginia, where they languished until the war ended eight months later. W. G. Duckett was among the few who avoided that fate. He stole away from his guards and hid for hours in the suffocating July heat underneath giant hay bales on a Maryland farm two days after his capture.

The Confederate wounded and many of the Union wounded were treated in temporary hospitals set up in houses and farm buildings on and around the Best, Thomas, and Worthington Farms. The Union wounded, the overwhelming majority of whom were left behind because of the hasty retreat, then were taken to the U.S. General Hospital in Frederick. Most of the Confederate wounded wound up in hospitals in Virginia. Those who were too severely hurt to travel were left behind in Frederick.

One of the many Confederate wounded, Lt. Col. John Hodges of the Ninth Louisiana, had taken a bullet in the upper arm, which shattered the bone and left him in excruciating pain. The members of the Worthington family found him in their backyard after they emerged from their cellar when the fighting ended. John Worthington told his two young sons, Glenn and Harry, to bring sheaves of wheat from the field to make a comfortable place for Hodges to rest and to put him up against a fence to shade him from the broiling sun.

"But so great was his suffering, so oppressively warm the weather that he fainted away just as he was being placed on his improvised bed," Glenn Worthington remembered years later. His father then gave Hodges a tablespoon of whiskey, "whereupon he soon revived." Later an ambulance took Hodges to Frederick.

"Whether his arm was amputated or not is not known," Glenn Worthington said, "but it is understood that he survived many years."

The Confederate troops buried their dead where they fell. Two days after the battle, Union troops returned to Monocacy and buried their dead. After the war many of the Union remains were dug up and taken to nearby Antietam National Cemetery. Many were unidentified. Those unknown Union remains of Monocacy, along with those of Union soldiers who perished at Antietam, South Mountain, and other actions in Maryland, lie in graves marked with small square stones. The remains of 4,776 Union identified and unknown dead are buried at that cemetery, which is administered by the National Park Service.

As for the CSA dead, the Ladies' Confederate Memorial Association of Frederick raised funds a few years after the war to disinter the remains from the battlefield and rebury them at historic Mount Olivet Cemetery in Frederick, the final resting place of Francis Scott Key and Barbara Frietschie, among many others. The identified bodies were buried in eighty-seven individual, marked graves. The bones of the others were interred in a mass grave. The marker at that grave reads: "This Stone Marks the Last Resting Place of 408 Confederate Soldiers Who Gave Their Lives in the Battle of Monocacy, July 9, 1864, Honor the Brave."

After Wallace and his surviving troops escaped, Early crossed the river and set up his headquarters at Monocacy Junction. It was late afternoon, probably around 5:30, and Early gave his men time off to rest. A few hours later, at sunset, the divisions set up camp on the former fields of battle, where they saw "the gastly forms" of "Yanks killed in the fight," North Carolina infantryman William Williams Stringfellow noted in his diary that night.

Gordon's men camped in the fields at the Thomas Farm. Terry's brigade set up "in an orchard near the road," Pvt. John Worsham of the Twenty-first Virginia wrote, "on the same ground over which we chased the enemy a few minutes before."

The field contained dead and wounded Union soldiers, many of the latter "groaning & shrieking with pain," as Confederate cavalryman Henry Trueheart put it in a letter home two weeks later. "The Yankee dead & wounded were very numerous," he said. "Saw them in almost every position—stiff & cold—& in the agonies of death. Saw them stripped of almost every rag of clothing mutilated by shot & shell in every part."

After the Confederate soldiers buried their own dead, he said, they "gathered up very many of their [Union] wounded and put them under the trees—gave them all the attention we could spare." Trueheart saw, he said, "wounded Yanks twenty-six hours after the fight lying in the broiling sun with no water & no attention & so concealed that they might never [be] found."

One of the wounded Yankees, Cpl. Roderick A. Clark of the Fourteenth New Jersey's F Company, was shot in the left ankle and shoulder on the Thomas Farm during Gordon's final charge. The first shot crushed his ankle joint; the second penetrated his right lung and remained lodged "just under the skin in my breast," Clark later said. It felt, he said, "about the size of a cannon-ball."

The young corporal passed out and came to with the battle still roaring and the "Rebels all around me," he said. When the battle ended a short time later, Clark said, he "was dying with thirst." Then "a big Rebel came along and pulled off my shoes; the pain caused was almost unbearable." When the big Confederate soldier saw that one of Clark's shoes had a bullet hole in it, "he threw it down with disgust," Clark said, "and said it was a d——n shame to spoil so good a shoe."

Soon another Confederate soldier took his watch, "telling me that I wouldn't be able to see what time it was very long." The soldier also took his empty wallet, knife, and picture album. "When I beseechingly held out my hand and asked for the latter," he said, "he threw it back with an oath."

Another soldier, "a mere boy," Clark said, came by, and Clark asked him for a drink of water. The boy soldier muttered that he would rather run a bayonet through Clark but relented and offered him his canteen, saying, "Drink. I will let you see that we are not as bad as you think us." Another Confederate soldier ministered to Clark throughout the night, giving him water and offering words of encouragement.

"All through the night the doctors of both sides and their assistants called on me frequently," Clark said. "The Rebel doctor gave me a drink of liquor, but the Union doctor had only a little for his own regiment." Later, that same doctor, with two stretcher-bearers, put Clark in an ambulance bound for Frederick.

He found no nurses in Frederick, but a young woman volunteer, Lizzie Ott, looked after him that day and for the next twelve weeks, "bringing me every delicacy that could be thought of, and sitting by me hour after hour, fanning me and speaking words of cheer." Roderick Clark and Lizzie Ott fell in love and married after the war.

Another wounded Union soldier asked John Worsham for some water.

He "stated he had had a canteen but one of our men had taken it from him," Worsham remembered. Feeling compassion for a brother in arms, Worsham went to a spring, filled one of his own canteens, and brought it to the enemy combatant.

"As I had two canteens, [I] gave him this one, and told him that in case some of our men wanted it, he must tell them what I had done for him, and I was sure none of our men would take it."

Worsham also carried "a full haversack," he said, that he had "taken from the body of a dead Yankee on the hill." He offered the wounded Union solider something to eat, but the man "said he had his own haversack, and it was full. He seemed to be very grateful for my little attention."

At the Thomas farmhouse the noncombatants who had waited out the battle in the cellar were taking care of a wounded Confederate soldier when the fighting ended. Not long after the last shots were fired, another rebel soldier entered the cellar to let everyone know the battle had been won.

"Imagine, if you can, the sight that greeted the eye when released from our prison cell," Mamie Tyler told a newspaper reporter fifty years later. We saw "the soft carpet of grass" around the house turned into a "resting place of dead and dying soldiers, a battlefield in verity and truth."

Many of the Confederate troops bathed off the grime of the day's fighting in the nearby Gambrill Mill pond. They then had something to eat. We "had plenty of Uncle Sam's coffee, sugar, pickled pork, and beans and crackers to do us several days," said one Confederate foot soldier. After their repast, the men slept under the stars on the former battlefield.

The officers of both sides that evening set about the grim job of counting the dead and wounded. "There was too many of them for us. Our company is pretty small now," Pvt. Charles McDowell of the Fourteenth New York Heavy Artillery wrote to his wife, Nancy, on July 18. "There is a good many killed and wounded and missing and I can't tell you who all was wounded now for there was a good many left on the battleground."

Ricketts's division, the general wrote in his after-action report, "lost heavily in killed, wounded, and missing." One of his regiments, the Fourteenth New Jersey, the "Monocacy Regiment," had come into the fight with some 350 men. When the smoke cleared, the Fourteenth New Jersey claimed the unwanted distinction of having suffered the highest casualties of any unit at the Battle of Monocacy. The count: 14 dead, 39 missing and presumed dead, 105 wounded. Of the Fourteenth New Jersey's fifteen officers who fought in the battle, four were killed and eight wounded. Two of the unit's seven men who carried the colors perished, and three were wounded.

On the Confederate side, Gordon's division, especially Evans's and York's brigades, which also took part in the heaviest fighting, suffered disproportionately large losses. Zebulon York's Consolidated Louisiana Brigade "lost fully one half of the men that went into the action, including several of our best officers," Capt. William J. Seymour wrote in his war memoir. Seymour called the conflict at Monocacy "one of the sharpest & most bloody fights of the war."

Clement A. Evans's Georgia brigade, which "had displayed such splendid courage in all the great battles of the war, was decimated by Gen. Lew Wallace's men," Pvt. E. G. Bradwell of the Sixty-first Georgia, a member of that unit, later wrote. The Union troops killed "nearly every officer in the brigade and many of our best soldiers."

"I regret to state that my loss was heavy in both officers and men," Gordon said in his after-action report, written on July 22. He reported that his losses amounted "in the aggregate" to 698. Historians who have studied the records believe that, altogether, all of Early's forces suffered between 700 and 800 killed and wounded at Monocacy.

Wallace's losses—which he called "heavy," illustrating "the obstinate valor of " his men—were just under 1,300 killed, wounded, and missing, out of some 5,800 who reported for duty on the morning of July 9. That included more than 700 killed and wounded and more than 500 missing in action among Ricketts's men, and 70 killed and wounded and 115 missing of Tyler's.

"The Confederate victory," John Brown Gordon wrote in his memoir, "was won at fearful cost and by practically a single division, but it was complete, and the way to Washington was opened for General Early's march."

Lew Wallace put his own spin on that assessment, writing in his August after-action report: "Orders have been given to collect the bodies of our dead in one burial ground on the battle-field, suitable for a monument upon which I propose to write, 'These men died to save the National Capital, and they did save it.' "

Those orders never were carried out, nor was Wallace's proposed monument erected.

Official Washington blamed Wallace for the defeat at Monocacy. The day after the battle, Sunday, July 10, the day when Early began his march on Washington, Henry Halleck relieved Lew Wallace of his command. General Order Number 228, issued by the War Department the following day, July 11, when Wallace was at Ellicott's Mills, assigned Maj. Gen. Edward O. C. Ord to command Wallace's Eighth Army Corps and "all of the troops in the Middle Department."

When Wallace received the news, he shot off a telegram to Secretary of War Stanton, asking: "Does General Ord report to me, or am I to understand that he relieves me from command of the department corps? If so, what am I to do?"

Stanton replied that Wallace was to report to Ord, but was to "remain in charge of the administration of the department," taking away his job and his power to issue orders with "respect to all military operations and movements."

The order came from Stanton, but Wallace blamed his old enemy Halleck for the demotion. The outcome at Monocacy, Wallace later told his son, gave Halleck "the opportunity he had looked for."

When Early moved his battle-weary men out early on Sunday morning, he left Ramseur's men at Monocacy temporarily with orders to do what John Garrett had feared: destroy the iron railroad bridge over the river. The Confederate troops torched and burned all the B&O Railroad buildings at the junction, including the agent's house, the telegraph office, and coal bins. But they failed to destroy the iron bridge.

"For want of sufficient powder," Kyd Douglas, who was on the scene, wrote, "the attempt was a failure. I noted a ludicrous attempt on the part of a battery of artillery to knock it to pieces with solid shot."

Five days later, on July 15, B&O repair crews came to Monocacy. It took them two days and some thirteen thousand dollars' worth of materials, but they repaired the bridge. The train carrying the crew then crossed the Monocacy, heading for Harpers Ferry.

TWELVE

Great Alarm in Baltimore and Washington

I infer they are marching on Washington.
—LEW WALLACE, JULY 10, 4:00 A.M.

When the citizens of New York City awoke on Sunday morning, July 10, 1864, and opened their copies of *The New York Times*, this is the front-page headline that screamed out to them:

THE INVASION.

HIGHLY IMPORTANT.

A BATTLE AT MONOCACY.

Our Forces Defeated with Severe Loss.

General Wallace Retreating to Baltimore.

The Enemy Twenty Thousand Strong.

General Tyler and Colonel Seward Captured.

GREAT EXCITEMENT IN BALTIMORE.

The Citizens All Ordered Under Arms.

Hagerstown Reoccupied by Our Cavalry.
THE WHEREABOUTS OF GENERAL HUNTER.

There was, indeed, "great excitement" in Baltimore. A small tide of Union-friendly Marylanders poured into the city as Baltimore residents prepared for what they thought would be an imminent attack by Confederate troops. Grant ordered General Ord that day to "press into service every able bodied man to defend the place." Union general Henry Hayes Lockwood in Baltimore put out the order that day for the streets of the city to be "barricaded as far as to prevent a dash of cavalry."

"The state of affairs in Baltimore is terrible," J. N. Du Barry, the general superintendent of the Northern Central Railway, said in a telegram sent from the city at 9:00 that morning.

"Bells were rung at 6:30 a.m. calling loyal citizens together to form companies to man fortifications for protection of the city," Du Barry said. Union scouts "report rebels within seven miles of Cockeysville" just north of the city.

When Alexander's Baltimore Artillery Battery arrived home from Monocacy that afternoon, the men "found the City in the greatest excitement," with "citizens and militia . . . under arms" awaiting a Confederate assault, Frederick W. Wild said in his 1912 memoir.

On the morning of July 9, after the firing had ended at Monocacy, Jubal Early had sent Bradley T. Johnson's 1,500-man-strong cavalry brigade to wreak havoc between Washington and Baltimore. Johnson's orders were to move toward the city of Baltimore, cut the railroad between that city and the North, then go south along the railroad to Washington, and head southeast to free the Confederate prisoners at Point Lookout. Johnson's men rampaged northward. They cut telegraph lines, burned railroad bridges, tore up railroad tracks, looted stores, farms, and homes, and spooked the local Union-supporting populace.

The "rebel cavalry" are "infesting" the area east of Frederick, a Union officer in nearby Gettysburg, Pennsylvania, informed Maj. Gen. Darius Couch, the Pennsylvania Department commanding officer, on July 10. The Confederate marauders, he said, are "stealing horses and creating much alarm."

Maj. Harry Gilmor, who formed the Confederate Maryland Cavalry soon after the war began, was particularly active in his—and his men's—backyard. "I was now where I knew pretty much every one, and very few did I meet but seemed glad to see me," Gilmor, twenty-six, wrote in his 1866 memoir. That included Gilmor's family. He took time out during the raid to spend several hours visiting with his mother, father, sisters, and brothers at Glen Ellen, the family estate in Baltimore County where he grew up.

That visit came the day after Gilmor, astride his "beautiful and very powerful black mare," and his 130 or so rough-around-the-edges men had raided the city of Westminster, Maryland, about twenty-five miles northwest of Baltimore on July 10. Expecting to face a Union force of 150 men, Gilmor took 20 men on horseback, counting on the element of surprise to oust the Union troops just before sunset.

"Trusting to their supposing we were well backed," Gilmor remembered, "we drew sabers, closed up the column, and charged through town at a fast gallop, with horses well in hand, and on the look-out for ambuscade in the cross streets." His men saw only a few Union troops, he said. When they did, his "boys gave an awful yell," which "brought every one to the doors and windows, and when a handkerchief was waved by a fair hand, the yelling was louder than ever."

The Union troops, he said, "took two or three rapid looks, fired two or three shots, and then made for Baltimore." At which point Gilmor's raiders seized the town's telegraph office and cut the lines. A courier arrived from Johnson with an order demanding 1,500 "suits of clothes, including boots and shoes" from the town. Before the town's mayor could assemble the dry goods, Johnson himself rode up, and Gilmor, he said, "persuaded him to say nothing more about it." Then Gilmor "shook hands with my friends, lots of whom I have there."

He then embarked on a burning and looting spree around the close-in northern and western suburbs of Reisterstown, Cockeysville, and Timonium. Gilmor, born and raised outside of Baltimore, Wild wrote, was "taking advantage of the situation, riding around the country taking horses and cattle and capturing Gen'l Franklin on a train going to Philadelphia."

Gilmor's men did, indeed, capture Union major general William Buel Franklin, a West Point grad, career army officer, and veteran of many Civil War battles. Franklin, who commanded a corps in the Union Department of the Gulf, had been convalescing at the Naval Academy Hospital in Annapolis after having been shot at the April 8 Battle of Mansfield in Louisiana.

Gilmor's men had taken over Magnolia Station, north of Baltimore near Joppatowne, early on Monday morning, July 11. When two passenger and mail trains rolled into the station at around 9:30 and 11:15 a.m., the Confederate cavalrymen stopped them, confiscated all the mail and the baggage, then set the trains on fire. The passengers included Franklin, who was wearing civilian clothes, and four other Union officers.

"Being informed that General Franklin was on board, I went into the car pointed out to me, and asked some officers who were in it which was General Franklin," Gilmor said in his memoir. "No reply. I then proceeded to examine each one's papers, and presently I came to him. He acknowledged himself to be the man." Impressed by Franklin's "blunt, though polite gentlemanly bearing," Gilmor nevertheless seized Franklin and the other officers and sent them under guard into the station's telegraph office.

The next day, after Gilmor had returned from a raiding party near Baltimore, he discovered that the wounded Union general had managed to escape at midnight while the men guarding him were sleeping. He swore at his men, he said, "with unusual energy," Gilmor wrote in his memoir. "Right glad I am that my pious friends were not there to *hear* me when I found that Franklin had indeed escaped. I fear they would have considered me somewhat *ruffled*."

Gilmor sent his men out to look for the Union general—"not, perhaps," he said, "so much because of his importance, as that I hated to be charged with carelessness." The men did not find Franklin.

Franklin, Early pointed out, "was permitted to escape, either by the carelessness or exhaustion of the guard placed over him, before I was informed of the capture."

A small party of First Maryland Cavalry under a Lieutenant Blackstone that day also burned the country home of Maryland governor Augustus W. Bradford in retaliation for Hunter's torching of Virginia governor Letcher's house in Lexington. While a squad of men carried out that task at dawn, the rest of Johnson's cavalrymen came upon several wagonloads of ice cream about to be loaded onto a Western Maryland Railroad car at Owings' Mills to be shipped to Baltimore. They did what any army would have done under the circumstances.

"The whole brigade engaged in feasting on this, to many, a novel luxury as the column moved along," Capt. George W. Booth of Johnson's staff remembered. "The men carried the ice cream "in their hats, in rubber blankets, in buckets and old tin cans," he wrote. "A number of the men from southwest Virginia were not familiar with this delicious food, but were not slow in becoming acquainted with its enticing properties and expressing themselves as being very much satisfied with the 'frozen vittles,' as they termed it."

Early again fooled the Union high command with Johnson's Baltimore feint. He never intended to invade Baltimore. His goal, as the Union high command was just then realizing, was to invade Washington.

Johnson's cavalry turned south and east during the afternoon of July 10 and headed toward Point Lookout. When they arrived at Beltsville, Maryland, just a few miles north of Washington in Prince George's County, Johnson's troops "found a large number of government mules, some seven hundred," Booth later wrote. "These would serve admirably to mount some of the prisoners, and they were at once driven up and secured."

Taking a rest before heading to Point Lookout, Johnson heard from Early the next day. Early's news: The raid on the prison camp would not take place.

"Johnson had burned the bridges over the Gunpowder [River], on the Harrisburg and Philadelphia roads, threatened Baltimore, and started for Point Lookout, but I sent an order for him to return," Early wrote in his autobiography.

He issued the order to abort the Point Lookout mission, Early said, because "the enemy had received notice of it in some way." John Brown Gordon, in his war memoir, saw it differently—which is not surprising in that Gordon, like many other Confederate officers, often disagreed sharply with Early.

Gordon believed that Early canceled the raid because he needed all the troops he could muster to threaten Washington. Gordon also said that communications and logistics problems played a role. "There was not time enough for the delicate and difficult task of communicating secretly with our prisoners so as to have them ready for prompt coöperation in overpowering the negro guards," Gordon wrote, "nor time for procuring the flotillas necessary silently to transport across the Potomac the forces who were to assault the fortress."

Another factor was that the newspapers in Richmond had learned of the impending raid and ran articles about it. When Jefferson Davis saw the newspaper accounts, he called off the naval portion of the raid, which would have provided weapons to the newly freed prisoners.

Even with the Confederate cavalry dispersing, things remained tense in Baltimore for at least another day. "The panic here is heavy and increasing," Lew Wallace reported to Halleck at around noon on Monday, July 11.

"It was an anxious Sunday throughout the North," Abraham Lincoln's secretaries John G. Nicolay and John Hay wrote twenty-five years later in their influential ten-volume biography of Lincoln. "Troops were everywhere called out, in various degrees of readiness. Every available man in Baltimore and Washington was put into the trenches."

Both Washington and Baltimore, Assistant Secretary of War Charles Dana reported from Washington to Grant that night, "are in a state of great excitement." Both cities, Dana said, "are filled with country people fleeing from the enemy. The damage to private property by the invaders is almost beyond description. Mills, workshops, and factories of every sort have been destroyed. From twenty-four to fifty miles of Baltimore and Ohio Railroad have been torn up."

The number of Confederate troops, Dana reported, "is everywhere stated from 20 to 30,000. The idea of cutting off their retreat would seem to be futile for there are plenty of fords & ferries now in their control where they can cross the Potomac & get off in spite of all our efforts to intercept them, long before our forces can be so concentrated as to be able to strike an effective blow."

Just before eleven on the night of July 10, Halleck, showing how desperate he was for troops, had sent an order to Maj. Gen. George Cadwalader, the Union commander of the District of Philadelphia.

"Send forward to Baltimore all convalescents fit for duty, armed or unarmed," Halleck said, "as may [be] most expeditious."

As Sunday, July 10, wore on, it began to dawn on many people that Early's aim was to attack Washington, not Baltimore. Lew Wallace figured as much. At 6:40 in the morning, Wallace sent a telegram to Lt. Col. Samuel B. Lawrence, the assistant adjutant-general at the Eighth Army's Middle Department Headquarters, with instructions to Lawrence to forward it to Old Brains Halleck in Washington. "I have been defeated," Wallace wrote en route from Ellicott's Mills to Baltimore. "The enemy are not pursuing me, from which I infer they are marching on Washington."

Wallace was correct. Early, as we have seen, did not pursue him. And he did begin his march on Washington at dawn on July 10, posing what would be by far the greatest Confederate threat to the nation's capital since the start of the Civil War.

———

Not all of Early's troops set out at dawn on what would turn out to be a broil-ingly hot and dusty day. Ramseur's division, as we have seen, stayed behind to try to destroy the railroad bridge, and didn't move out until after mid-night. McCausland's cavalry led the way down the Georgetown Pike—the present-day Route 355—on a straight line aimed at Washington, just forty miles away.

Gordon's men followed, after Gordon took time to bury the two highest-ranking officers in his division who had perished at Monocacy, Col. John H. Lamar and Lt. Col. James D. Van Valkenburg. "On the morning of July 10th we marched early, passing through Urbanna, Hyattstown, and Clarksburg" on Georgetown Pike, John Worsham wrote in his memoir.

"The day was a terribly hot one and the men straggled a great deal, al-though it was reported that the enemy's cavalry we left at Harper's Ferry were following us, and picking up all they could reach from our stragglers."

Those reports were exaggerated. Union general Albion Howe, who had taken over Sigel's men at Maryland Heights and had moved into Harpers Ferry after Early's men moved east, emulated Sigel's less-than-aggressiveness. Howe stayed put and did not come after Early from the rear. What Wor-sham referred to were the actions by Company C of the First Potomac Brigade, a group of Maryland Union cavalrymen under Col. Henry Cole. Cole's cavalry, which fought at Monocacy but did not retreat to Baltimore, had circled back west of Frederick, where they captured a few of Early's stragglers.

As the day wore on, however, McCausland's cavalry did run into more aggressive Union cavalrymen. The attackers: some five hundred mounted troops under Union major William H. Fry of the Sixteenth Pennsylvania Regiment, who rode out from Washington, along with Maj. Levi Wells's small contingent of Eighth Illinois Cavalry. McCausland's men faced "hard and severe skirmishing on the main road to Rockville," Lt. Thomas Feam-ster of the Fourteenth Virginia Cavalry wrote in his diary that day.

The Union cavalrymen kept up their attacks. They hit parts of the miles-long Confederate line of men and supply wagons, livestock, and Union pris-oners from the Battle of Monocacy intermittently the entire day.

At 4:00 Fry wired his commanding officer, Maj. Gen. Christopher C. Augur, who headed the Union Department of Washington: "My rear guard is fighting the enemy near Rockville." Fry suggested to Augur that the forts in northwest Washington "be strongly guarded as the enemy's column is a mile long."

At nightfall the Union cavalry attacks ended, and Early rested his weary men. They bedded down alongside the Georgetown Pike, strung out along a five-mile stretch from Gaithersburg to Rockville. In 1864 those small towns were barely in Washington, D.C.'s, outer orbit. Today Gaithersburg and Rockville are heavily populated, close-in commuter suburbs of the nation's capital.

Early arrived in Rockville at around eight o'clock. On the steaming Sunday of July 10, 1864, he and his men had marched more than twenty miles, the day after battling through the intense, all-day fight at Monocacy—not to mention having spent the last three weeks nearly constantly on the go.

After arriving in Rockville, Early "occupied the Clerk's office of the Court-house for a few minutes, in conversation with his officers," a *Baltimore Sun* correspondent wrote a few days later. The correspondent described the wiry, forty-seven-year-old Early as "a stout man, of at least sixty years, with gray hair and beard, red face, and very round shouldered."

His uniform, the reporter said, "was of the commonest character, and had been much soiled and worn—his hat, for instance, being a high crowned drab slouch, adorned with a single dusty black feather." Early "appeared to be all the time in deep, abstracted study."

Word of Early's army closing in on Washington had reached the capital that morning. At 9:20 President Lincoln wired former mayor Thomas Swann and other prominent leaders in Baltimore, evidently in response to their request to send troops north from Washington. "By latest accounts, the enemy is moving on Washington," Lincoln said. "I have not a single soldier but who is being disposed by the military for the best protection of all."

The Confederate troops, the president said, "cannot fly to either place. Let us be vigilant, but keep cool. I hope neither Baltimore nor Washington will be taken."

Grant reported to Meade early that morning that "great alarm" was being "felt in Washington" following Wallace's having been "whipped at Monocacy bridge, and driven back in great confusion."

Although Grant did not say so then, or in his memoirs, it appears as though some members of his staff in his camp at City Point also were alarmed about the situation. "The war fever is once more at high heat," Capt. Ely S. Parker, Grant's military secretary, wrote in a letter the day before, on Saturday, July 9, from City Point.

"The news from Washington and other northern points have considerably agitated the even tenor of our camp. We cannot tell with any degree of certainty how large a force the rebs have up there. Nor can we guess to what extent Lee has diminished his forces in our immediate front."

Grant's aide-de-camp, Gen. Horace Porter, said in his war memoir that "directions for executing the plans for checkmating" Early's move on Washington "fully occupied every one on duty" at Grant's headquarters after July 4 when Grant received "definite information" about what Early was up to.

That news brought about "several days of serious perplexity and annoyance at [Grant's] headquarters," Porter said. Twice "the wires of the telegraph line were broken, and important messages between Washington and City Point had to be sent a great part of the way by steamboat," Porter remembered. A rumor, soon proved false, that Lee had sent an additional corps to help Early, Porter said, produced "some anxiety."

Porter described Grant himself as resolute and in complete control during the entire episode. "The general had occupied himself continually during this anxious and exciting period in giving specific instructions by wire and messengers to meet the constantly changing conditions which were taking place from day to day and hour to hour," he said, "and no dispatches were ever of greater importance than those which were sent from headquarters at this time."

Grant's "powers of concentration of thought were often shown by the circumstances under which he wrote," Porter said. "Nothing that went on around him, upon the field or in his quarters, could distract his attention or interrupt him. Sometimes when his tent was filled with officers, talking and laughing at the top of their voices, he would turn to his table and write the most important communications."

Another eyewitness at City Point, *Boston Journal* war correspondent Charles Carleton Coffin, painted a more sanguine picture of the mood there on the day he visited, Sunday, July 10. "There was no commotion at General Grant's head-quarters," Coffin wrote in 1866. "The chief quartermaster was looking over his reports. The clerks were at their regular work."

When Coffin arrived that morning, Grant himself "was out, walking leisurely about, with his thumbs in the arm-holes of his vest, smoking his cigar so quiet and apparently unconcerned, that, had it not been for the three stars on his shoulders, a stranger would have passed him without a thought of his being the man who was playing the deepest game of war in modern times."

The members of Grant's staff, Coffin reported, "were not in the least excited." Col. Theodore Shelton "Joe" Bowers, whom Coffin found "attending to the daily routine," told the reporter: "They are having a little scare at Washington and in the North. It will do them good."

When Coffin asked Bowers, Grant's adjutant general, how many Confederate troops were in Maryland, he replied: "Somewhere about twenty-five thousand—possibly thirty." Early, Bowers said, "has raked and scraped all the troops possible which are outside Richmond. . . . It will not affect operations here. Lee undoubtedly expected to send Grant post-haste to Washington; but the siege will go on."

Coffin noticed a map on Bowers's wall that contained the "various gauges of the railroads" throughout the South. "Grant came in," Coffin said, looked at the map, "said, 'Good morning,' and went out for another stroll about the grounds, thinking all the while."

The alarm in Washington and Baltimore and whatever the mood was at City Point contrasted with rejoicing in the South—and wild rumors of Confederate triumphs—when word arrived of Early's victory at Monocacy and his army's march to Baltimore and Washington. There were breathless reports that the Union troops put up a feeble fight at Monocacy and fled in terror; that Baltimore fell to the Confederate troops; even that Early had taken Washington. Richmond "is in great excitement and joy," J. B. Jones, a clerk in the Confederate War Department in Richmond, wrote in his diary on July 13.

"Gen. Early has gained a victory in Maryland, near Frederick, defeating Gen. Wallace, capturing Gen. Tyler and Col. Seward (son of the secretary), besides many prisoners," Jones wrote. "The slaughter was great, and the pursuit of the routed army was toward Baltimore." Grant, Jones said, "is certainly sending away troops."

The people of Richmond remained excited through the following day, July 14. "The excitement on the news of our successes in Maryland is intense," Jones wrote in his diary that day, "and a belief prevails that great results will grow out of this invasion of the country held by the enemy. Twice before but little if any benefit resulted from crossing the Potomac."

Surgeon James Holloway, writing to his wife in Mississippi that day, described Richmond as a city "wild with excitement over the Northern news." Washington and Baltimore, he said, are "threatened and the greatest terror prevails. Would that every hamlet in the North could be made to feel this terror."

Events, he said the next day, "are so thrilling and occur in such rapid succession that I have presumably to hold my breath, so great is the suspense."

The *Richmond Daily Whig* could not help but crow about Early's victory. "Silently a body of troops, which the Yankees say is large, at least it is too large for any force they have ready to meet it, is hurled into Maryland," a July 14 editorial noted, "and after having destroyed railroad bridges, viaducts, commissary stores, and in fact everything they pleased, are now threatening the Federal Capital and the City of Baltimore."

Grant, the newspaper said, "is asleep or stupefied by Virginia juleps in front of Petersburg, waiting for something to turn up that will save him from the disgrace he merits."

One thing that turned up was a telegram that Lincoln sent to Grant at 2:00 on the afternoon of July 10 suggesting that his top general leave City Point outside Richmond and come to Washington to lead the defense of the city. Speaking of the "present emergency," Lincoln told Grant that Halleck had notified him that he had "absolutely no force here fit to go to the field."

Halleck reported, Lincoln said, that the hundred days' men and recuperating wounded soldiers in Washington, known as the Veteran Reserve Corps, "can defend Washington," but "scarcely Baltimore." In addition to those men, Lincoln said, "there are about eight thousand not very reliable, under Howe at Harper's Ferry, with Hunter approaching that point very slowly with what number I suppose you know better than I."

Wallace, Lincoln said, "was so badly beaten yesterday at Monocacy that what is left can attempt no more than to defend Baltimore." What we "can get from Penn. & N.Y.," Lincoln said, "will scarcely be worth counting, I fear."

He went on to ask Grant to bring troops to Washington "and make a vigorous effort to destroy the enemy's force in this vicinity." I think, Lincoln concluded, "there is really a fair chance to do this if the movement is prompt."

Lincoln, though, as was his wont, stopped short of issuing Grant a direct order to come north to defend the nation's capital. "This is what I think," he told Grant, "and is not an order."

At least one member of Grant's staff, Lt. Col. Cyrus Ballou Comstock (West Point Class of 1855), thought Lincoln was right in asking Grant to come to the nation's capital. "Did my best to get general [Grant] to go to Washington & catch Early," Comstock wrote in his diary that night. "There seems to be no head there. Think he does not wish to go till he goes from Richmond."

Comstock was correct. Grant—who on July 9 had wired Halleck saying that if Lincoln thought it "advisable that" he "should go to Washington in person," he would "start in an hour after receiving notice leaving everything here on the defensive—changed his mind the next day and declined to leave City Point."

"I think on reflection it would have a bad effect for me to leave here," Grant cabled Lincoln at 10:30 on the night of July 10. The commanding Union general said that he had faith in the Union commanders around Washington, including the hapless Hunter, and that his presence there "would do no good."

At 3:30 that afternoon Old Brains Halleck had given Grant an earful about how woefully underdefended Washington was. "We have no forces here for the field," Halleck said.

Halleck reminded Grant—as if he needed to be reminded—that virtually all of the able-bodied troops that had been posted to Washington had been "sent to you long ago." All that was left, Halleck told his commanding general, "are raw militia, invalids, convalescents from the hospitals, a few dismounted batteries, and the dismounted and disorganized cavalry sent up from the James River."

Halleck said that that motley crew probably could defend the "immense depots of stores and the line of intrenchments" around Washington. But, he said, "what can we do with such forces in the field against a column of 20,000 veterans?"

Half of the troops in Washington, Halleck said, "cannot march at all. The only men fit for the field was Ricketts's division, which has been defeated and badly cut up under Wallace."

THIRTEEN

Sunday, July 10: A Strange Sabbath Day

[Washington,] seriously menaced, was incapable of self-defence—that much was clear.

—LEW WALLACE

Washington, D.C., became the nation's capital in July of 1790 when Pres. George Washington chose the site, which he carved out of territory belonging to the states of Maryland and Virginia. Washington, which the first president modestly called "Federal City," grew into the nation's fourteenth largest city with a population of some 61,000 on the eve of the Civil War in 1860.

By July of 1864, when Early's troops began their march on Washington, the population had mushroomed as the city took on the color of a national capital in wartime. In the previous three years tens of thousands of government workers, legislators, lobbyists, journalists, and others had flocked to the national capital. As the war dragged on and casualties mounted, Washington's hospitals overflowed with wounded recuperating Union soldiers. By 1870 the city's population had swollen to nearly 110,000. Many of the wounded soldiers had to be housed in public buildings, including the ornate U.S. Patent Office, City Hall, classroom buildings at Georgetown University, and in the Capitol itself. Many private homes, churches, schools, and hotels also served as makeshift medical facilities for the sick and wounded.

Nurses, doctors, and other caregivers, including family members of the wounded, flocked to the city to care for the growing number of convalescing soldiers. Those who ministered to the wounded included hundreds of compassionate people whose names are lost to history, as well as some who became national figures. The latter group included Dorothea Dix (1802–87), the famed mental health facilities reformer; Clara Barton (1821–1912), the founder of the American Red Cross; the novelist Louisa May Alcott (1832–88), the author of *Little Women*; and the acclaimed poet Walt Whitman (1819–92).

Whitman arrived in Washington from his home in Brooklyn in December of 1862, searching for his brother George, who had been severely wounded serving with the Fifty-first New York Infantry at the Battle of Fredericksburg. The forty-three-year-old poet found his brother on December 29 at a camp in Falmouth, Virginia, completely recovered from his wounds. Whitman, whose classic work, *Leaves of Grass*, was published in 1855, volunteered to accompany other wounded soldiers from Falmouth, about fifty miles south of Washington, to the capital. When he arrived, Whitman decided to stay. He spent the rest of the war ministering to the needs of the sick and wounded.

Washington's Civil War hospitals "are not like other hospitals," Whitman wrote in a February 26, 1863, dispatch to *The New York Times*. "By far the greatest proportion . . . of the patients are American young men, intelligent, of independent spirit, tender feelings, used to a hardy and healthy life; largely the farmers are represented by their sons—largely the mechanics and workingmen of the cities."

Walt Whitman found work in the Army Paymaster's Office and penned freelance newspaper articles. But his main occupation was visiting soldiers. He engaged them in conversations. He helped them write letters home, giving them writing paper, envelopes, stamps, and pens and pencils. He brought them food such as strawberry jam, oranges, apples, and pickles, and supplies such as books, newspapers, and chewing tobacco.

Whitman estimated that from late 1862 to February of 1866 he made "600 visits or tours" and went "among from some 80,000 to 100,000 of the wounded and sick, as sustainer of spirit and body in some degree, in time of need."

His visits varied, he said, "from an hour or two, to all day or night; for with dear or critical cases I always watc'd all night." Sometimes, he said, he "took up my quarters in the Hospital, and slept or watch'd there several nights in succession. Those three years I consider the greatest privilege and satisfaction, (with all their feverish excitements and physical deprivations and lamentable sights,) and, of course, the most profound lesson and reminiscence, of my life."

During the war Washington had genteel neighborhoods and a staid, bureaucratic federal government enclave. But the city also had a profusion of barrooms and brothels and several crime-ridden neighborhoods. Many saw the capital "as a sink of iniquity, where weak-minded bachelors were exposed to the temptations of saloons, gambling hells and light women," as Margaret Leech put it in *Reveille in Washington*, her renowned portrait of the city during the Civil War.

The city also sat directly across the Potomac River from the then Confederate state of Virginia, and just 105 miles from Richmond, the capital of the Confederacy. There were plenty of Confederate sympathizers in the neighboring state of Maryland, as we have seen. The District of Columbia itself, while a haven for freed blacks, also was the home of slave-owning whites, and had the ambience of a Southern city.

When it became apparent early in 1861 that war soon would break out, government officials began planning for an attack on the capital. Lt. Gen. Winfield Scott, who commanded the Union army, ordered army regulars to move into the city beginning in February. More troops arrived in April after the war started. By the end of April, some eleven thousand Union troops had come to protect Washington. They set up makeshift camps in nearly every available space, including the Treasury Building, the Patent Office, City Hall, the Navy Yard, and in the U.S. Capitol Building.

In late May many of those troops went to work building a series of forts and interconnected rifle pits and trenches—what would become known as the Civil War Defenses of Washington. The big impetus for building the defenses came late in July of 1861, following the unexpected and disastrous Union defeat at the first Battle of Manassas in Virginia. That shocking Union loss, also known as the Battle of Bull Run, took place just thirty miles southwest of Washington, raising new fears in the capital about an impending Confederate invasion.

The stunning defeat at Manassas "left no longer room to doubt" the need for "a chain of fortifications" around Washington, Gen. John G. Barnard, the Army of the Potomac's chief engineer, said late in 1861. "With our army too demoralized and too weak in numbers to act effectually in the open field against the invading enemy, nothing but the protection of defensive works could give any degree of security."

Maj. Gen. George B. McClellan—West Point Class of 1846, Mexican War hero, and the former chief engineer of the Illinois Central Railroad—took over as commander of the Army of the Potomac on July 27, just after First Manassas. He immediately ordered that the fort and fortification building effort be stepped up significantly. McClellan gave the job to Bernard, who had fought at Manassas.

Construction continued at a feverish pace all summer under Bernard's day-to-day supervision. He oversaw the construction of earthen forts, many of them two- or three-sided structures called lunettes and based on seventeenth-century French field forts. The bigger forts also contained artillery emplacements, wooden blockhouses, infantry parapets, stockades, and so-called defensive barracks. Most of the forts were built on hills and high ground, and all were connected by rifle pits and trenches, along with barricades across the bridges of the Potomac and Anacostia Rivers. Union troops and hired laborers did the work.

By the end of 1861, Bernard reported, the "aggregate perimeter" of all the works stretched nearly nine miles and the forts were armed with 480 pieces of artillery. By the end of 1862, fifty-three forts and twenty-two artillery batteries encircled virtually the entire city in a horseshoe shape from the northwest banks of the Potomac all the way around to the river's shoreline opposite the city of Alexandria, Virginia. Bernard built forts on the Virginia side of the Potomac, as well, stretching from Fort Marcy in the west to Alexandria in the southeast.

By July of 1864 the defenses of Washington were complete. They consisted of a formidable interconnected, thirty-seven-mile-long string of sixty-eight forts and nearly one hundred open artillery batteries and blockhouses, linked together by some twenty miles of contiguous rifle pits and trenches.

The northernmost structure, Fort Stevens, guarded the entrance to the city at the Seventh Street Pike, the main thoroughfare from the north. It originally was named Fort Massachusetts by the men of the Thirty-seventh Massachusetts Regiment, who began building it in October of 1861. The fort was enlarged in 1862 and 1863, primarily by the men of the Eleventh Vermont Regiment, and its name changed on April 1, 1863, to honor Maj. Gen. Isaac Ingalls Stevens of the Seventy-ninth New York Highlanders.

A view of a parapet at Fort Stevens, the northernmost of the thirty-seven-mile-long string of sixty-eight forts and fortifications that made up the defenses of Washington. *Credit: The Library of Congress*

The Massachusetts-born Isaac Stevens, West Point Class of 1839, was a former governor of the territory of Washington, and a two-term (1857–61) member of Congress. He died on September 1, 1862, at the Battle of Chantilly in Virginia, a bloody engagement in which Jubal Early also took part.

Fort Stevens was built in a section of Northwest Washington where the city's first free blacks had settled in the 1820s. Known then as Vinegar Hill—and today as Brightwood—the section was home to many black landowners, most of whom were women and many of whom operated small subsistence farms.

To build Fort Stevens, the U.S. military requisitioned land owned by Emory Methodist Church—which still stands today on Georgia Avenue—as well as property owned by Elizabeth Thomas, a free black woman. According to the then forty-year-old Thomas, known as "Aunt Betty," the army confiscated her house and tore it down without her permission—and without compensating her.

"The soldiers camped here at this time were mostly German," Thomas said. "I could not understand them, not even the officers, but when they began taking out my furniture and tearing down our house, I understood." Hours later, she said, she was sitting under a sycamore tree "with what furniture I had left around me. I was crying, as was my six-months-old child, which I had in my arms, when a tall, slender man, dressed in black, came up and said to me, 'It is hard, but you shall reap a great reward.' "

That tall, slender man, Thomas said, "was President Lincoln, and had he lived I know the claim for my losses would have been paid."

Thomas never received her compensation, but lived at Fort Stevens until the day she died in 1917.

Whether or not the Lincoln story is apocryphal, the fact remains that Fort Stevens, when it was finished, included several structures and featured a vast, 375-yard perimeter overlooking mostly open terrain. Rifle trenches surrounded the front of the three-sided lunette fort. Inside, the fort had nineteen artillery pieces, including ten twenty-four-pound cannons. The Fort Stevens complex also included a stockade, a blockhouse, barracks, and officers' quarters, as well as two bomb-proof magazines for the storage of ordnance.

During the war, several Union units from Massachusetts, Vermont, New York, Rhode Island, Maine, and Ohio camped in and around Fort Stevens. Among the Ohioans who spent time at Fort Stevens in 1864 were Pvt. George K. Nash of the 150th Ohio National Guard, who went on to become governor of Ohio from 1900–1904, and 2nd Lt. Marcus Alonzo Hanna. After the war, the lieutenant, then known as Mark Hanna, became a powerful Ohio industrialist. As the campaign manager for William McKinley in 1896, Hanna is credited with inventing the modern political campaign. He later served as a U.S. senator from Ohio from 1897 to 1904.

By the summer of 1864, everyone agreed that the physical earthwork defenses were, metaphorically speaking, rock solid. The big problem, as Halleck had reminded Grant, was that Washington was virtually bereft of able-bodied Union soldiers; nearly all of them had been sent to Grant.

Halleck had sent Bernard's aide-de-camp, Lt. Col. Barton Alexander, to inspect the forts along the Potomac River on July 5, the day that Early's men had crossed that same river into Maryland some sixty miles north at Shepherdstown. Alexander's report to Halleck the next day was less than encouraging.

Alexander (West Point Class of 1842), an engineer, found one lieutenant and sixty-three Veteran Reserve Corps men defending Washington

Credit: Liz Weaver

at Chain Bridge, the northernmost entry point over the Potomac into the city. Only one man, a Private Spink of the 147th Ohio National Guard, manned the artillery batteries on the Washington side of the bridge.

Acting Ordnance Sergeant Spink, Alexander reported, "knows nothing about ordnance or artillery. In fact no one at the bridge knows how to load the guns." Spinks's job, he said, was cleaning the guns, "airing" the ammunition, and sweeping the platform.

New York Herald war correspondent Sylvanus Cadwallader, who had arrived in Washington at 10:00 on Monday morning July 11 and then toured the defenses, had a similar assessment of the entire defenses. "The armament was insufficient, the ordnance supplies limited, and all of [the forts] were so weakly manned as to make any protracted resistance impossible," he wrote in his memoir.

Washington's defenders that day amounted to a relative handful of newly recruited hundred days' men and troops of the Veteran Reserve Corps, a group of soldiers Lew Wallace called "invalids and convalescents."

The Veteran Reserve Corps began life on March 20, 1863, with the inauspicious name of the Invalid Corps. Formalizing a practice that had begun a year earlier, the Invalid Corps consisted of "experienced soldiers who were simply disabled for the march," as Capt. J. W. De Forest, a Veteran Reserve Corps officer, put it in an official postwar report.

The corps was organized into detachments under the aegis of officers acting as military commanders. The men served in Northern cities as military policemen, and as nurses, cooks, hospital attendants, security guards, guards at Union prison camps (including Point Lookout), as clerical workers in recruiting centers and army camps, and in other noncombat, behind-the-lines capacities.

In contrast to the dark blue Union uniform, the Invalid Corps men sported a special uniform featuring a sky blue jacket for enlisted men and sky blue frock coat and trousers for officers. The uniforms turned out not to be a good idea.

"The men did not like to be distinguished from their comrades by a peculiar costume," Captain De Forest pointed out. "They wanted to keep the dark-blue blouse and dress coat in which they had learned their profession and received their honorable disabilities."

De Forest also took note of another problem caused by the distinctive uniforms: the "inevitable jealousy between field and garrison regiments, which ripened into something like bitterness between the soldiers of the Invalid Corps and the ranks in which they had so lately marched and fought."

The old uniforms went. So, too, did the corps' name. On March 18, 1864, the army's Adjutant General's Office ordered that the name "Invalid Corps" be replaced by the "Veteran Reserve Corps" and the newly named organization be divided into regiments.

The main reason for the name change, De Forest said, was "the bitter prejudice of field troops," which resulted in "a multitude of sarcasms and jeers that made the title of Invalid Corps a burden. Men frequently begged to be sent back to their old regiments in the field rather than remain in garrison at the price of being called invalids."

The experiences of Pvt. Alfred Bellard of the Fifth New Jersey Volunteer

Infantry typify those of the average Veteran Reserve Corps trooper in the spring and summer of 1864. Bellard had joined the Union army in August 1861 when he was eighteen and fought in several big battles, including Second Manassas and Fredericksburg.

Bellard was shot in the right leg at the Battle of Chancellorsville in May 1863, a severe wound that put him out of action. After nearly six months of recuperation, he joined the Veteran Reserve Corps in December, and spent the rest of the war in the unit's Twelfth Regiment.

Bellard's regiment came to Washington early in 1864. Its assignment: escorting captured Union deserters to prisons in the city and serving as military policemen. The Twelfth's main mission was trying to keep order among the Union soldiers as they took part in the pleasures of Washington's saloons, theaters, and houses of prostitution.

On July 8 the men of the Twelfth VRC Regiment were each issued thirty-five rounds of ammunition. The next day they reported to brigade headquarters, where they "were ordered to sleep in our uniforms and be ready to move in five minutes," the young New Jersey man wrote in his war journal.

On Sunday, July 10, the order came. The men left their camp at 7:00 a.m., and "forming a brigade on Pen. Ave. we marched through Georgetown and Tennallytown [the neighborhood north of Georgetown now known as Tenleytown] with bands playing and colors flying," Bellard said, "the streets being thronged with people to see us off."

The reserve men marched to Fort Reno, located just off present-day Nebraska Avenue, Northwest. The men of the 119th Pennsylvania had built it in the winter of 1861. Fort Reno stood (it no longer exists) at the highest point in Washington and not far from the then Georgetown Pike—the road Early's men were marching on that very day.

Fort Reno, less than a mile west of Fort Stevens, was the most heavily fortified of all of the forts ringing Washington. It was armed with a dozen big artillery pieces and had been designed to be defended by some three thousand men.

As was the case with all the other forts in Washington on July 10, 1864, though, Reno was seriously undermanned. That is why Bellard and the other Veteran Reserve Corps men marched there that morning and deployed in the rifle pits of Reno's advanced battery.

"Orders were given to keep awake and have an eye on the supposed rebels in front," the twenty-one-year-old Bellard said.

"We remained there all night, but as for keeping awake, I for one did not, for I had several cat naps during the night. Had the rebs made an attack on Was. that night, nothing could have saved it, as [there] was no troops round the city but our brigade, and we were supposed to be unfit for active service."

There were other Union troops "round the city." But there weren't a great deal of them. In his December 1861 report, Bernard estimated that the number of troops needed to man the Defenses of Washington was 34,125. The actual number in July of 1864 probably was closer to 10,000, nearly all of whom were physically incapacitated in some way or had never fired a weapon.

"That is to say, eight or nine thousand inefficients were in the works proper," Wallace later wrote accurately, if hyperbolically, "ready upon alarm to take to the guns and do the duty of forty thousand trained specialists." Washington, he wrote in retrospect, "seriously menaced, was incapable of self-defence—that much was clear."

Not much else was clear as late as July 10 to Secretary of War Stanton and other higher-ups at the War Department. Gideon Welles, the navy secretary, wrote in his journal that day that he learned from one of his clerks that advance Confederate troops (known as pickets) were "on the outskirts of Georgetown, within the District lines."

There "had been no information to warn us of this near approach," Welles said, so he immediately "sent to the War Department to ascertain the facts."

What he found, Welles said, was that Stanton and his staff at the War Department "were ignorant—had heard street rumors, but they were unworthy of notice—and ridiculed my inquiry."

Stanton may have pooh-poohed talk of an imminent invasion. But many of Washington's citizens on Sunday July 10 believed that the nation's capital soon would be under attack for the first time since the war began.

Washington "was in an uproar," U.S. Army second lieutenant Frank Wilkeson of the Fourth U.S. Artillery later wrote; ". . . pale-faced, anxious men solemnly asserted that certain information had been received at the War Department that at least fifty thousand veteran soldiers were marching with Early."

Men, that day, "stood in groups on street corners, in hotel lobbies, in newspaper offices, and in drinking saloons, and discussed the military situation," the then sixteen-year-old Wilkeson, who had lied about his age and joined the Union army, remembered. "Officers rode furiously up and down the streets, and swarmed around the War Department."

"Bands of music, bodies of infantry and little clouds of cavalry begin to pass across the city," *Chicago Evening Journal* military correspondent Benjamin F. Taylor wrote that day. "Hard riders dash through the streets; engines are harnessed to the trains; steamers draw heavy breaths and give symptoms of waking; the treble of newsboys flaunting their second extra, and singing out 'rebels a marchin' on to Washington!' again startles you. . . ."

The city, Taylor said, "leans out of windows; it comes fairly out of doors; it ties itself in knots on street corners; it buys 'extras' and reads them; it hears rumors and believes them; it whistles a little and tries to look unconcerned. We have the defeat of Wallace at Monocacy yesterday," while "the enemy . . . appears at Rockville on the Frederick turnpike, sixteen miles distant. . . ."

There is "Excitement in the city," Pliny Fiske Sanborne, an Ohio-born Presbyterian minister volunteering with the Christian Commission, wrote in his diary that day. "Rebels in force near [Baltimore and Washington]. Army wagons in long trains passing through the city. Regiments mustering and marching."

That evening, Reverend Sanborne wrote, there was more "great excitement. Troops moving. War Department busy. Citizens drilling . . . A thousand rumors. A strange Sabbath day."

FOURTEEN

Monday, July 11: Greatly in Need of Privates

The Rebels are upon us.

—Navy Secretary Gideon Welles, July 11, 1864

At 8:45 on the night of July 9, just a few hours after Wallace's defeat at Monocacy, Halleck relayed an order from U.S. Grant to Maj. Gen. Horatio Wright, the forty-four-year-old commander of Grant's Army of the Potomac's Sixth Corps outside Richmond. The order: Bring the remaining two divisions of the Sixth Corps "at once" to City Point, get them onto troop transport ships, and report to Halleck once they arrived in Washington.

The Connecticut-born Horatio Gouverneur Wright had graduated from West Point in 1841 and began his army career in the engineers. Soon after the Civil War began, on April 20, 1861, Wright was captured (and released four days later) during the burning and evacuation of the Gosport Navy Yard in Norfolk, Virginia. Wright came to Washington later that year to help superintend the building of the city's defenses.

He went on to serve as an engineer at the Battle of First Manassas, and in the summer of 1862 took command of the Department of Ohio. Wright took over the First Division of the Sixth Corps in May 1863 and fought at Wilderness, Spotsylvania Courthouse, and Cold Harbor. When the Sixth

Commanding general Horatio Wright brought two divisions of
Sixth Corps troops to Washington. They arrived on Monday, July
11, just as Early and the lead elements of his army had come
within sight of the U.S. Capitol dome. *Credit: The Library of
Congress*

Corps commander, Maj. Gen. John Sedgwick, succumbed to a sharpshooter's bullet to the head at Spotsylvania Courthouse on May 8, Wright
was promoted to major general and took over as the head of the entire Sixth
Corps.

Wright's First and Second Divisions moved out from their encampments
near Petersburg on the night of July 9 at around 11:00, less than an hour after he received his orders. "We had become too much accustomed to sudden
movements to require long preparations for breaking up camp," George

Stevens, a surgeon with the Seventy-seventh Regiment of New York Volunteers, explained in his war memoir.

The men marched for fourteen miles that hot, dusty night to City Point, speculating what their mission would be. "We could not tell where we were going," Thomas W. Hyde, a twenty-three-year-old lieutenant colonel serving on Wright's staff, wrote in his war memoir. "Some had it to take Wilmington [North Carolina], some that riots had broken out in New York, and some that we were to join the Western Army; but no one knew that one Jubal Early was on the warpath in Maryland with his corps of seasoned veterans. . . ."

The Sixth Corps didn't particularly bother disguising its exit. "When leaving," the men "made a great deal of noise, beating marches, blowing calls, and making bonfires of their camps," General Meade complained to Grant the next day.

"This attracted the attention of the enemy, and this morning at daylight they advanced on a portion of the Second Corps pickets, crying out 'The Yankees are gone,'" Meade said. Union pickets, he said, "received them with brisk fire, driving them back."

The noisy Sixth Corps troops appreciated the fact that they didn't have to make the march to the river during daylight hours. The night march "was far more tolerable than it could have been by day," Stevens said. "For although the roads were composed of dry beds of dust in which the men sank almost ankle deep at every step, and the cloud which rose as the column moved along filled their throats and eyes and nostrils, yet they were not forced to endure the misery of a long march under a burning sun."

It was "an all-night march from the dust of Petersburg and the stones . . . stubbed our sleepy toes," B. F. North of the 122nd New York remembered years later.

North and the rest of Wright's men reached City Point at daylight on Sunday, July 10. By early evening the two divisions, with about one hundred horses and a small mountain of baggage, had boarded the transports, which were waiting for them when they arrived at the James. As was the case with Ricketts's men a few days earlier, most of Wright's men felt relaxed and relieved once they made their way onto the ships and their sea voyage north began.

"Enjoyed a shower, the first we have experienced in forty days," Lt. Col. Mason Whiting Tyler of the Thirty-seventh Regiment of Massachusetts Volunteers wrote in his diary that day. "The trip was enlivened by singing in the afternoon."

"Great satisfaction was felt by all," Stevens said, "at the prospect of leaving the region whose natural desolation was heightened by the devastation of war and going to a country of plenty, with which so many pleasant remembrances were associated."

Each man, Stevens said, "breathed more freely as the steamer swung out upon the river, and our brigade band sounded a good-bye to the scenes of our recent labors and privations."

A fellow Union surgeon, forty-five-year-old Daniel M. Holt, a small-town doctor from Herkimer, New York, described the experience similarly. "The trip, taken together, was a rather pleasant one," Holt, who served with the 121st New York Volunteer Infantry, wrote home to his wife a few days later. "At least it was a change from marching on dusty roads to cool and comparatively shady quarters."

Holt said, though, that he found "little real comfort" on "such a packed and crowded vessel." Two regiments, he said, "without the use of saloons or State rooms were piled in promiscuously together—officers and men—upon the decks of a not over-large boat." Holt took refuge on top of the boat's pilothouse with "eight or ten other officers," where they spent a mostly uncomfortable night without bedding, blankets, or overcoats.

The weather, he said, "was chilling enough after getting fairly out to sea." The wind "came cutting and cold—nothing overhead but blue sky and beneath blue water." Holt spotted a discarded bass drum and decided to use it for shelter from the wind that night. He appropriated a "small coil of rope" for a pillow.

"I crawled into [the drum, which was missing one head] and there lay until my limbs became so stiff with cold that I could not stir," Holt wrote. "Next day, of course, I paid well for the unusual luxury in a burning fever and divers other ills too numerous to mention."

As his ship passed Mount Vernon just south of Washington, Holt paused to contemplate what George Washington might have made of the sight of Union troop ships steaming toward the nation's capital to face an invading military force led by a Virginian. "I could not repress the thought that the spirit of the departed sage and patriot was tearfully beholding these transports filled with troops to put down an effort to crush out and extinguish a government for which he battled and bled and left to generations unborn the blessed heritage of a free people."

At around 1:00 in the afternoon on July 11, not long after the ships carrying the two Sixth Corps divisions had steamed off en route to Washington, the steamer *Crescent* arrived at City Point. It was the first of a flotilla of ships carrying an entire division of the Union's army's Nineteenth Corps under Ohio-born major general Quincy Adams Gillmore (West Point Class of 1849). A week earlier Grant had ordered those Louisiana-based troops to come to his aid at Petersburg. Their ships departed the port of New Orleans on July 3. Once the Nineteenth Corps troops reached City Point, however, Grant immediately changed their orders. They, too, were sent to Washington to meet Jubal Early's threat.

Grant relayed the good news to Lincoln at 10:30 that night, in the same telegram in which he told the president that he had decided not to come to Washington. "One div of XIX Corps, 6,000 strong, is now to Washington, one steamer loaded with these troops having passed Fort Monroe to-day," Grant told his commander-in-chief. "They will probably reach Washington tomorrow night."

Grant said that he was confident that the veteran fighters of the Sixth and Nineteenth Corps "should be able to compete" with the invading Confederate army, which he continued to mistakenly believe was commanded by Lt. Gen. Richard S. Ewell (West Point Class of 1840), who had lost a leg after the August 1862 Battle of Groveton, had performed poorly at the Bloody Angle at Spotsylvania Court House, and had been out of action—and out of favor for his lackluster leadership—since Lee had relieved Ewell of his field command in May.

Grant continued to express his belief that Hunter would extricate himself from West Virginia and come to Washington's rescue. "Before more troops can be sent from here," Grant told Lincoln, "Hunter will be able to join Wright in rear of the enemy with at least 10,000 men besides a force sufficient to hold Maryland Heights."

Before the Sixth and Nineteenth Corps troops reached Washington beginning around noon on Monday, July 11, wild rumors and a mounting sense of panic swept the citizenry. Adding to the confusion: a horde of refugees that streamed into the city from the west and north on a day that Henry H. Atwater of the U.S. Military Telegraph Corps called "one of the hottest" he had "ever experienced." The dust was so thick, he said, that it "rose in clouds blinding the vision."

On the outskirts of Georgetown, Atwater said, "we met a great number of people coming into Washington with their household effects, some driving cattle and leading horses."

The "panic-stricken people from Rockville, Silver Spring, Tennallytown, and the other Maryland villages" came "flocking into Washington by the Seventh Street road," the *Sacramento Daily Union* correspondent Noah Brooks later wrote, "flying in wild disorder, and bringing their household goods with them."

In "a general way," Brooks remembered, "we understood that the city was cut off at the north and east, and that the famine of market-stuff, New York newspapers, and other necessities of life, was due to the cutting of railway lines leading northward. For two or three days we had no mail, no telegraphic messages, and no railway travel. Our only communication with the outer world was by steamer from Georgetown, D.C., to New York."

Farmers "living in the path of the coming enemy," Frederick William Seward, the son of Secretary of State William H. Seward who was in Washington serving as assistant secretary of state, remembered, "fled to the city for refuge. By every northern road their wagons were coming in, loaded with their household goods, accompanied by cattle hastily gathered and driven before them."

"I can give you but a faint idea of the panic which [Early's troops'] advent created," Maj. John H. Brinton, a physician from Philadelphia who worked in the U.S. Army Surgeon General's Office in Washington, wrote in his war memoir.

Washington "had no garrison of trained or experienced troops, either regular or volunteer," Brinton said. "We all whistled to keep our courage up, and whistled, too, very loud."

Throughout the city, he remembered, "everybody tried to appear very busy. Not one would admit ideas of danger, but yet everyone was at heart afraid." One widely believed rumor, Brinton said, was that Secretary of War Stanton "thought so gravely" of Early's threat that he had sent "his silver and valuables aboard a gunboat."

Brinton also said that he doubted "if many persons in the North ever knew, or knowing, realized the true state of insecurity in Washington." I "really believe," he said, that "five hundred, yes, one hundred, of Early's horses could have ridden into Washington and captured whom they chose, the president or his Cabinet, or even *myself*."

The "most alarming feature of the whole affair," a Union soldier wrote in a long, unsigned dispatch that appeared in the July 18 *New York Times*, came at midnight on July 10 when Washingtonians learned "that the enemy were massing their columns against Fort Stevens," the "weakest point of defense." The "terror of the citizens," the soldier said, "amounted almost to paralysis."

Washington, *New York Herald* correspondent Sylvanus Cadwallader said, "never was more helpless. Several wide turnpikes led directly to it. Any such cavalry commander as [Philip] Sheridan . . . , [Wade] Hampton or [J.E.B.] Stuart could have ridden through all its broad avenues, sabred everyone found in the streets, and before nightfall could have burned down the White House, the Capitol, and all public buildings."

One citizen, who identified himself as E. Harman, took it upon himself to write to President Lincoln, suggesting how to defend Washington.

"Never has danger so menaced us before," Harman wrote to the president on July 10. "Permit me to suggest the expediency of barricading the City as an additional safeguard against surprise and attack." The barricades, Harman said, "would hold an army in check, which may have overpowered the outer defences of the City. . . ."

"If the rebels make an attack on the Forts at all, I think that it will be by tomorrow morning," Horatio Nelson Taft, a U.S. Patent Office examiner, wrote in his diary that day. "It is said today that they are Forty thousand strong now in Maryland and threatening the City. Should they make an attack, it will be a bloody fight." The city, Taft said, "has been in great excitement all day."

Assistant Secretary of War Charles A. Dana arrived in town that day, after a two-day trip from Grant's headquarters. When he entered the city, Dana said, he also found the citizens "in a state of great excitement" and "all sorts of rumors came in." Washingtonians could see "clouds of dust in several quarters around the city, which we believed to be raised by bodies of hostile cavalry."

Taft said he "never saw such a crowd of people" on Pennsylvania Avenue as he did that afternoon. "Excited crowds," he said, "were listening to some new comer from the northern Forts or surrounding a soldier or swallowing the most absurd stories from some sober faced wag."

The authorities, Dana noted, "had utilized every man in town for defense."

Dr. Robert Reyburn, the surgeon in chief of the Union defenses in Washington, received orders at midnight the night before to take ten doctors to Fort Reno, "accompanied by appropriate medical supplies for the care of the wounded, as the enemy were in force and rapidly approaching Washington by way of Rockville, Md.," he remembered forty years later.

Upon arriving at Fort Reno on Monday morning, July 11, Reyburn faced "a scene of dire confusion." Fortifications, he said, "we had in abundance, but we had very few men to man them and a very insufficient supply of the munitions of war."

The halt and infirm manning the forts, Maj. John Brinton said, after riding out from Washington to take a look for himself, were "all looking and feeling very uncomfortable, and distressed at the idea of passing the night in the open air, and that, too, within sight of their own boarding houses, within touch almost of their very beds."

A July 12 *New York Times* editorial called for calm amid the sea of "many wild and exaggerated reports." There "is no necessity whatever for any public panic about the matter," the staunchly pro–Lincoln Administration *Times* editorialized. "But still we urge all loyal and gallant young men who love the Union and would repel the enemy from the Union capital, to hasten forward at the call of the Government to drive away this insolent rebel foe."

Washington had more than a few nonloyal men and women. Those Southern partisans greeted the news of Early's march on Washington with joy. The city's "large secession element," former Republican Ohio congressman Albert G. Riddle later wrote, "had never been so moved as on Early's approach at the head of a numerous, well-appointed, and presumably conquering army."

Confederate sympathizers in Washington, Riddle (who was in Washington working as a lawyer at the time) said, had had little to be happy about for the previous year, but took heart at "this sudden, unexpected advance and successful invasion." Hope, he said, "had overcome uncertainty and doubt" and "all contributed to create a crisis of confused emotions in their circles."

A secessionist, Riddle said, "was now known by the radiance of his face— 'At last, at last, thank God!' was quoted, as exclamatory bursts from them." Many, he said, "had already sought the enemy's camps and forces, to aid as they best could in the reduction of the Capital. . . . It was the long-sighed-for, unattainable liberation, now about to be consummated."

Noah Brooks reported that Union troops confiscated a half-sewn Confederate flag from a "nest of secessionists" in Georgetown on Sunday, July 10. "The men were marched over to the guard-house, and the unfinished colors, probably intended to be presented to Early, were promptly confiscated,"

Brooks later wrote. "This was not the only flag made to be presented to the rebels when they should effect their triumphal entry into Washington."

Halleck, meanwhile, taking note of the city's less-than-ideal military personnel situation, wrote later that night: "We have five times as many generals as we want, but are greatly in need of privates. Any one volunteering in that capacity will be thankfully received."

In addition to his commanding officer, Lt. Gen. Ulysses S. Grant, who called all the strategic shots from his base at City Point in Virginia, Halleck had eight generals in Washington in charge of various phases of the hastily organized operation to defend the city. To wit:

- Maj. Gen. Quincy Gillmore of the Nineteenth Corps, assigned to command the line from Fort Lincoln in northeast Washington (the site of the present-day Fort Lincoln Elementary School) to Fort Totten (off present-day North Capitol Street) southeast of Fort Stevens.

- Brig. Gen. Montgomery Cunningham Meigs (West Point Class of 1836), the quartermaster general of the army, to command the line from Fort Totten westward to Fort De Russy, including Fort Stevens.

- Brig. Gen. Martin Davis Hardin (West Point Class of 1859), a twenty-six-year-old Illinois native who happened to be in Washington recovering from the amputation of his left arm a year earlier, to command the line from Fort De Russy westward to Fort Sumner, just over the district line in Maryland and just north of the Potomac River.

- Horatio Wright of the Sixth Corps, to be held in reserve.

- Major General Augur, the commander of the entire Department of Washington.

- Brig. Gen. Richard Delafield (West Point Class of 1818), the army's sixty-five-year-old chief engineer, who took charge of army engineer officers constructing seacoast batteries north and east of Washington.

- Maj. Gen. Abner Doubleday (West Point Class of 1842), who had commanded the First Corps at Gettysburg and was performing administrative duties in Washington, was assigned on July 11 to take command of the front east of Fort Stevens to Fort Slemmer near the present-day site of Catholic University. Doubleday, a native of upstate New York, sometimes is given credit for inventing the game of baseball in 1839 at Cooperstown, New York, while a West Point cadet.

- Maj. Gen. Alexander McDowell McCook (West Point Class of 1852), who had arrived in the city on the morning of July 10 and whom Halleck put in charge of the entire line of troops along the city's northern defenses.

It doesn't take a military historian to deduce that this improvised command structure—which also included Col. Moses N. Wisewell, the military governor of Washington—was not exactly conducive to decisive decision making. Halleck, as the Union army chief of staff, outranked all of the generals in Washington. He should have taken command, which Grant trusted him to do. But Halleck balked and would not make any moves without instructions from Grant.

"There was no head to the whole," Charles Dana wrote in his memoir. "General Halleck would not give orders, except as he received them from Grant; the president would give none; and, until Grant directed positively and explicitly what was to be done, everything was practically at a standstill."

After meeting with Old Brains Halleck that morning, McCook took off to assess the personnel situation at the northernmost forts. McCook, one of fourteen brothers and first cousins of the "fighting McCook" clan who served in the Union army in the Civil War, was not happy with what he saw.

He "discovered the fact that the only troops on the north of Washington were the small garrisons in the forts, small detachments of the cavalry" and a smattering of Veteran Reserve Corps men, McCook wrote in his official after-action report. Only 209 Union troops were garrisoned at Fort Stevens, for example: 78 hundred days' men of Company K of the 150th Ohio National Guard Regiment; 79 men from the Thirteenth Michigan Battery; and

52 men described by the commander of Fort Stevens, Lt. Col. John N. Frazee, as "convalescents," commanded by Lieutenant Turner of the 150th Ohio's Company K.

With the enemy fast approaching, McCook took action early the next morning, Monday, July 11.

All reserves "were brought forward and posted in the rifle pits," he said, and "several additional regiments" of Veteran Reserve Corps troops were called to the front.

That night, the forty-eight-year-old Montgomery Meigs—an engineer who had helped design and construct parts of the wings and dome of the U.S. Capitol Building, among other structures in Washington—showed up at Fort Stevens with some 1,500 civilian employees of the War and State Departments, "armed and equipped," as McCook put it.

Henry Atwater of the Military Telegraph Corps had arrived at Fort Reno that afternoon. He found General Hardin's temporary headquarters in a nearby building. "On the roof in the blazing sun," Atwater later wrote, "signal-men were wigwagging their despaches. To the northeast we could see the dust of the enemy as they moved back and forth."

At 11:00 that night, Atwater said, General Hardin handed him a worrisome dispatch. "A scout just reports that the enemy are preparing to make a grand assault on this fort to-night," Hardin's message said. "They are tearing down fences, and are moving to the right, their bands playing. Can't you hurry up the Sixth Corps?"

"The Rebels are upon us," navy secretary Welles wrote in his diary that day. "The truth is that the forts around Washington have been vacated and the troops sent to General Grant, who was promised reinforcements to take Richmond."

Grant was "resting, apparently," Welles complained. Lee "has sent a force threatening the National Capital, and we are without force for its defense. Citizens are volunteering, and the employees in the navy yard are required to man the fortifications left destitute."

Stanton and Halleck, Welles said, "are now the most alarmed men in Washington."

The alarmed Stanton "directed that all orderlies, messengers, military riffraff, the invalids, veteran reserve and indeed every man in Government employ who could put on a uniform, or carry a musket, should turn out in defence of the capital of his country," John Brinton wrote in his war memoir.

What "a sorry lot they were," Brinton said. "They laid down their pens, and off they went to 'report' for military duty. My clerks went too, from my office, but they were a mild-mannered set, and I assume they would never have hurt anybody, not even in self-defence."

The mild-mannered set included, among many other civilians, Simon Newcomb, who was working as a professor of mathematics and astronomy at the U.S. Naval Observatory. "I became a member of a naval brigade, organized in a hurried manner by Admiral [Louis M.] Goldsborough, and including in it several officers of high and low rank," Newcomb, who went on to become one of the nineteenth century's most accomplished astronomers, wrote in his memoir.

The "rank and file" of that hastily organized unit, Newcomb said, "was formed of the workmen in the Navy Yard, most of whom were said to have seen military service of one kind or another." The ad hoc brigade formed up at the Navy Yard in the middle of the afternoon and marched a couple of miles out to Fort Lincoln in Northeast Washington. That fort stood on a hill protecting the Baltimore and Ohio Railroad and the Baltimore Pike. Today, the appropriately named Fort Lincoln Elementary School sits on the site.

Newcomb's new brigade took up positions in the six-foot-deep trenches that lined the front of the fort, while a small number of army men manned the guns inside Fort Lincoln. "I was not assigned to any particular duty, and simply walked around the place in readiness to act whenever called upon," Newcomb remembered. The men "bivouacked that night, and remained the night following awaiting the attack of the enemy," which never came to Fort Lincoln.

Newcomb's brief military experience started off badly, but ended well, he said. "I was surprised to find how quickly one could acquire the stolidity of a solider," he wrote. "During the march from the Navy Yard to the fort I felt extremely depressed, as one can well imagine, in view of the suddenness with which I had to take leave of my family and the uncertainty of the situation, as well as its extreme gravity."

That depression, though, Newcomb said, "wore off the next day, and I do not think I ever had a sounder night's sleep in my life than when I lay down on the grass, with only a blanket between myself and the sky, with the expectation of being awakened by the rattle of musketry at daybreak."

Young second lieutenant Frank Wilkeson, assigned to Fort Totten to the west of Fort Stevens, watched in consternation that evening as "the motliest crowd of soldiers I ever saw came straggling out from Washington to man the rifle pits which connected the forts." The motley crowd, Wilkeson said in his war memoir, "was composed of quartermaster's employes, clerks from the War, Navy and State departments, convalescents from the military hospitals, and veteran reserves."

The latter group, he noted, were "clad in the disheartening, sickly uniform of pale blue, which was the distinctive dress of that corps. The Confederates aptly characterized these disabled soldiers as 'Condemned Yankees'."

The veteran Union army soldiers at Fort Totten looked at the newcomers "with open-eyed astonishment," Wilkeson remembered. They "were evidently trying to keep up their courage by talking loudly and boastfully of their determination to hold the rifle pits at all hazards. I smiled sorrowfully as I thought of the ease with which the Confederates, veterans of twenty pitched battles, would drive them out of their earthworks."

Later that night some 2,800 "convalescents and men from hospitals," as McCook characterized them, were pressed into service and sent as a reserve force to the rear of Fort Slocum. The next morning, Monday, July 11, according to Bellard, about 3,000 more men, "both black and white," arrived at Fort Reno, including "a squad from hospitals and several companies of the Second battalion V.R.C." One Union soldier called the assemblage a collection of "counter jumpers, clerks in the War Office, hospital rats and stragglers."

That motley crew never could have fought off Early's veteran troops, no matter how tired the rebel soldiers were. Luckily for the Union, help arrived at almost the very last minute.

The first ships carrying Wright's Sixth Corps troops docked at the old Sixth Street wharf on the Potomac River in Southwest Washington at about noon on Monday, July 11—just about the time that Early himself and the advanced elements of his army had made their way into Washington and within sight of Fort Stevens.

By 2:00, all of the Sixth and Nineteenth Corps troop ships had arrived. Their commander in chief was among the happy and relieved citizenry of Washington on hand to greet the men as they disembarked.

"President Lincoln stood upon the wharf chatting familiarly with the veterans," George Stevens remembered, "and now and then, as if in compliment to them, biting at a piece of hard tack which he held in his hand."

Volunteers with the U.S. Sanitary Commission also hailed the arriving troops. "At the landing we were met by some Sanitary Commission agents

who gave the regiment a lunch of good coffee and bread (butter too!),"
Capt. John William de Forest of the Nineteenth Corps' Twelfth Connecti-
cut Volunteers wrote in his memoir. The food and drink "seemed great lux-
uries after the starvation on the transport, where most of the officers went
hungry for lack of money."

The embarking troops quickly formed a column and began marching
through Washington to the forts on the northern and western edges of the
city. Wright's men initially set out, under Halleck's orders, marching west
along the Potomac toward Chain Bridge. But soon thereafter Halleck changed
his mind after learning that Early's men were outside Fort Stevens.

"Please stop Gen Wright's movement up the Potomac," Halleck wired
Augur at 1:40, "and send his command up 7th St."

Wright, who fumed about Old Brains's indecisiveness, nevertheless obeyed
the new order.

"We marched up Seventh Street, past the Smithsonian Institute, the
Patent Office and the Post Office," Stevens wrote, "meeting on the way old
friends and hearing the people who crowded upon the sidewalks exclaiming,
'It is the old Sixth corps! . . . The danger is over now!'"

The heat "was appalling," Lieutenant Colonel Hyde remembered. "But
under the banners of the Greek Cross [the Sixth Corps emblem] was disembarked a ragged and bronzed lot of soldiers in very business-like haste, and
soon a sturdy column of twelve thousand veterans was going up the avenue
and out Seventh Street, through applauding crowds."

We found the citizens of Washington "in a state of great and not surprising consternation," Lt. Col. Aldace F. Walker of the Sixth Corps' Eleventh
Vermont Regiment said. The "sight of the Veterans of the Sixth Corps,"
Walker wrote in his 1869 war memoir, "was an intense relief to the consti-
tutionally timid Washingtonians."

As the Vermonters "passed through crowded streets," Walker said, "cheers,
good wishes, and fervent God-speeds were heard on every side. Citizens ran
through the lines with buckets of ice-water, for the morning was sultry;
newspapers and eatables were handed into the column, and our welcome
had a heartiness that showed how intense had been the fear."

The men of the Sixth Corps, Stevens said, "never before realized the
hold which the corps had upon the affection of the people. Washington an
hour before was in a panic; now as the people saw the veterans wearing the
badge of the marching men through their streets, the excitement subsided
and confidence prevailed."

Stevens's fellow surgeon, Daniel Holt, reported a similar reception. "All sorts of rumors—vague and ridiculous—filled the city when we landed," he wrote to his wife two days later. "However, confidence—*perfect confidence*—appeared to possess the people that we should save the Capital from spoliation and fire. Never were men more cordially greeted than we."

President Lincoln—whom Holt, like many other Northerners, called "Father Abraham"—along with his "wife and son followed us in a carriage to the walls of the fort," Holt said. The men, he said, learned "to love him as well as he appears to love his boys in blue, and we all would be willing to sacrifice anything for such a man and such a government."

Thomas Scott of the 122nd New York also used the words "great excitement" to describe the scene as he disembarked on the Sixth Street wharf. "The attempt to capture Washington had thrown the population into a state of great excitement," Scott remembered in 1890. "They greeted the passing troops heartily, and brought ice water to them without limit."

The weather, Scott said, "was intensely warm" and it affected the Sixth Corps men, despite their two-day river voyage and the ocean of proffered ice water. The "very bad water" the men drank on the transports "caused hundreds to fall on the march to the fortifications," he wrote. "'God bless you,' and 'You will save us,' greeted the worn and sweltering troops as they passed through the streets."

The Reverend Pliny Sanborne, volunteering with the Sanitary Commission, was among the troop greeters. He saw "the 19th Corps pass the city from Louisiana via City Point," Sanborne wrote in his diary that night, "immence body, hot and sweltering, gave one oranges." Later that evening, he wrote, he saw "regiments constantly passing north. Rebels within five miles—some fighting—wounded brought in . . . Went to the War Department by White House . . . Cavalry passing—Squads of infantry—To our rooms and bed—An interesting and exciting day!"

President Lincoln had made a short tour of some of the northern and western forts on Sunday, July 10, accompanied by Asst. Adj. Gen. James A. Hardie of the Department of Washington, along with an armed mounted escort. Lincoln had planned to spend that night with his family at the presidential cottage at the Soldiers' Home (today known as Anderson Cottage at the Armed Forces Retirement Home), his summer residence on the northern suburban outskirts of the city, not far from Fort Stevens. But at 10:00

that night when Secretary of War Stanton finally realized that Early's army was on the march and heading for the city, he sent word that the president should get back to the White House.

"The enemy are reported advancing towards Tennallytown and Seventh street road," Stanton told Lincoln. "They are in large force and have driven back our Cavalry. I think you had better come to town tonight."

Lincoln protested, but Stanton insisted, and Lincoln finally took Stanton's advice and hustled his family back to the Executive Mansion in downtown Washington.

The next morning, Monday, July 11, though, Lincoln spent an active day moving about the city. "The President concluded to desert his tormentors today & travel around the defenses," Lincoln's secretary John Hay wrote in his diary that day.

At around 9:00, Lincoln set out toward Tennallytown and Fort Reno, accompanied by his wife and entourage. They then headed north and east to Fort Stevens, where shortly after his arrival Confederate pickets began firing on the Union troops. Lincoln, his wife, and several other civilians watched the short-lived action standing on a parapet, but they soon took themselves out of the line of fire and returned to the White House, then went to the wharf to greet the newly arrived Sixth and Nineteenth Corps troops.

"His tall form must have been a conspicuous target for the enemy's sharp-shooters," David Homer Bates, the manager of the War Department's telegraph office, wrote in his memoir. "It was a matter of remark at the time that he did not seem to realize the serious risk incurred in going to the front of our line while skirmishing was in progress."

Lincoln went to the War Department after his visit to Fort Stevens. At the telegraph office he sketched a diagram that "showed the relative positions of the two bodies of troops, and where the skirmish took place," cipher operator Albert B. Chandler remembered, "all of which he explained to" the other operators and their commanding officer, Maj. Thomas J. Eckert. All "were, of course, extremely interested in his picturesque description," Chandler said.

Abraham Lincoln's short appearance on the Fort Stevens parapet on July 11, 1864, marked the first—and only—time in American history that a sitting president came under hostile fire in a military engagement. Until the following day, that is.

FIFTEEN

Monday, July 11: A Desperate Engagement

*We expected to move forward immediately and drive the few frightened defenders
out of the works, enter the city, capture Lincoln, and demand of him peace or more
humane treatment of helpless prisoners in the hands of his government.*

—Pvt. I. G. Bradwell, Thirty-first Georgia Volunteer Infantry

Jubal Early had set out his order of march to Washington sometime
during the night of Sunday, July 10. Rodes's division would take the lead, departing at 3:30 in the morning the following day, followed by a battalion of
Brig. Gen. Armistead L. Long's artillery. Ramseur's division was supposed to
be next, but stayed behind to destroy the Monocacy railroad bridge. More
artillery followed Long's men, after which came Gordon's division, and yet
more artillery. The wagon trains would come next, with Breckinridge's division under Brig. Gen. John Echols bringing up the rear.

Among the regimental commanders serving under Echols was thirty-
one-year-old Col. George Smith Patton of the Twenty-second Virginia Infantry Regiment, the grandfather and namesake of the legendary World
War II army general George S. Patton.

The 3:30 departure didn't happen. But at 6:20 on the already steamy
morning of Monday, July 11, Early led his men down the Georgetown Pike
heading directly for Washington. At Rockville, Early took most of his corps
along what is now Viers Mill Road, past Rock Creek Park, through

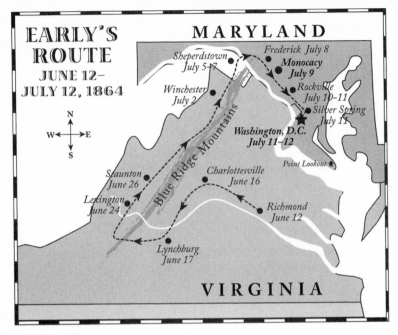

EARLY'S ROUTE
JUNE 12–
JULY 12, 1864

MARYLAND

Sheperdstown
July 5–7

Frederick July 8

Monocacy
July 9

Winchester
July 2

Rockville
July 10–11

Silver Spring
July 11

Washington, D.C.
July 11–12

Staunton
June 26

Charlottesville
June 16

Point Lookout

Lexington
June 24

Richmond
June 12

Blue Ridge Mountains

Lynchburg
June 17

VIRGINIA

Credit: Liz Weaver

Wheaton (then called Leesborough) and into Silver Spring, where they reached the Seventh Street Road (now Georgia Avenue), which led directly to Fort Stevens. McCausland's cavalry stayed on Georgetown Pike and headed toward Fort Reno.

That route of march took McCausland and his men past a small eighteenth-century cabin in Bethesda on the pike (now Old Georgetown Road) known then as the Riley House. The cabin stood on a large farm owned by George Riley and was the former longtime home of Josiah Henson (1789–1883), a Riley slave. Henson in 1830 had escaped to Canada via the Underground Railroad. He'd learned to read and write and published one of the first autobiographies written by a former American slave.

Josiah Henson's autobiography inspired Harriet Beecher Stowe to create the title character of her famed novel *Uncle Tom's Cabin*, which was published in 1852. It went on to become the bestselling novel of the nineteenth century and an important factor in fostering abolitionist sentiment in the United States. History does not record whether or not any of the Confederate troops were aware of the cabin's significance as they rode by it on July 11, 1864.

The corps of troops that Early led that day was markedly different than it was two days earlier at the start of the Battle of Monocacy. The biggest difference: the number of his able-bodied infantrymen had dwindled to about what Early claimed to be just 8,000 men—compared to the 11,700 foot soldiers who had marched down the Shenandoah Valley toward Maryland.

Why the precipitous drop-off? First, as Early put it in his autobiography, "the rapid marching" that he had subjected the men to since they left Gaines's Mill on June 13 had "broken down" many men "who were barefooted or weakened by previous exposure." Those weakened men had been left behind "in the Valley and directed to be collected at Winchester," Early said.

Many of Early's men, as John Worsham noted in his war memoir, had been "barefooted and footsore" since early in May. "I was still barefooted, my feet being too sore to wear my boots," Worsham said of his condition on July 11. "The scars made on that march are on my feet to this day. Many men, like myself, marched right along without shoes, but many of them were physically unable to keep up."

Second, his ranks were thinned by the hundreds of men killed or severely wounded at Monocacy and at the previous days' skirmishes at Harpers Ferry, Maryland Heights, and Middletown.

Of those remaining, large numbers were unfit for battle because they suffered from exhaustion after marching two days after the fight at Monocacy in what Union prisoner of war W. G. Duckett called the "almost suffocating" heat. Some of the men, Early said, had "fallen by sunstroke." By the time he reached Fort Stevens at around noon on July 11, Early said, he believed that "not more than one-third of my force could have been carried into action."

Not long after Early's men set out on Monday morning from Gaithersburg and Rockville, they exchanged fire with Union pickets, who soon retreated back toward Washington. At noontime, Col. George H. Smith's Sixty-second Virginia Mounted Infantry, made up mostly of men from the Shenandoah Valley and present-day West Virginia, crossed the Maryland border into the District of Columbia. They halted amid the orchards and farmland about two miles from Fort Stevens.

The day, Early said, "was an exceedingly hot one, and there was no air stirring." During their march from Rockville, his men "were enveloped in a suffocating cloud of dust, and many of them fell by the way from exhaustion." His progress, Early said, "was therefore very much impeded, but I pushed on as rapidly as possible, hoping to get into the fortifications around Washington before they could be manned."

Early rode ahead of Smith's men and he made it "in sight of Fort Stevens on the road a short time after noon." He could see the dome of the U.S. Capitol in the distance. He also could see that Fort Stevens and the surrounding fortifications were, as he put it, "but feebly manned."

Robert E. Lee's audacious, risky plan, conceived four weeks before, had worked. Early had driven Hunter from the Shenandoah Valley. He then marched an entire army into Maryland without the Union high command realizing it. Five days earlier, when Halleck and Grant finally discovered that Early was on the way to Washington, Lee's final piece of strategy fell into place when Grant detached the Sixth Corps from his army besieging Petersburg and Richmond and rerouted the Nineteenth Corps to Washington.

The Confederate military brain trust abandoned one element of the plan, releasing the Confederate prisoners at Point Lookout. But now, Jubal Early stood at the gates of a feebly defended Washington, D.C. Would the Confederate army's arguably most aggressive general do what he'd promised Lee he would do in his June 28 message—"to threaten Washington, and if I find an opportunity—to take it"?

Many of his troops, including the level-headed John Brown Gordon, thought Early would. "We were nearer to the national capital than any armed Confederates had ever been, and nearer to it than any Federal army had ever approached to Richmond," Gordon wrote in his memoir. "I myself rode to a point on those breastworks at which there was no force whatever. The unprotected space was broad enough for the easy passage of Early's army without resistance."

The few Union regulars defending Washington at noontime on July 11, Gordon said, "could not have manned any considerable portion of the defences. Undoubtedly we could have marched into Washington. . . ."

That feeling also held sway among many of the men in the ranks.

"I believe," Charles T. O'Ferrall of the Twenty-third Virginia Cavalry, which was among the leading elements of Early's force, wrote in his war memoir, "we could have ridden into the works."

All along the march from Monocacy "our guards had jokingly told us of the gay time expected by them on their entering Washington," Union prisoner Alfred Roe of New York later wrote, "remarks we took more in the spirit of banter than otherwise, hardly thinking it possible that Early would have the temerity to beard the lion in his den."

Many of Early's men "were bloated with extravagant notions with regard to the easy capture of the capital," a *Baltimore Sun* correspondent observed at the time. As they headed to Washington on July 11, the Confederate troops "frequently could be heard to indulge in little controversies as to what buildings should be allowed to stand, and what should be destroyed."

"Our army is very anxious to enter Washington City," Pvt. William Williams Stringfellow of the Sixty-ninth North Carolina wrote in his diary on July 11. "I fear for the people if [we] ever do enter there. So much misery has been brought upon our people by vile miscreants living there that [we] could not be restrained. If the proper ones were the only sufferers I would say [let] them loose upon the city. . . ."

"Long before we came in sight of the defenses, we knew that the city was protected by militia, or home guards, from the way they handled the big guns," I. G. Bradwell of the Thirty-first Georgia wrote fifty years later. "Someone jokingly remarked that the enemy was shelling our wagon train, which was at that time many miles in the rear, and their wild shooting produced in our minds a great contempt for the 'melish.' "

Early's men, Bradwell said, "expected to move forward immediately and drive the few frightened defenders out of the works, enter the city, capture Lincoln, and demand of him peace or more humane treatment of helpless prisoners in the hands of his government."

But Jubal Early hesitated. Several factors weighed on his mind. For one thing, the bulk of his army was scattered for miles and miles behind him. And every one of his troops labored under the intense heat. "I did not arrive in front of the fortifications until after noon on Monday, and then my troops were exhausted and it required time to bring them up into line," Early pointed out in his autobiography.

Rodes's division, the first to arrive, deployed into a line of battle that ran through farms, orchards, and the occasional house, and sent out pickets to act as scouts to see how well Fort Stevens was defended. The battle line moved forward to within about three hundred yards of Fort Stevens.

"Before us were the tremendous and almost impregnable fortifications of the city," Capt. Seaton Gales of Gen. William R. Cox's brigade of six North Carolina infantry regiments remembered, "while the minarets of the metropolis gleamed in the distance, the massive dome of the capitol, capped with the colossal statue of Liberty, towering eminently among them. A shout of exultation rang along the lines. . . ."

Rodes's men also saw "a cloud of dust in the rear of the works toward Washington," Early later wrote, "and soon a column of the enemy filed into them on the right and left." Soon thereafter Union troops went out to challenge Rodes's pickets, and Union artillery batteries at Fort Stevens and the nearby Forts DeRussy, Slocum, and Totten opened up on the Confederates— a situation Gales described as "a storm of monster shells from the titanic siege guns in the forts."

The yelling and shelling "defeated our hopes of getting possession of the works by surprise," Early said, "and it became necessary to reconnoiter."

The lead elements of Gordon's division didn't reach the Seventh Street Road until around 3:00 in the afternoon—just about the time that Gen. Horatio Wright had galloped up to Fort Stevens to report that his men were right behind him, marching up from the Washington wharf along the very same road, Seventh Street, on the other side of the fort. That was the time, too, when the Union artillery opened up.

"The enemy were shelling the road at this point with their big guns," John Worsham of Gordon's Twenty-first Virginia wrote in his memoir. "We soon came in sight of the Soldiers' Home, where the enemy had a signal station, and we were really at Washington City. We could see their fortifications and the men marching into them on each side of the road on which we were. Their dress induced us to think they were the town or city forces, some of them looking as if they had on linen dusters, and there being none in regular uniform."

The day, Worsham said, "was hotter than the preceding, and we had been marching faster too. Consequently there was more straggling. Our division was stretched out almost like skirmishers, and all the men did not get up until night."

Gordon's men waited for orders that afternoon. "Our division stacked arms on the side of the road, the men broke ranks and looked around," Worsham remembered. "A house between the two lines was burning. I went to Silver Springs, the country home of Mr. [Montgomery] Blair, one of Lincoln's cabinet, and got water, and examined the place. It was a splendid home."

Worsham had two small details wrong about the Blair residence. The name of the palatial, French-château-like estate on the Seventh Street Road just over the Maryland line was Silver Spring (not Springs). It was built in 1845 by Francis Preston Blair (1791–1876), a powerful politician who had been a close political ally of Pres. Andrew Jackson and later had helped start the Republican Party. Francis Preston Blair's son, postmaster general and trusted Lincoln adviser Montgomery Blair, owned Falkland, the estate next door.

Blair father and son had gone on a fishing trip to Pennsylvania early in July. Jubal Early took advantage of the empty mansion, and made Silver Spring his headquarters when he reached the town of Silver Spring on July 11. The elder Blair also owned an elaborate town house on Pennsylvania Avenue in Washington, across the street from the White House. The residence, known as Blair House, has been owned by the government and used as the official guesthouse of the president of the United States since 1942.

When Worsham and Gordon's other men returned to the front on Monday afternoon, July 11, they had a good look for the first time at the defenses of Washington.

"As far as my eye could reach to the right and left there were fortifications, and the most formidable looking I ever saw!" Worsham said. "In their front the trees had been cut down so that the limbs pointed towards us and they were sharpened. About midway of the clearing was a creek that seemed to run near the fortifications and parallel with them. The enemy had a full sweep of the ground for at least a mile in their front, and if their works were well manned, our force would not be able to take them. . . ."

Worsham's commanding general had a similar reaction. After Rodes's men had driven the Union pickets back, "we proceeded to examine the fortifications in order to ascertain if it was practicable to carry them by assault," Early said. "They were found to be exceedingly strong, and consisted of what appeared to be enclosed forts of heavy artillery, with a tier of lower works in front of each pierced for an immense number of guns, the whole being connected by curtains with ditches in front, and strengthened by palisades and abattis."

Early also saw that the Yankees had cut down trees outside their lines, "making a formidable obstacle, and every possible approach was raked by artillery." He noted that Rock Creek ran between him and the forts "through a deep ravine which had been rendered impassable by the felling of the timber on each side, and beyond were the works on the Georgetown pike which had been reported to be the strongest of all."

To his left, "as far as the eye could reach, the works appeared to be of the same impregnable character," Early lamented. "The position was

Once the shelling began around Fort Stevens on July 11, farmhouses and fields and trees in the neighborhood became the victims of often-severe collateral damage. *Credit: The Library of Virginia*

naturally strong for defence, and the examination showed, what might have been expected, that every appliance of science and unlimited means had been used to render the fortifications around Washington as strong as possible."

McCausland found a similar situation as he approached Fort Reno on the Georgetown Pike. He "reported the works on the Georgetown pike too strongly manned for him to assault," Early said. "We could not move to the right or left without its being discovered from a signal station on the top of the 'Soldiers' Home,' which overlooked the country, and the enemy would have been enabled to move in his works to meet us."

Early decided not to attack. He believed, he said later, that "to have rushed my men blindly against the fortifications, without understanding the state of things, would have been worse than folly."

Early knew he had fought against some Sixth Corps soldiers at Monocacy. But he didn't know when he made the fateful decision not to attack that two Wright's divisions of the Sixth Corps had left Petersburg and were at that moment headed for the Washington forts. Lee had sent him a telegram that day telling him of that development, but Early did not receive it.

"We may," Lee said, "assume that a corps or its equivalent has been sent by General Grant to Washington."

Lee, as usual, had assumed correctly. And, in light of that news, he gave Early an excuse to call off the invasion of Washington. "I send a special messenger to apprise you of this fact," Lee told Early, so "that you may remain on your guard and take this force into consideration with others that may be brought to oppose you. In your further operations you must of course be guided by the circumstances by which you are surrounded . . . and must not consider yourself committed to any particular line of conduct, but be governed by your good judgment."

Early judged not to make an assault on July 11, but he did not order a retreat. His men encamped outside Fort Stevens and periodic fierce fighting erupted outside the fort throughout the afternoon and evening. The most intense fighting came after the Sixth Corps troops arrived at Stevens at around 4:00.

At 5:00 Rodes's men pushed the ragtag Union outer picket line of clerks, civilians, and Veteran Reserve Corps troops back toward the fort. Five hundred newly arrived troops of the Sixth Corps' First Brigade, Second Division, under thirty-one-year-old brigadier general Frank Wheaton quickly moved out of the fort and into the fray. Within two hours they had pushed back Rodes's troops and regained the skirmish line.

Men of the Ninety-eighth, 102nd, and 139th Pennsylvania Veteran Volunteers "drove the enemy's advance back to their main lines," Wheaton wrote in his after-action report. Wheaton, a Rhode Island native who had joined the U.S. Cavalry in 1855 and stayed in the military, reinforced his line after sunset with men from the Ninety-third Pennsylvania and the Sixty-second New York.

"Skirmishing," Wheaton said, "continued through the night and the following day."

Troops of the Second Division's Third Brigade also took part in what Thomas H. Scott of the 122nd New York characterized as "a desperate engagement" outside Fort Stevens. Confederate troops, in position behind a board fence, aimed "well directed" fire at the Union line, Scott said, "and in the gathering darkness (for it was getting dark at 8:30) our men were directed to concentrate their fire on the lower board of the fence at short range."

The Union line of men from the Forty-third and 122nd New York and the Sixty-first Pennsylvania, he said, "was getting thinned, but the men protected themselves as best they could and poured such an incessant fire on the prostrate enemy that it compelled them to retreat in disorder." The "well officered" Sixth Corps' "double skirmish line of disciplined troops," Scott said, "met and drove back, after a severe engagement, a full line of battle. In no other engagement of our three years' service did we witness so many acts of individual valor and daring. . . ."

The fighting "occurred chiefly on the skirmish line," Dr. Robert Reyburn, who was there, later wrote. "Each man flattened himself upon the ground, seeking to cover himself from the enemy by every inequality of the ground or little hillock and singly each soldier fired upon the antagonist nearest to him. Every now and then the Union troops would make a rush, and were evidently driving the Confederates back from their positions."

The fighting went on all night, Reyburn remembered.

"After dark," he said, "the firing became more continuous and the flash of the musketry firing as each piece was discharged temporarily illuminated the scene." During the entire time the artillerymen at Fort Stevens poured out a constant barrage of long-range shelling.

"You could watch the progress of the shells as they ascended, looking exactly like gigantic rockets," Reyburn said, "then as they fell, we could see the chasm in the earth made by their explosion. If you could divest yourself of the idea that people were being wounded and killed during this time, it seemed to look exactly like an exhibition of gigantic fireworks."

Maj. John Brinton also took in the scene that afternoon, sitting on his horse just outside of Fort Stevens. "We had quite a sharp fight," he wrote to his mother three days later. "I saw all the fighting here; it was quite brisk and very exciting, bullets whizzing all around."

Navy secretary Welles also rode out to Fort Stevens that evening. "Could see the line of pickets of both armies in the valley, extending a mile or more," Welles wrote in his diary that night. "There was continual firing, without many casualties as far as I could observe, or hear. Two houses in the vicinity were in flames, set on fire by our own people because they obstructed the range of our guns and gave shelter to the Rebel sharpshooters. Other houses and buildings had also been destroyed. A pretty grove nearly opposite the fort was being cut down. War would not spare the tree, if the woodman had."

After watching the action that night, Welles believed that Early would not mount a full-scale attack on the city. The Confederates, he said, "have lost a remarkable opportunity" because of what the hypercritical Welles called the War Department's "neglect, ignorance, folly [and] imbecility in the last degree." Early's troops, Welles said, "might easily have captured Washington. Stanton, Halleck, and Grant are asleep or dumb."

At that point on Monday night Early had not made up his mind about what he would do on the following day. He therefore convened a council of war with his commanding generals—Breckinridge, Rodes, Gordon, and Ramseur—that night at the Silver Spring mansion. John Breckinridge, a distant Blair cousin, had been a guest at Silver Spring during his days in Washington as vice president. As the generals dined, smoked cigars, and drank wine liberated from the Blair larder, Early laid out the pros and cons of invading. Then he heard what his generals had to say.

John Brown Gordon, who earlier in the day had favored an invasion, changed his mind that night. He and the other commanders lobbied not to invade on Tuesday. There "was not a dissenting opinion as to the impolicy of entering the city," Gordon wrote in his memoir.

Gordon also wrote that the generals joked about what would have happened if they had invaded. They discussed "the propriety of putting Gen. John C. Breckinridge at the head of the column and of escorting him to the Senate chamber and seating him again in the Vice-President's chair," Gordon said.

As the generals joked around, some of their "sore-footed men," Gordon said, "were lazily lounging about the cool waters of Silver Spring, picking blackberries in the orchards of Postmaster-General Blair, and merrily estimating the amount of gold and greenbacks that would come into our possession when we should seize the vaults of the United States Treasury."

Gordon overheard two privates discussing the merits of invading Washington. It was "evident," Gordon said, "that neither of these soldiers believed in the wisdom of any serious effort to capture Washington at that time."

Despite the views of his generals, Early claimed that he came out of the Silver Spring council of war inclined to order the invasion the next day.

"After interchanging views with them, being very reluctant to abandon the project of capturing Washington, I determined to make an assault on the enemy's works at daylight next morning," Early said in his autobiography.

But Early had one caveat. He would not launch an invasion if he received information that night "showing its impracticability."

Later that night, in fact, Early heard from Bradley Johnson, who was between Washington and Baltimore. Johnson said that he had found out "from a reliable source" that "two corps had arrived from General Grant's army, and that his whole army was probably in motion." That was nearly the same information that Lee had cabled to Early that day, but that in all likelihood never reached Silver Spring.

With that new news, Early decided to delay his decision about attacking until he took one more close look at the defenses on Tuesday morning, July 12, "as soon as it was light enough to see."

Henry Halleck, among others, continued to worry as late as Tuesday morning that a Confederate assault had a decent chance of succeeding. Washington, he told Grant in a cable that morning, "is now pretty safe," unless, that is, "the forces in some parts of the intrenchments, and they are by no means reliable, being made up of all kind of fragments, should give way before they can be re-enforced from other points. A line thirty-seven miles in length is very difficult to guard at all points with an inferior force."

Charles Dana, Halleck's assistant secretary of war, also expressed his pessimism about the situation on the ground that morning. Dana's main concern was the disjointed Union command structure and how it would affect the course of events if Early decided not to attack.

"Nothing can possibly be done here toward pursuing or cutting off the enemy for want of a commander," Dana said in an 11:30 a.m. cable to Grant. "General Augur commands the defenses of Washington, with McCook and a lot of brigadier-generals under him, but he is not allowed to go outside. Wright commands his own corps. General Gillmore has been assigned to the temporary command of those troops of the Nineteenth Corps in the City of Washington."

That command structure was fragmented enough, Dana said. To make matters worse, he complained to Grant, "there is no head to the whole, and it seems indispensable that you should at once appoint one." Dana said that the elusive Hunter, who was dallying west of Frederick, would be the ranking officer "if he ever gets up, but he will not do." Halleck, Dana said, "directs me to tell you in his judgment Hunter ought instantly to be relieved, having proven himself far more incompetent than even Sigel."

Dana ended with this plea to the Union army's commander:

"General Halleck will not give orders except as he receives them; the president will give none, and until you direct positively and explicitly what is to be done, everything will go on in the deplorable and fatal way in which it has gone on for the past week."

SIXTEEN

Heavens Hung in Black

*War, at the best, is terrible, and this war of ours, in its magnitude
and in its duration, is one of the most terrible.*

—ABRAHAM LINCOLN, JUNE 16, 1864

Abraham Lincoln seemed not to share Halleck and Dana's
fears about the military situation. Nor was he outwardly gripped by the
panic that had overcome so many people in Washington on July 10, 11, and
12. "The President is in very good feather this evening," twenty-five-year-
old presidential secretary John Hay wrote in his diary on July 11. "He seems
not in the least concerned about the safety of Washington. With him the
only concern seems to be whether we can bag or destroy this force in our
front."

The next day—the second day of fighting within five miles of the White
House—Lincoln "seemed in a pleasant and confident humor," Hay wrote.

"Even with the sound of hostile guns in his ears," Hay, with fellow presidential secretary John Nicolay, wrote in 1890, Lincoln wrote "with the utmost calmness to General Grant at Petersburg, thinking only of the chance
of crushing the army which [had] ventured so far from its base. . . ."

Gideon Welles, on the other hand, saw signs that Lincoln felt the danger
much more acutely than Hay observed. "The President has been a good deal

incredulous about a very large army on the upper Potomac," Welles wrote in his diary on July 8. "Yet he begins to manifest anxiety."

Welles thought that Halleck and Lincoln's other military advisers in Washington deliberately kept Lincoln in the dark about Early's progress and the invasion threat so as not to burden the president unnecessarily with unsettling news. Lincoln "is under constraint, I perceived, such as I know is sometimes imposed by the dunderheads at the War Department," the caustic Welles wrote, "when they are in a fog, or scare, and know not what to say or do."

Lincoln, he said, "is now enjoined to silence, while Halleck is in a perfect maze, bewildered, without intelligent decision or self-reliance, and Stanton is wisely ignorant."

Abraham Lincoln had a great deal on his mind in July of 1864. The Civil War had been raging for more than three years. The loss of life and limb on both sides stunned citizens, soldiers, and war managers north and south. More than five hundred thousand on both sides had died, and untold hundreds of thousands were wounded, many seriously. War weariness was particularly acute in the North.

"The awful fighting in the Wilderness and at Cold Harbor had fairly startled the country by the enormous loss of life sustained by the Army of the Potomac, apparently without any corresponding gain in position," the journalist Noah Brooks, a Lincoln confidant, later wrote.

Nothing showed the deteriorating morale in the North more clearly than Lincoln's emotional and political states. On July 11 and 12, with Early's men at the gates of Washington, Lincoln's emotional condition—despite what Hay reported—and the president's political fortunes were precariously close to bottoming out.

"All familiar with him will remember the weary air which became habitual during his last years," the painter Francis B. Carpenter, who spent many days in the White House from March to July of 1864 working on a portrait of Lincoln, said. "This was more of the mind than the body, and no rest and recreation which he allowed himself could relieve it. As he sometimes expressed it, the remedy 'seemed never to reach the *tired* spot.'"

Even in the best of times, Abraham Lincoln exhibited symptoms of what was at the time called "melancholy." Today the condition is described as

Extreme war weariness is evident on the face of
President Lincoln in this, the last photograph of
him, which was taken on April 10, 1865, by
Alexander Gardner. *Credit: The Library of Congress*

depression. "No element of Mr. Lincoln's character," said Henry Clay Whitney, a lawyer and Lincoln confidant, "was so marked, obvious and ingrained
as his mysterious and profound melancholy."

Lincoln "was a sad looking man; his melancholy dripped from him as he
walked," his former law partner and early biographer, William H. Herndon,
said in 1865. "He was gloomy, abstracted, and joyous—rather humorous—
by turns. I do not think he knew what real joy was for many years."

Lincoln's state of mind and the state of his political future in July of 1864
hinged on the relentless and depressing war news of the spring and early summer, namely the fact that an astounding sixty thousand Union soldiers were

killed or wounded in Grant's Wilderness Campaign. And no end was in sight for the slaughter.

"Who shall revive the withered hopes that bloomed at the opening of General Grant's campaign?" a July 12 editorial in the *New York World* asked on the very day that Early's troops were at the gates of Washington.

"This war, as now conducted, is a failure without hope of other issue than the success of the rebellion," the pro-peace, Democratic *World* lamented three weeks later.

The seemingly unrelentingly bad war news did nothing to alleviate Lincoln's chronic melancholy.

"War, at the best, is terrible, and this war of ours, in its magnitude and in its duration, is one of the most terrible," Lincoln said in a June 16, 1864, speech at the Great Sanitary Fair in Philadelphia. "It has deranged business, totally in many localities, and partially in all localities. It has destroyed property, and ruined homes; it has produced a national debt and taxation unprecedented, at least in this country. It has carried mourning to almost every home, until it can almost be said that 'heavens are hung in black.'"

When will the war end? Lincoln asked rhetorically.

"This war has taken three long years," he said. "It was begun or accepted upon the line of restoring the national authority over the whole national domain, and for the American people, as far as my knowledge enables me to speak, I say we are going through on this line if it takes three years more."

As for politics, Lincoln on June 8 had won the Republican presidential nomination, but only after a contentious two-day national convention in Baltimore, which Lincoln did not attend. When he learned from Major Eckert at the War Department telegraph office that the delegates had chosen him, Lincoln reportedly exclaimed, "What! Am I renominated?"

When Eckert assured Lincoln that that was indeed the case, the president asked him "if he would kindly send word over to the White House when the name of the candidate for vice president should have been agreed upon," Noah Brooks wrote. Trying to appeal to a fractured electorate, the Republicans chose a Democrat, Sen. Andrew Johnson of Tennessee, as Lincoln's running mate.

Lincoln and his advisers on July 10 and 11 had faint hope that he would be reelected to a second term in November in what would be the first and only national election held in a democracy during an all-out Civil War. A large part of Lincoln's political problem: his Republican Party was beset by internal strife.

Radical Republicans chafed at any Lincoln gesture that did not advance the cause of continued all-out war. Moderate Republicans, on the other hand, argued that it was in the nation's best interest to come to some kind of accommodation with the Confederacy. Lincoln completely rejected that idea.

Then there were the Democrats. The opposition also was bitterly divided among those who wanted an immediate end to the carnage—the Peace Democrats—and those who wanted the war to continue. The Democrats, though, were united on one thing: their vehement disdain for the president and his leadership in fighting the War of Rebellion. One wing of the party, the deservedly nicknamed Copperheads (after the venomous snake and the copper pennies that some wore as ID badges), worked hand in glove with Confederate political operatives to try to sabotage Lincoln at every turn.

Later that summer the Democrats would choose as their 1864 presidential nominee former Union army commander in chief Gen. George B. McClellan, whom Lincoln had relieved of his command after he failed to capitalize on the Union position following the Battle of Antietam in November of 1862. McClellan had retired to his New Jersey home, where the Democrats courted him and convinced him to run against Lincoln. McClellan's running mate, Rep. George H. Pendelton of Ohio, was an out-and-out Peace Democrat.

War weariness and his shaky political future weighed on Lincoln's psyche during the spring and summer of 1864. "The immense slaughter of our brave men chills and sickens us all," Gideon Welles wrote in his diary on June 2. "It is impossible," he wrote on July 11, "for the country to bear up under these monstrous errors and wrongs."

Welles later elaborated on the despondency that hung over the North in the late spring and summer of 1864. "An accumulation of disheartening difficulties, internal and external in the free States—differences such as loyal and disloyal, democrat and republican, republican and radical, personal and sectional—had clouded the administration," Gideon Welles wrote in 1878, "with scarcely a cheering ray to lighten or encourage the government in the mighty struggle to suppress the rebellion."

Lincoln's "ability and energy in prosecuting the war were questioned," Welles said, "his conciliatory policy toward the rebels and his disinclination to confiscate their property were denounced, and his amnesty and reconstruction measures were censured and condemned. . . . Military failures and inactivity everywhere rendered the summer gloomy and disheartening."

Lincoln, Welles said, "was blamed and held responsible for the killed and wounded by a large portion of his countrymen."

There is little doubt that Lincoln considered the political and military ramifications of what would have happened if Early had invaded Washington on July 11 or 12. He knew that if Early's men had broken through the defenses, Confederate veterans would have been running loose on the streets of Washington, D.C., that the U.S. Treasury, virtually undefended, was sitting ready for looting, and that tons upon tons of brand-new, desperately needed war supplies, from blankets to rifles, were there for the taking.

Washington's "capture and possession for a day would have been disastrous to the cause of the Union," U.S. Treasury Department official Lucius Chittenden wrote in his war memoir. "Early would have seized the money in the Treasury; the archives of the departments, the immense supplies of clothing, arms, and ammunition in store; he would have compelled General Grant to raise the siege of Richmond; he would have destroyed uncounted millions in value of property. . . ."

Confederate sympathizers in Maryland, Chittenden said, "would have swarmed to [Early's] assistance, and he could certainly have held the capital long enough to give Great Britain the excuse she so much desired, to recognize the Confederacy and break the [Union] blockade" of Southern ports.

Lincoln himself also was a target of opportunity, not to mention the U.S. Capitol and dozens of other government buildings, as Chittenden noted. Without Lincoln's knowledge—and later to his great annoyance—assistant navy secretary Gustavus Vasa Fox had arranged to have the Baltimore, a small ordnance steamship, waiting on the Potomac to spirit the president out of town had Early's men broken through into the streets of Washington.

Lincoln knew that, even if he had escaped Early's men, his already low chances of winning the presidential election in November would have been even lower. It is quite possible that a Confederate incursion into Washington on July 10, 11, or 12 would have led to a Democrat—maybe even a Copperhead—winning the White House in November.

An invasion almost certainly would have changed the course—and perhaps the outcome—of the Civil War. As Lucius Chittenden put it in 1891: such a "loss of prestige and property, compared with which previous disasters would have been trifling," easily could have been "a blow fatally destructive to the Union cause."

An invasion remained very much an option for Jubal Early at daylight on Tuesday, July 12, when he rode from Silver Spring back to Fort Stevens to make his final decision about whether or not to move into Washington. The last of his men had finally made it to Washington late Monday night. Ramseur's, Rodes's, and Gordon's divisions were arrayed just outside the range of the heavy Fort Stevens artillery. Confederate pickets and sharpshooters formed a rough line closer in to the fort just in front of the Union skirmish line.

Early, like Lincoln, realized the high stakes involved. The decision he made did not come lightly as he took one last look at Fort Stevens through his field glasses that morning.

"The parapets," he saw, were "lined with troops."

He knew that thousands of the troops lining the parapets there and at Fort Reno and the other Northern Union forts were experienced Sixth Corps soldiers. And he knew how physically strong the forts and fortifications were.

Jubal Early, for one of the few times in his military career, did not make the aggressive move. Then and there he gave up "all hopes of capturing Washington," he said in his autobiography, after having arrived "in sight of the dome of the Capitol, and given the Federal authorities a terrible fright."

Early abandoned the idea of invading, but he decided to cause other kinds of trouble that day. "I determined," he said, "to remain in front of the fortifications during the 12th, and retire at night, as I was satisfied that to remain longer would cause the loss of my entire force."

Halleck that morning had made an uncharacteristically decisive move. At 6:15 a.m., having determined that Early had concentrated his force outside Fort Stevens, Halleck ordered all of Wright's Sixth Corps troops to that fort and gave Wright the authority to take command there.

Wright had beseeched Augur the night before to let his veteran Sixth

Corps men loose on the Confederate troops. "The enemy has been close to Fort Stevens, and although driven back, is still not far distant," Wright cabled Augur at 10:00 p.m. "I believe it to be only a very light skirmish line, and with your permission will send a brigade out against it and try to clean it out."

McCook's men, Wright said bluntly, "are not as good as mine for this purpose."

Augur replied later that night with his own blunt, one-sentence dismissal of Wright's request. "I do not consider it advisable to make any advance," Augur said, "until our lines are better established, perhaps tomorrow."

South and west of Fort Stevens, one-armed general Martin Hardin decided to take matters into his own hands on Tuesday morning. Just before dawn he sent Col. Charles Russell Lowell (the Harvard-educated nephew of the famed poet James Russell Lowell) and Lt. Col. Casper Crowinshield and their Second Massachusetts Cavalry Regiment after McCausland in front of Fort Reno. The Second Massachusetts, armed with seven-shot Spencer repeating rifles, drove off McCausland's men.

Outside Fort Stevens, Union shelling, Confederate sniping, and occasionally strong skirmishing took place all day. During a day that dawned "bright and glorious," George Stevens remembered, "from the parapets of Fort Stevens could be seen the lines of rebel skirmishers, from whose rifles the white puffs of smoke rose as they discharged their pieces at our pickets."

Confederate cavalry, Frank Wilkeson at nearby Fort Totten remembered, "rode aimlessly to and fro along the edge of a wood, about five miles from our fort. We saw their artillery glisten in the sun."

Portions of the Confederate skirmish line, he said, "were within range of the forts, and heavy guns opened on it away off to our left." The Union artillery performance from Fort Stevens "was the poorest I ever saw," he said. "It was evident that the department clerks or the 100-day men were serving the guns. The Confederates did not pay the slightest attention to this fire."

Wilkeson, of course, was correct about who was manning the guns. Ironically, the experienced artillerymen of the Eleventh Vermont, who were stationed at Fort Stevens earlier in the war, sat in reserve watching the inept firepower demonstration. "Long practice" had made the Eleventh Vermont's "officers and men entirely familiar with the range and capacity of every gun, howitzer, and mortar" at Fort Stevens, the unit's commanding officer Aldace Walker said after the war.

His men, sitting idle behind the fort, "had the mortification of seeing the artillery entrusted to troops who could hardly load heavy ordnance with safety. When, by the lucky chance of [the unit's] return to what seemed like home, great good might have been secured as the fruit of its early labors— unfortunately no use was made of the skill its members longed to exercise."

The Union skirmish line that day, Alfred Bellard reported, "was on a range of hills that surrounded the city." That afternoon Bellard's Ninth Veteran Reserve Corps Regiment, which had moved from Fort Reno to Fort Stevens, received an order to man the line.

"Advancing to the edge of the hill, we were deployed as skirmishers with our company on the extreme left," he said. "After we had scrambled over lots of brush wood, we finally reached our position on the crest of the hill, and saw the rebel skirmishers posted on a range of hills just in front of us, but out of range so far as we were concerned, as we were armed with smooth bore muskets, while the rebels had long range rifles."

Soon thereafter, Bellard's regiment received the order to go back to the rifle pits closer to the fort. "During the day," he said, "our artillery fire set fire to a mansion that was between the lines, and a company of rebels who had taken possession were dislodged. What with the burning houses, the bursting of shells and the rattle of small arms, it looked and sounded very much like old times, but with this exception, that very few men were killed or wounded."

Alfred Roe, the Union prisoner who witnessed the fighting behind the Confederate lines, also likened the sound of the battle to earlier fighting. "The noise of the encounter on the 12th was great," Roe wrote in 1890, "and the rebel yell, varied by Union shouts, seemed as vivid as ever."

Dr. Stevens, who was assigned to a rear barracks at Fort Stevens that had been converted into a hospital, remembered the day as one in which he treated dozens of dead and severely wounded Union soldiers. Following a Union artillery barrage, Wright, taking advantage of Halleck's order that morning overriding Augur's hesitancy to take action, ordered Col. Daniel Bidwell and his Second Division's Third Brigade to attack the rebels at 4:00.

"The pseudo-soldiers who filled the trenches around the Fort were astounded at the temerity displayed by these war-torn veterans in going out before the breastworks and benevolently volunteered the most earnest words of caution," said Aldace Walker of the Eleventh Vermont.

After that short, fierce fight, "the commanding officer of every regiment

Members of the Third Massachusetts Heavy Artillery manning the big guns at Fort Stevens in 1865. *Credit: The Library of Congress*

in the brigade was either killed or wounded," Stevens wrote in his war memoir.

The "big guns boomed," Pvt. B. F. North of the 122nd New York said in 1891, "the Johnnies ran; we ran after them." The Union men advanced smartly; Early's men retreated, but then fought back. We "were having it all our way when, presto, they halted, rallied, turned and under sharp fire advanced to gobble us," North remembered.

"Just then one of their balls crashed into poor [Private Snediker's] left shin and flattened there. I pitied him but he grinned and bore it like a hero."

The Confederate fire "was so hot that in the little time required for this manoeuvre one third of the men of this brigade were killed or wounded," Lucius Chittenden, who witnessed the fight, later wrote. "I had supposed that a battlefield was filled with the shrieks and groans of the wounded and dying. There was nothing of the kind, scarcely a spasmodic action, and in the majority of cases those who had been struck by the enemy's balls seemed rather to be lying quietly down."

The fight, Stevens said, "had lasted but a few minutes, when the stream of bleeding, mangled ones began to come to the rear. Men, leaning upon the shoulders of comrades, or borne painfully on stretchers, the pallor of their countenances rendered more ghastly by the thick dust which had settled upon them, were brought into the hospitals by scores, where the medical officers . . . were hard at work binding up ghastly wounds, administering stimulants, coffee and food, or resorting to the hard necessity of amputation."

The "little brigade," Stevens said, "numbering only a thousand men when it went into action, had lost two hundred and fifty of its number."

Early's men also suffered, primarily under a withering Union artillery barrage. "One could follow the course of the shells by their burning fuses," Chittenden remembered. "They rose in long, graceful curves, screaming like demons of the pit, then descending with like curves into the crowds of running men, they appeared to explode as they touched the ground."

The rebel troops "swayed outward with the explosion, but many fell, and did not rise again," Chittenden said. "After the retreat of the last Confederates, the bodies lay so near each other that they almost touched. It was beautiful artillery work, but its results were horrible." The "odor of burning flesh filled the air; it was a sickening spectacle!"

The Reverend Pliny Sanborne had volunteered that day to work in the makeshift Union hospital at Fort Stevens. His account written that night jibes with Stevens's. "Labored all day in hospital and grounds," Stevens wrote in his diary. "Dead—dying and wounded. Saw skirmishing.—skirmishing extends forty-eight miles—Whissing of balls and crack of rifles."

Many other civilians came out to Fort Stevens, not to lend a hand as Sanborne did, but simply to get a firsthand look at the action. "It is a wonder that more men were not wounded or killed there, as the grounds in and near the fort were crowded with citizens, whose curiosity had induced them to be so venturesome," Andrew Wilkins of the Sixth Corps' 122nd New York later recalled.

"I was much amused to see the 'cits,' as the boys call them, duck their heads and even go through the very undignified performance of hugging mother earth as an occasional bullet came whizzing by. The 'rebs' could have picked off very many of them had they chosen as their white summer costumes formed a good, conspicuous mark, but they humanely refrained, and when a 'stray' bullet did come over it seemed always to pick out some poor soldier as its victim."

The fighting that day raised fears among many Union troops manning the forts. "We grew anxious," Frank Wilkeson wrote in his memoir. "I knew that Early, who had eighteen thousand veteran soldiers with him, could break our line whenever he saw fit to strike it. I knew that he could capture Washington in two hours, if he determined to take the national capital. How we fumed and fretted!"

SEVENTEEN

————·••·————

Scared as Blue as Hell's Brimstone

President Lincoln and Secretary Seward, accompanied by one or two cavalry officers and a cavalry escort, visited the threatened defenses on Monday and yesterday.

— *WASHINGTON DAILY NATIONAL INTELLIGENCER*, JULY 13, 1864

Grabbing the president by the arm, [Oliver Wendell Holmes] dragged him under cover, and afterwards, in wave upon wave of hot misgiving, was unable to forget that in doing so he had said, "Get down, you fool!"

—ALEXANDER WOOLCOTT, FEBRUARY 1928

Abraham Lincoln took in the fighting at Fort Stevens on Tuesday, July 12, just as he had done the day before. Lincoln's "interest in the progress of affairs was intense and ardent," his secretaries Nicolay and Hay noted in their 1890 biography of the president, "and his presence among the soldiers roused the greatest enthusiasm."

As he did the day before, the six-foot, four-inch Lincoln stood on the parapet on July 12, wearing his customary frock coat and tall stovepipe hat. And for the second consecutive day, he made an inviting target and came under fire. Amid the firing on Monday, according to Hay (who was not there and heard the story either from the president or from a third party), "a soldier ordered him to get down or he would have his head knocked off."

Something similar happened on Tuesday—something that later evolved into something of a folk legend. The story goes that during the afternoon fighting, a rebel sharpshooter out on the skirmish line climbed onto the roof of an abandoned house, took aim, and shot a Union surgeon, Dr. C. C. V. A.

This plaque marks the spot on the rebuilt Fort Stevens parapet where Lincoln came under fire on July 11 and 12—the only time in American history that a sitting president was fired upon during a war. *Credit: Michael Keating*

Crawford of the 102nd Pennsylvania. The bullet tore through Crawford's leg. Crawford was standing on the parapet right next to Lincoln.

One of the bystanders to the shooting was Horatio Wright's twenty-three-year-old aide-de-camp, Capt. Oliver Wendell Holmes Jr. of the Twentieth Massachusetts Infantry Regiment. Holmes had earned his staff assignment, having fought at the Battles of Antietam, Wilderness, Fredericksburg, and many others. When Crawford was hit, Holmes—who went on to become one of the nation's most celebrated Supreme Court justices—turned to Lincoln and shouted, "Get down, you fool!"

Or so the much-repeated story goes.

Did Oliver Wendell Holmes utter those famous words? A close examination of at the primary source evidence indicates strongly that the story is apocryphal. Many eyewitnesses have attested to the fact that Lincoln did go to Fort Stevens on July 12, that he did, indeed, stand on the Fort Stevens parapet to watch the war, that he came under fire, and that he was urged in strong terms to climb down out of harm's way. But none of the witnesses mentioned Oliver Wendell Holmes nor the "Get down you fool" remark.

Nor did any contemporary newspaper accounts mention the incident. The Holmes story did not become public until February of 1928, when the famed *New Yorker* critic and commentator Alexander Woolcott recounted the incident in an article in the *Atlantic Monthly* magazine. Woolcott's source: what Holmes himself told friends had happened that day.

"Grabbing the president by the arm," Woolcott wrote, Holmes "dragged him under cover, and afterwards, in wave upon wave of hot misgiving, was unable to forget that in doing so he had said, 'Get down, you fool!'"

The ubiquitous navy secretary Gideon Welles was among those at Fort Stevens that day who later wrote about what they'd seen and experienced. Welles had ridden out to the fort that afternoon from downtown Washington. Inside the fort, Welles wrote in his journal that night, "we found the President, who was sitting in the shade, his back against the parapet towards the enemy."

Welles did not see Lincoln on the parapet.

But many others at Fort Stevens did, including Pvt. David T. Bull of the 147th Ohio National Guard, who placed Lincoln on the parapet facing the enemy. In a letter to his wife dated July 14, Bull wrote that a "large force" of Confederate troops "gathered around a house in front of the Fort and there was a sharp shooter got up in the top of the house and thought he would kill some of our men that was on the parapets."

Lincoln, whom Bull called "Old Abe," and "his doctor was standing up on the parapets," Bull wrote, "and the sharp shooter that I speak of shot the doctor through the left thigh, and Old Abe ordered our men to fall back."

Bull made no mention of Holmes or his strong verbal warning.

Nor did another eyewitness, Dr. George Stevens. "President Lincoln and his wife drove up to the barracks" at Fort Stevens "unattended, except by their coachman," Stevens wrote in his 1870 memoir. "The carriage stopped at the door of the hospital, and the President and his affable lady entered into familiar conversation with the surgeon in charge, praising the deeds of the old Sixth corps. . . ."

The Lincolns stayed for about an hour, Stevens remembered, "when General Wright and his staff arrived on the ground, accompanied by several ladies and gentlemen from the city."

Lincoln and his entourage watched the sharp fight that took place at 4:00 that afternoon, Stevens said. During the action, he wrote, "President Lincoln stood upon the parapet of the fort watching, with eager interest, the scene below him. Bullets came whistling around, and one severely wounded a surgeon who stood within three feet of the President. Mrs. Lincoln entreated him to leave the fort, but he refused. He, however, accepted the advice of General Wright to descend from the parapet and watch the battle from a less exposed position."

Stevens made no mention of Oliver Wendell Holmes.

Dr. Robert Rayburn, who also was on the scene, put Lincoln on the parapet with Secretary of War Stanton in a newspaper article that Rayburn wrote in 1906. Lincoln, Rayburn said, "watched the conflict from the ramparts of Fort Stevens, and rather recklessly exposed himself to the enemy's fire. His tall, conspicuous figure as he stood there made him an excellent mark for the Confederate sharp shooters.

"My recollection is that Gen. Wright, in rather a brusque manner, almost forcibly insisted that he should get down from his exposed position and said he was not going to have the President of the United States shot in that way."

Rayburn did not mention Oliver Wendell Holmes.

Lt. Col. Thomas Hyde of Wright's staff, writing in his 1894 war memoir, said he was sitting on the Fort Stevens parapet—Hyde called it "the rampart"—watching "our people get into position, and looking at the flight of shells from a few great guns firing," when he "saw the President standing on the wall a little way off."

Bullets, Hyde said, "were whizzing over in a desultory manner, and the puffs of smoke in the woods opposite were growing in number." Just then "an officer standing on the wall between me and Mr. Lincoln suddenly keeled over and was helped away. A lot of people persuaded Mr. Lincoln to get down out of range, which he very reluctantly did."

Hyde did not mention his fellow staff officer Oliver Wendell Holmes, although it is conceivable that Holmes was one of the people Hyde spoke of who "persuaded" Lincoln to get down from the parapet.

George A. Armes, then a lieutenant with the Veteran Reserve Corps, also was at Fort Stevens. Lincoln, Armes said in his 1900 memoir, insisted on climbing upon the parapet, thus exposing himself to the fire of the enmy. The president, he said, was "frequently cautioned by the commanding officer," that is, General Wright, "not to make a target of himself." Lincoln "was finally told," Armes said, "that if he again exposed himself he (the officer) would be forced to place him under arrest."

To which, Armes said, "Lincoln smilingly replied: 'Well, I reckon I had better obey orders, then.'"

Armes did not mention Holmes in his account.

The unit history of the Thirty-seventh Massachusetts—which had helped construct the fort in 1861 and which arrived at Fort Stevens that day—contains an account of the incident that also does not mention Holmes. A Confederate bullet, the history recounts, "struck a wheel of the siege gun and wounded the surgeon standing almost directly behind and close to the President. The latter was then induced by General Wright to sit down out of range, and a chair was placed for him against the parapet."

A few minutes later, according to this account, one of Lincoln's cabinet members addressed the seated president. "Mr. President," he said, "if you will look over in that direction, you can see just where the rebels are."

To which Lincoln replied: "My impression is that if I am where I can see the rebels, they are where they can see me."

Nicolay and Hay, in their authoritative 1890 biography of Lincoln, offer an account of the incident that has Wright—not Holmes—inducing Lincoln to get out of the line of fire. Their version is among the few that says that Crawford, the surgeon, was killed by the Confederate sharpshooter.

Lincoln "stood, apparently unconscious of danger, watching, with that grave and passive countenance, the progress of the fight amid the whizzing bullets of the sharp-shooters, until an officer fell mortally wounded within three feet of him," the secretaries' account goes. "General Wright peremptorily represented to him the needless risk he was running."

Wright himself provided a detailed account of the incident in 1870 in a letter he wrote to Dr. Stevens, following the publication of his memoir. Lincoln, Wright recalled six years after the fact, "evinced a remarkable coolness and disregard of danger" that day. Wright said he "invited" Lincoln "to see the fight in which we were about to engage, without for a moment supposing he would accept."

The president, Wright said, "took his position on my side of the parapet, and all my entreaties failed to move him, although in addition to the stray shots that were passing over, the spot was a favorite mark for sharpshooters. When the surgeon was shot after I had cleared the parapet of everyone else, he still maintained his ground till I told him I should have to remove him forcibly."

The "absurdity" of "the idea of sending off the President under guard seemed to amuse" Lincoln, Wright said, "but in consideration of my earnestness in the matter, he agreed to compromise by sitting behind the parapet instead of standing upon it."

Wright said that he "could not help thinking" that "in leaving the parapet," Lincoln "did so rather in deference to my earnestly expressed wishes, than from any consideration of personal danger, though the danger had been so unmistakably proved by the wounding of the officer alluded to. After he left the parapet, he would persist in standing up from time to time, thus exposing nearly one-half of his tall form."

Wright recollected his exact words to Lincoln during a visit Wright made to Fort Stevens in 1897. After asking Lincoln to come down from the parapet and finding that his "entreaties failed to make an impression" on the president, Wright said: "Mr. President, I know you are commander of the armies of the United States, but I am in command here, and as you are not safe where you are standing, and I am responsible for your personal safety, I order you to come down."

President Lincoln, Wright said, "looked at me, smiled, and then, more in consideration of my earnestness than from inclination, stepped down and took position behind the parapet."

Maj. Henry Kyd Douglas was among the Confederate soldiers on the other side of the skirmish line when Lincoln stood upon the parapet and when Wright's Sixth Corps attacked on Tuesday afternoon. "I saw [the attack] coming and thought we were 'gone up,'" Douglas, who was on Early's staff, wrote in his memoir. The attack, though, "proved to be little more than a heavy skirmish," Douglas said.

Said heavy skirmishing lasted until dark, when Early gave the order for his men to pull out.

That night, Early, in the company of Breckinridge and Gordon back in Silver Spring, sent for Douglas. The following conversation ensued:

"Major, we haven't taken Washington," Early told Douglas in his "falsetto drawl," but "we've scared Abe Lincoln like hell!"

"Yes general," Douglas replied, "but this afternoon when that Yankee line moved out against us, I think some other people were scared as blue as hell's brimstone!"

"How about that, General," Breckinridge laughed.

"That's true," Early replied, "but it won't appear in history."

EIGHTEEN

———·•·———

An Egregious Blunder

The great rebel raid is over.
— *THE NEW YORK TIMES*, JULY 15, 1864

It did appear in history. Two weeks after Jubal Early marched on Washington, England's newspaper of record, *The Times* of London, reported that Early's "operations in the neighborhood of Washington are the most dramatic part of the history."

To "be told that the President of the Republic was very nearly taking refuge in a gunboat, and that he was expected in New York, is not likely to raise the Federal spirits," *The Times* opined. "For a time it appeared as if the Confederates would penetrate, at least temporarily, the Federal capital."

The historical record also shows that while the fighting outside Fort Stevens was a relatively minor affair in a war in which the worst battles counted casualties in the tens of thousands, as many as 370 Union men were killed or wounded in Washington's outskirts between July 10 and 12. The Sixth Corps' First and Third Brigades bore the brunt of the casualties; they suffered 59 men killed and 145 wounded in the skirmishing against Early's forces.

Figures for Early's losses do not appear in any official CSA records. The best estimate is that the Union artillery barrages and the skirmishing outside Fort Stevens cost some 500 Confederate dead, wounded, and captured.

The history books also recorded that the last shots fired in the Fort Stevens fighting came at around 10:00 on Tuesday night, July 12. The "remainder of the night," General Wheaton said, "was occupied in strengthening the position, burying the dead, and caring for the wounded. . . ."

A few hours earlier, Early had led his men away from Washington. At "about dark" that night, Early said in his autobiography, "we commenced retiring and did so without molestation."

Lincoln wanted the Union army to make every effort to pursue Early. "The President," John Hay wrote in his diary on Wednesday, July 13, "thinks we should push our whole column up the river road & cut off as many as possible of the retreating raiders."

That morning, however, the Union generals, emulating what their brethren did after many earlier Civil War battles, did not order an all-out effort to go after the retreating Southern forces, the last of whom by then had quietly left the skirmish lines in front of Fort Stevens.

The main reason: disorganization among the Union high command. Grant, directing things a hundred miles away outside Richmond, waited until just before midnight to assign Wright the "supreme command of all troops moving against the enemy, regardless of the rank of the other commanders."

Wright, Grant told Halleck, "should get outside of the trenches with all the force he possibly can and should push Early to the end, supplying himself from the country." But by that time, Early's men had been moving steadily away from Washington for at least three or four hours.

What did the on-site commanders do on Wednesday morning? Maj. Gen. Montgomery Meigs, for one, was content to take in the quiet outside Fort Stevens pensively and do little more than order his pressed-into-service men to eat breakfast.

"The gray dawn spread over the landscape widely extended in sight," Meigs wrote in his official report three days later. "An occasional shot from a suspicious picket and the low of a cow or the bray of a mule alone broke the stillness of the morning, and at last the sun arose and all remained quiet."

A few Union cavalry "were sent out," Meigs said, and "reported the rebel positions abandoned." The Union troops at Fort Stevens, he said, "remained in position till full daylight," at which time he "sent the men to their breakfast and continued our work of clearing off obstructions to our fire and completing our intrenchments." Then he sent the men back to their civilian jobs.

Meigs's "irregulars," Assistant Secretary of War Charles A. Dana later wrote, "were withdrawn from the fortifications, General Meigs marching his division of quartermaster's clerks and employees to their desks; and Admiral Goldsborough, who had marshaled the marines and sailors, returned to smoke his pipe on his own doorstep."

McCook did send two companies of men out to chase Early that morning. They caught up to the rear guard of the Confederate troops, and managed to return to Washington with captured prisoners; to wit, a group of wounded and sick rebel soldiers left behind by Rodes in makeshift hospitals in Silver Spring and Leesborough.

McCook's men brought in "a few prisoners," John Hay, who was on the scene, wrote in his diary that day. They "were ragged & dirty but apparently hearty & well-fed of late. Most of them expressed themselves anxious to get out of the army. Said they had been watching for a chance, &c &c."

Lowell's 750 cavalrymen left Fort Reno that morning and also chased after the Confederates. They engaged in a sharp skirmish with a much larger force of rearguard Confederate cavalry under Col. William B. Jackson in Rockville. It did not go well for Lowell. Jackson's men charged Lowell's advance guard, who were driven back "nearly through the town," Lowell reported that afternoon. His men then dismounted and managed, barely, to hold off Jackson's men.

"My regiment in the town, I fear, was mostly enveloped by the enemy," Lowell reported, "and are severely whipped."

Charles A. Humphries, the Second Massachusetts's chaplain, gave a much more positive spin on the engagement in his 1918 war memoir. When Lowell's advance guard came upon Johnson's men, Humphries said, the Massachusetts men "charged upon them gallantly." The Confederates "were soon provoked to turn, resolved to *wipe out* our regiment."

A "heavy counter-charge," Humphries said, overwhelmed the "advance squadron, hurling it back upon the rest of the regiment just as it was being led by Colonel Lowell through the centre of town."

Lowell—"not the man thus to give up the day," Humphries noted—rallied the troops. "At the very first favorable position, with a splendid audacity, and a voice sure to be obeyed, he shouted the order—'Halt! Dismount!'" Lowell's men, inspired by his strong leadership, "in a moment sprang from their saddles, in another moment they were in line, and in the next moment poured such a hot volley into the pursuing column that it recoiled in confusion."

The Confederates regrouped and made "four impetuous charges" at Lowell's "small force," Humphries said, "till the enemy were forced to retire without dislodging him from his position."

Both Jackson and Lowell, in point of fact, retired. What Humphries didn't mention in his breathless account was that about thirty Massachusetts cavalrymen were killed or wounded and some were taken prisoner before Lowell—who would be fatally wounded at the Battle of Cedar Creek on October 19—returned to Washington.

While the Union forces halfheartedly chased Early, cleared out obstructions around Fort Stevens, touched up their trenches, and went back to their desk jobs, Early and his men had made their way back through Silver Spring and Rockville, then turned south at Poolesville. Early's army had with them a good number of Union prisoners taken at Monocacy, what was left of the $220,000 in tribute they had collected in Hagerstown and Frederick, supplies they had purchased with those funds, as well as what Early called "quite a large number of beef cattle," horses, and mules his men had confiscated in the previous two weeks.

They left behind a trail of ransacked civilian property. Noah Brooks, who rode out to Washington's Maryland suburbs after the battle with other correspondents, later wrote that he saw "traces of rebel occupation five or six miles from Washington." Horses, he said, "had been picketed in the orchards; fences were torn down and used for firewood; books, letters, and women's wearing-apparel were scattered about the grounds, showing that the raiders had made the best use of their time in looting the houses where they had been quartered."

Brooks described one "comfortable family mansion" that was "in a sad state of wreck" as "if a wild Western cyclone had swept through the building." Furniture, he said, "was smashed, crockery broken, and even a handsome piano was split up in the very wantonness of destruction. Obscene drawings covered the walls." Someone had scrawled in charcoal on a wall of the house the words: "Fifty thousand Virginian homes have been devastated in like manner."

On Thursday, July 14, Early took his army back across the Potomac River and into Virginia at White's Ford, just north of Leesburg. It was a very quiet crossing with no Union troops in sight.

Wright had assured Augur the night before that "there will be no delay on my part to head off the enemy, and that the men I have will do all that the number of men can do." But Wright did delay and all that he and his men did was make contact with the slowest stragglers among the Confederate troops.

"The pursuit of Early proved, on the whole, an egregious blunder," Dana later said. "Wright accomplished nothing, and drew back as soon as he got where he might have done something worth while. As it was, Early escaped with the whole of his plunder."

Everybody, presidential secretaries Nicolay and Hay later wrote, "was eager for the pursuit to begin." Why then did the pursuit come too late? Nicolay and Hay blamed a series of circumstances: Grant, they said, "was too far away to give the necessary orders." Lincoln, "true to the position he had taken when Grant was made general in chief, would not interfere, though he observed with anguish the undisturbed retreat of Early." And Halleck, "whose growing disposition to avoid responsibility had become only too apparent, merely told Augur what Wright [ought] to do to strike the retiring column. . . ."

The caustic Gideon Welles placed the blame primarily upon his bête noire, Henry Halleck. Welles met with Halleck at 11:00 on Wednesday morning, July 13, the navy secretary wrote in his diary. While Welles sat in his office, Halleck received a telegram informing him that Early's men had passed through Rockville at around three o'clock that morning.

"They are making, I remarked, for Edwards Ferry and will get off with their plunder if we have no force there to prevent [them]," Welles told Halleck.

Halleck "said it was by no means certain they would cross at Edwards Ferry," Welles wrote in his diary that night. "There was harshness and spite in his tone."

The Confederate forces around Washington, Welles said, were "defiant and insolent, our men were resolute and brave, but the . . . generals were alarmed and ignorant, and have made themselves and the Administration appear contemptible."

Abraham Lincoln shared that assessment, according to several close as-
sociates. When John Hay asked the president on Thursday night, July 14,
what news he had heard about Early, Lincoln told his secretary: "Wright
telegraphs that he thinks the enemy are all across the Potomac but that he
has halted and sent out an infantry reconnaissance, for fear he might come
across the rebels and catch some of them."

Lincoln, Hay said, "is evidently disgusted."

He had learned from Lincoln's "own lips," the newspaper correspondent
Noah Brooks later wrote, that Lincoln's "chief anxiety" about Early's move
into Maryland "was that the invading forces might not be permitted to get
away." Lincoln blamed Halleck, Brooks said, for what happened.

Halleck's "manifest desire to avoid taking responsibility without the immediate sanction of General Grant was the main reason why the rebels,
having threatened Washington and sacked the peaceful farms and villages
of Maryland, got off scatheless," Brooks said. For months afterward Lincoln
"frequently referred to the escape of Early as one of the distressing features
of his experience in the city of Washington."

Grant, barely disguising his disgust, told Halleck on July 12 that he
wanted Halleck to go after Early's men with everything Old Brains could
muster. Early "should have on his heels, veterans, Militiamen, men on
horseback and everything that can be got," Grant said. The object: "to follow, to eat out Virginia clear and clean as far as they go, so that Crows flying
over it for the balance of this season will have to carry their provender with
them."

Mary Todd Lincoln, the First Lady, shared the opinion that Halleck was
to blame for not sending troops after Early.

Later that summer, according to a story that circulated widely in Washington, Halleck paid a visit to the president and Mrs. Lincoln at their retreat
at the Soldiers' Home. Halleck, in jest, said to Mrs. Lincoln: "I intend to
have a full-length portrait of you painted, standing on the ramparts of Fort
Stevens overlooking the fight."

To which Mary Todd Lincoln supposedly replied: "That is all very well,
and I can assure you of one thing, Mr. Secretary. If I had a few *ladies* with
me, the Rebels would not have been permitted to get away as they did."

NINETEEN

The Verdict

[It] was hoped that by threatening Washington and Baltimore Genl Grant would be compelled either to weaken himself so much for their protection as to afford us an opportunity to attack him, or that he might be induced to attack us.

—ROBERT E. LEE, JULY 19, 1864

The "great rebel raid," *The New York Times* correspondent William Swinton reported on the front page of the July 15 editions, "is over." It "abruptly ends the boldest, and probably the most successful of all the rebel raids," Swinton said. "There is much in the whole affair that time alone can clear up. It is too early yet for a verdict. That 'some one has blundered' is obvious; but who he is must be left for time to disclose."

Assistant Secretary of War Dana, who had witnessed much of the fighting in Washington on July 11 and 12, had a long list of blunderers topped by Halleck, Augur, and McCook. I "do not exaggerate in the least when I say that such a lamentable want of intelligence, energy and purpose was never before seen in any command," Dana said, in a scathing appraisal of the Union military's performance that he sent at 9:00 on the night of July 12 to Brig. Gen. John A. Rawlins, one of Grant's top aides.

Dana began his evisceration of the generals' performance—in a telegram that he stressed was for Rawlins's "eye and that of [Grant] alone"—with a lament over the state of the Union's intelligence. "It would be difficult to

give you an idea how little we know respecting this force which has been before Washington now for nearly three (3) days," Dana told Rawlins. "It is
still undetermined how much infantry there is in it or whether there is more
than one battery of Artillery."

Dana harshly criticized McCook for doing little or nothing in the way of
reconnaissance until Wright had taken over at Fort Stevens and said that
Hardin was, "if possible, a bigger fool than McCook. . . ." No reconnaissance, Dana said, "had been undertaken from our lines—nor had any skirmishers been pushed forward to any considerable distance." Until Wright
arrived, he said, "McCook had had no skirmishers out at all but had allowed
the rebel sharpshooters to get up near [the] line and pick the men off at the
embrasures of the fort."

Dana then reiterated his disgust at the confused Union command structure. There "was no general commander—no real knowledge of what was
in the front—nothing but wild imagination and stupidity." Dana faulted
Augur because he had not "personally visited any part of the lines." I am
sure, he said of Augur, "that he knows as little respecting them as I did before I went out."

As for Halleck, Dana spared the beleaguered army chief of staff no
venom. "Halleck seems to be about as well informed as Augur," Dana said,
"and I judge that he contributes quite as much as the latter to the prevailing
confusion & inefficiency."

The army chief, Dana told Rawlins the next night, "strenuously opposed sending Wright out and the President was unwilling to take any
responsibility—Senators [Benjamin Franklin] Wade & [Zachariah] Chandler
were nearly frantic at the impossibility of getting anything done but found the
President unwilling to overrule the obstinate prudence of Gen. Halleck."

Dana went on to accuse Halleck of an extremely serious dereliction of
duty: being too drunk to do his job. Basing his charge on "testimony of those
best informed," Dana told Rawlins that Halleck's mind "has been seriously
impaired by the excessive use of liquor, and that as [a] general thing it is regularly muddled after dinner every day."

Whether or not Halleck was too drunk to command effectively—no
other witness publicly accused him of that type of malfeasance—the fact remains that even though Early did not take Washington, the defense of the
city from July 10 to 12 was far from the Union command's finest hour.

Strong differences of opinion, however, remain about the big decisions involved in Jubal Early's great rebel raid into Maryland and up to the forts in Northwest Washington, D.C. The biggest contentious question has been whether or not Early could have—and should have—invaded Washington.

Then there is the question of whether or not Lew Wallace's stand at Monocacy did, indeed, "save Washington" by delaying Early for just enough time for Grant to bring experienced troops to stop the invasion.

Finally, there is the overriding question of what impact Early's invasion of Maryland, Wallace's stand at Monocacy, and Early's march on Washington had on the course of the Civil War—and on American history. There is no disputing the fact that Lee forced Grant to part with the Sixth and Nineteenth Corps, something Grant did not want to do. Nor is there any doubt that moving two corps of troops away from Richmond in the first week of July altered Grant's strategic timetable for a final push to end the war.

Some observers, primarily but not exclusively Northerners, believed at the time that Washington was there for the taking when Early arrived on July 11. Lt. Col. Aldace Walker of the Eleventh Vermont, for example, wrote in his 1869 war memoir that he had "little doubt" that Early "might have taken [Washington] on either of the two days he spent in its neighborhood before" the Sixth Corps' "arrival from Petersburg."

Sylvanus Cadwallader, the war correspondent who was in Washington on July 11 and 12, agreed. "I have always wondered at Early's inaction throughout the day [of Monday, July 11], and never had any sufficient explanation of his reasons," Cadwallader wrote in his 1896 war memoir. "Our lines in his front could have been carried at any point, with the loss of a few hundred men."

Cadwallader said that he did not believe Early backed off because of the presence of the Sixth Corps. "It has been stated that Early supposed it was fairly protected by federal troops. But this is a very poor excuse," the former war correspondent said. "As an army commander, it was his business to inform himself in such cases. His spies and Provost Marshals could have given him all these facts. Yet he spent the day supinely; and when he was about ready (in his own mind) to swoop down upon it, he found it strongly and sufficiently reinforced."

Cadwallader said that since he was "present and personally inspected the whole field," he saw that Early "might have entered the capital at any time before midnight of July 11th . . . without having the march of his columns delayed a half hour, and without any loss of men worth a moment's consideration, when playing for such a stake."

Early "passed the night of the 10th within five miles of Washington," Treasury official Lucius Chitteden wrote in his memoir. "Presumptively, he could have attacked the next morning, when a considerable portion of his force was at Silver Spring and above Georgetown, within two miles of the defences."

Had Early attacked on the morning of July 11, Chittenden said, "he would have found the city in the condition supposed by General Lee when the campaign was projected. The Confederate army would have met with no resistance except from the raw and undisciplined forces, which, in the opinion of General Grant, and it was supposed of General Lee also, would have been altogether inadequate to its defence."

Union lieutenant general Nelson A. Miles, who as a colonel had commanded the Twenty-second Massachusetts Volunteer Infantry at Petersburg during the third Confederate invasion of Maryland, accused Early of squandering a golden opportunity in Washington. "Had Stonewall Jackson been in command of that force," Miles wrote in his 1911 memoir, "the result would undoubtedly have been very serious, if not disastrous, to the Union cause."

Early was "largely checked by a motley force composed largely of convalescents and employees of the departments at Washington," Miles said, stretching the truth more than a little, "until the fortunate arrival of reinforcements."

Robert E. Lee's effort "to cause the Army of the Potomac to withdraw from its menacing position near Richmond and Petersburg by sending Early's corps on its fruitless mission to capture Washington had failed."

Presidential secretaries Nicolay and Hay, in their biography of Lincoln, accused Early of making "a serious error" on July 10 "in regard to the troops in front of him." When he arrived at the gates of Fort Stevens that day, they said, Early underestimated the number of able-bodied men under his command and mistook the inexperienced mixture of hundred days' men and civilians pressed into service at Fort Stevens for the veteran Sixth Corps troops.

Early "always looked at his own force through the wrong end of his field-glass," Nicolay and Hay wrote. Acting on what he heard from captured Sixth Corps soldiers at Monocacy and from reading newspaper reports, they said, Early "saw the improvised levies of General Augur moving into the works in the afternoon," and "came, not unnaturally, to the conclusion that he had to deal with the veterans of the Army of the Potomac."

That caused Early to pause, they said, and make "the most careful preparation." But "before the preparations were completed, what he had imagined had become true: Wright with his two magnificent divisions had landed at the wharf, being received by President Lincoln in person amid a tumult of joyous cheering. . . ."

The mercurial Horace Greeley, the passionately antislavery, pro-Union editor of the *New York Tribune*, also believed Early could have "taken the city," but only if he had "rushed upon Washington by forced marches from the Monocacy, and at once assaulted with desperate energy" on July 10. Even in that case, Greeley wrote two years after the war, Early "might have lost half his army."

If Early had broken through into the city and "attempted to hold it," Greeley said, he would have "lost *all* his army. . . ." Had Early waited and invaded on July 12, Greeley postulated, he would have been "confronted and crushed" by the Sixth and Nineteenth Corps troops.

Early's lieutenant Dodson Ramseur also held that view. "Natural obstacles alone prevented our taking Washington," Ramseur wrote to his wife on July 15. "The heat & dust was so great that our men could not possibly march further. Time was thus given the Enemy to get a sufficient force into his works to prevent our capturing them." By Tuesday morning, July 12, Ramseur said, the Union had "more men behind the strongest built works I ever saw than we had in front of them."

The "trip into [Maryland] was a success," Ramseur wrote to his wife a week later. He noted that the Richmond newspapers were " 'pitching into' Gen'l Early for not taking Washington." But he said, if Early "had attempted it, he would have been repulsed with great loss," Ramseur said, "and then these same wiseacres would have condemned him for recklessness."

Maj. Jedediah Hotchkiss, the topographical engineer on Early's staff, echoed Ramseur's words in a letter Hotchkiss wrote to his wife on July 15. On "Monday [July 11] we went up to the fortifications, & within 6 miles of the President's House, but our Men were so much exhausted by the intense heat (I have never experienced warmer weather) that we could not go on to the assault of the works that morning. . . ."

The Confederates "found the enemy's works of a very formidable character," Hotchkiss later wrote in his official report, "the whole country cleared off and exposed in every part to fire from their numerous forts and batteries that crowned the heights in our front."

By that evening, Hotchkiss said in his July 15 letter, "the enemy had been re-inforced by a Corps from Grant's Army, so we only spent the next day skirmishing. . . ." Early's army, Hotchkiss went on to say, has "been over ¾ of the state of Md, scared 'Old Abe' so that he has ordered a good portion of his force away from Richmond, captured thousands of horses & cattle—whipped the enemy in a regular battle & with small loss returned safely to a position that threatens Washington and Pa. at the same time."

Hotchkiss called the endeavor "the most successful expedition we have ever made into the enemy's country."

The journalist and close Lincoln friend Noah Brooks also characterized Early's campaign as a strategic success. If "the invasion of Maryland was designed to create a diversion from Grant's army, then in front of Richmond, that end was successful," Brooks wrote in 1895. "And while a great force of effective men was kept at bay within the defenses of Washington, the bulk of Early's army was busy sweeping up all available plunder, and sending it southward across the Potomac."

Brooks went on to say that the news of Early's invasion also had an impact on Northern morale. "In the country at large," he said, "the effect of this demonstration was somewhat depressing. The capital had been threatened; the President's safety had been imperiled; only a miracle had saved treasures, records, and archive[s] from the fate that overtook them when Cockburn seized the city during the War of 1812."

The journalist and author Edward A. Pollard (1818–72), a Southern partisan, wrote in 1866 that "the results" of Early's mission to Maryland "fell below public expectation [in] the South, where again had been indulged the fond imagination of the capture of Washington." But, Pollard said, "the movement was, on the whole, a success."

Why? Because "Early brought off five thousand horses and twenty-five hundred beef cattle; and the primary object of the march had been accomplished when he retreated and posted himself in the Shenandoah Valley—a standing threat to repeat the enterprise upon Washington. . . ." Grant, moreover, Pollard said, "had been weakened, and the heavy weight upon Gen. Lee's shoulders lightened."

Former Union private Alfred Roe, who as a POW had witnessed the fighting outside Fort Stevens, and who later wrote extensively about his experiences, also had words of praise for Early's operation. Early, Roe wrote in 1890, "personally told me that he found, on facing Fort Stevens, that the purpose for which he was sent by Lee had been subserved; *i.e*, some troops, he knew not how many, had been drawn from Petersburg, and this very arrival, while it blocked his entrances, lessened Lee's danger." Early "had not," Roe said, "from the moment of finding 6th Army Corps men there, entertained the possibility of getting into Washington."

Opposed as he "was to the case of the Rebellion," Roe said, "I think we can afford a little praise for this affair, though an unrelenting foe, in his leading his men by forced marches over many hundreds of miles, through a not over friendly country in some cases, down to the very Capital of the nation. Nothing but the final success was wanting to make him the Alaric of the century."

In his memoirs, U.S. Grant agreed with the essence of Hotchkiss's and Roe's assessments, although Grant did not address the success or failure of Early's mission. Grant spoke of "the gravity of the situation" in Washington on July 10 as Early "started on his march to the capital of the Nation." Grant came to believe, he said, that Washington was only vulnerable on July 10 before Early had arrived, but not on July 11 or 12.

"If Early had been but one day earlier," Grant said, "he might have entered the capital before the arrival of the reinforcements I had sent."

Jubal Early himself—not surprisingly—sounded off about his reasons for not pushing into Washington soon after the affair ended. His version of his mission, which he continued to expound throughout his life, in the main agreed with Ramseur's, Hotchkiss's, Grant's, and that of others who argued that an attack on July 11 or 12 would have been foolhardy.

Beginning on July 14, 1864, the day after he crossed back into Virginia and up to his dying day thirty years later, Early considered his four-week campaign a great success. He also maintained throughout his life that the reason he did not invade Washington on July 11 was because his men were near exhaustion and that he didn't invade on July 12 because he would have faced a force of numerically superior, entrenched veteran Union troops.

In his after-action report sent to Robert E. Lee, written in Leesburg, Virginia, on July 14, Early laid out his main points for the first time:

First, it wasn't that he mistook the ill-equipped troops for the Sixth Corps men when he arrived at the outskirts of Fort Stevens at noontime on Monday, July 11, but that his men could not physically have attacked at that time. The "men were almost completely exhausted and not in a condition to make an attack," Early said.

Second, that same day he saw for himself that the Washington defenses were nearly impregnable. The fortifications, he said, "we found to be very strong and constructed very scientifically."

Third, despite points one and two, Early decided to attack on Tuesday morning, July 12, but changed his mind only at the last minute when he saw that the Sixth Corps troops had made it to the Washington forts. After "consultation with my division commanders, I became satisfied that the assault, even if successful, would be attended with such great sacrifice as would insure the destruction of my whole force," he said. "If unsuccessful," Early said, it would have "resulted in the loss of life of the whole force."

Said loss, Early said, "would have had such a depressing effect upon the country, and would so encourage the enemy as to amount to a very serious, if not fatal, disaster to our cause."

On July 14, 1864, Early declared his campaign a victory. "An immense amount of damage has been done the enemy," he told Lee. "Our cavalry has brought off a very large number of horses. Over 1,000 have been brought off and $220,000 in money was levied and collected in Hagerstown and Frederick. . . ."

Early stuck to that argument for decades in countless newspaper and magazine articles, in speeches, in letters to newspaper editors, and in his two war memoirs, *A Memoir of the Last Year of the War for Independence in the Confederate States of America* and *Autobiographical Sketch and Narrative of the War Between the States.* The latter book, which Early published in 1866, was the first Civil War memoir written by one of the war's prominent figures.

In that volume, Early said that on leaving Monocacy on July 10 he had hoped "to get into the fortifications around Washington before they could be manned." He said he found the fortifications on July 11 to be "exceedingly strong" and that "a very large number" of his men were "greatly exhausted by the last two days of marching. . . ."

Under "the circumstances," he wrote, "to have rushed my men blindly against the fortifications, without understanding the state of things, would have been worse than folly."

Early said that on the night of July 11 he was "very reluctant to abandon the project of capturing Washington," but when he saw the thousands of Sixth Corps troops on the parapets the next morning he "reluctantly" had "to give up all hopes of capturing" the city.

He then went on to rebut charges in "some of the Northern newspapers" that he could have taken Washington between July 9 and 11 before the Sixth Corps had arrived. On Saturday, July 9, Early said, "I was fighting at Monocacy, thirty-five miles from Washington." After winning that battle, and "moving as rapidly as it was possible for me to move," he said, "I did not arrive in front of the fortifications until after noon on Monday," with a group of "exhausted" troops.

Adding up all those factors, Early said, "will cause the intelligent reader to wonder, not why I failed to take Washington, but why I had the audacity to approach it as I did, with the small force under my command."

Early added a new wrinkle to the story in a letter to the editor he wrote that appeared in the December 14, 1874, *Richmond Sentinel:* that Robert E. Lee did not ask him to invade Washington. Lee, Early said, "did not expect that I would be able to capture Washington with my small force; his orders were simply to threaten the city."

Early said that his only chance of capturing Washington "depended upon its being found without garrison."

The "object" of his entire four-week campaign, Early said, was not to invade Washington but to influence Grant to send significant numbers of troops away from Richmond and Petersburg. Lee, he said, "would have been gratified if I could have taken Washington, but when I suggested to him I would take it if I could, he remarked that it would hardly be possible to do so. . . ."

Lee, in fact, did from the beginning stress that getting Grant to move troops out of Richmond—along with pushing Hunter out of the valley—was his main goal on June 13 when he sent Early to Lynchburg. It "was hoped," Lee wrote to his secretary of war, James A. Seddon, on July 19, "that by threatening Washington and Baltimore Genl Grant would be compelled either to weaken himself so much for their protection as to afford us an opportunity to attack him, or that he might be induced to attack us."

Lee also listed several "collateral results" of Early's mission, mainly "obtaining military stores and supplies." Lee's overall assessment of Early's performance was positive. So "far as the movement was intended to relieve our territory in that section of the enemy, it has up to the present time been successful," he told Seddon.

Jefferson Davis also espoused that sentiment. "I have been asked," Davis said in a September 23, 1864, speech in Macon, Georgia, "why the army sent to the Shenandoah Valley was not sent here? It was because an army of the enemy had penetrated the Valley to the very gates of Lynchburg and General Early was sent to drive them back."

Early "not only successfully did," Davis said, "but, crossing the Potomac, came well-nigh capturing Washington itself, and forced Grant to send two corps of his army to protect it." That action, the Confederate president said, "the enemy called a raid. If so, Sherman's march into Georgia is a raid."

Davis believed that Early's success against Hunter in the valley, Grant's sending troops to Washington, and Early's move back into the valley staved off the fall of Richmond. "What would prevent them now," he said, "if Early was withdrawn, penetrating down the valley and putting a complete cordon of men around Richmond?"

Early addressed the Washington invasion question many other times, including a speech he gave at Confederate Memorial Day ceremonies on June 6, 1889, at the Stonewall Cemetery in Winchester, Virginia. "There has been some criticism on the part of some would-be strategists of my failure to capture Washington City, on my appearance before its strong fortifications," he said. Those fortifications, he reminded his audience, "were manned by a force more than double my own, to whose aid two corps from Grant's army arrived before all my force reached the front of the fortifications."

The irascible Early could not resist skewering his critics as "wiseacres" whose "views of the art of war were conceived while they were exempt from the disturbing elements of whistling bullets and bursting shells." It is "a pity," he said, "that those who undertake to criticize my conduct of the operations entrusted to me did not give me the benefit of their counsel in time to be of avail to me."

Still, Early had vowed to Lee, as we have seen, on June 28 that he intended "to threaten Washington" and if he could "find an opportunity to take it." And he certainly had the opportunity—albeit only for a brief period of time in the early afternoon of Monday, July 11. And there is little doubt that Lee would have been overjoyed to see Early move into Washington if for no other reason than the morale boost it would have meant for the Confederate cause.

Jefferson Davis defended Early's actions outside of Washington for decades after the war ended. "The exhaustion of our force, the lightness of its artillery, and the information that two corps of the enemy's forces had just arrived in Washington, in addition to the veteran reserves and hundred days-men, and the parapets lined with troops," Davis wrote in a history of the war published in 1881, "led us to refrain from making an assault, and to retire during the night of the 12th."

Fitzhugh Lee, the Confederate cavalry commander and nephew of Robert E. Lee, also believed that Early did the right thing in not invading Washington. "General Early could not have held Washington if he had entered its gates with his small force," Fitzhugh Lee wrote in an 1894 book that focused on his illustrious uncle's actions in the war. "No reenforcements were nearer to him than Richmond, and from the North and General Grant's army a large force could have been speedily assembled."

Lee also believed that Early greatly helped the Confederate war effort after leaving Washington and going to the northern Shenandoah Valley. "Early's presence in the lower valley," Lee said, "was menacing to Washington, preserved a threatening attitude toward Pennsylvania and Maryland, prevented the [Union's] use of the Baltimore and Ohio Railroad and the Chesapeake and Ohio Canal, and kept a large force from Grant's army to defend the Federal capital."

Although Grant and Halleck demoted Lew Wallace after the defeat at Monocacy, the Union army's commanding general soon changed his opinion 180 degrees about Wallace's performance. At Grant's urging—and presumably against the wishes of Old Brains Halleck—Secretary of War Stanton on July 28, 1864, reinstated Wallace as the commander of the Middle Department.

In his official report written a year later after the war's end, Grant said that Wallace, with "a force not sufficient to insure success," fought "the enemy nevertheless, and although it resulted in a defeat to our arms, yet it detained the enemy and thereby served to enable General Wright to reach Washington with two divisions of the Six Corps, and the advance of the Nineteenth Corps."

Grant expanded on his praise for Wallace in his memoir, which he wrote in the early 1880s. "Whether the delay caused by the battle [of Monocacy] amounted to a day or not, General Wallace contributed on this occasion, by the defeat of the troops under him a greater benefit to the cause that often falls to the lot of a commander of an equal force to render by means of a victory."

Did the Battle of Monocacy—ironically, the only Confederate victory north of the Mason-Dixon line—and Early's military move on the nation's capital change the course of the Civil War? Adding up all the evidence, a strong case can be made that Wallace's stand and Early's raid on Washington did just that. Delaying Early and preventing him from invading Washington on July 10 when Washington was ripe for the taking certainly had an impact—albeit a temporary one—on the contentious 1864 presidential election in the North.

"Many in the North saw [Early's] raid as evidence of northern military mismanagement and the impossibility of ever winning the war," the eminent Civil War historian James McPherson said. "It gave a boost to the hopes of northern Peace Democrats—the Copperheads—to gain control of the party and defeat Lincoln's re-election."

"Had Wallace failed to intercept Early," the Civil War historian Gary Gallagher wrote, "the Army of the Valley might have fought its way to Washington on July 10." No one can say exactly what would have happened next. But, as Gallagher put it, "it can be said with confidence that Wallace's troops spared the Lincoln government a potential disaster, and for that reason the battle of the Monocacy must be considered one of the more significant actions of the Civil War."

It is not at all far-fetched to postulate that Early's invasion of Maryland including the battle of Monocacy prevented Grant from undertaking what easily could have been a winning, all-out assault on Petersburg or a drawing out of Lee from his dug-in position in Richmond to fight on Grant's terms in the late spring or early summer of 1864. Grant, with Lincoln's backing, was ready to take decisive action that he strongly believed would hasten the end of the war.

Grant, Lincoln said in his June 16 speech at the Philadelphia Sanitary Fair, is "in a position from whence he will never be dislodged until Richmond is taken." Grant "is reported to have said," Lincoln said, "'I am going through on this line if it takes all summer . . .' I say," Lincoln added, "we are going through on this line if it takes three years more."

Before he learned of Early's move into the Shenandoah and Maryland, Grant "had been planning some important offensive operations in front of Richmond," his aide-de-camp, General Horace Porter, wrote in his war memoir. But Early's move into Maryland caused the Union commander "to postpone these and turn his chief attention to Early."

Grant boasted on July 5, the day that Early's troops crossed the Potomac into Maryland, that he had "the bulk of the Rebel Army" besieged in Richmond and was "conscious that they cannot stand a single battle outside their fortifications with the Armies confronting them."

The "last man in the Confederacy is now in the Army," Grant said in a letter that day to his friend the steamboat magnate J. Russell Jones of his hometown of Galena, Ill. "They are becoming discouraged, their men deserting, dying and being killed and captured every day. We [lose, too] but can replace our losses. If the rebellion is not perfectly and thoroughly crushed, it will be the fault and through the weakness of the people North."

In a telegram Grant wrote to Halleck from City Point four days later, on July 9 (the day Early fought Wallace at Monocacy), Grant spoke of his desire to complete assembling "a large force" outside Richmond by the 20th of that month. The object: to mount "aggressive operations" against Petersburg. But, Grant said, he would be willing to "postpone" said aggressive operations if "the rebel force now North can be captured or destroyed."

That is almost exactly what happened. Lee's bold move in sending Early to the Shenandoah Valley forced Grant to part with the Sixth and Nineteenth Corps—and to put off whatever "aggressive operations" he had envisioned—perhaps a final assault that may just have crushed Lee's army and ended the Civil War sometime in the summer or fall of 1864. At the very least, without Lee's risky strategic move, chances are that it would not have taken Grant until April of 1865 to win the war.

Lee's "strategy in sending Early down the Shenandoah prolonged the defence of Richmond for nine months," Thomas L. Livermore, who served on the staff of Union Second Corps commander Gen. Andrew Humphreys, wrote. That's because Lee's move, Livermore said, "led Grant to reduce his force so much that he could not force a conclusion."

Livermore calculated that the number of able-bodied Union troops arrayed outside Richmond and Petersburg dropped from 137,454 on June 30 to 93,542 on July 31 and to just 69,206 on August 31. The precipitous falloff was due to the departure of the Sixth Corps to Washington, as well as to casualties, illnesses, and the fact that many Union soldiers simply went home when their terms of enlistment ended.

Those factors reduced the number of Grant's troops around Richmond and Petersburg by 25 percent in August, Livermore said, a number that "remained for a long time below the danger line for a besieging force." The number of Confederate troops facing Grant, Livermore said, dropped from 65,562 on June 30 to 55,622 on August 31.

———

The July 9, 1864, fight at Monocacy has come to be known as "the battle that saved Washington." It was. It also very possibly was the battle that played a pivotal role in the series of events that started with Lee's June 12, 1864, order to send Early to the valley. That series of events prolonged the Civil War for as many as nine long months.

Epilogue

The Civil War went on for eight months after Jubal Early crossed the Potomac at White's Ford on the morning of July 14, 1864, and then headed back to the Shenandoah Valley of Virginia. Early had initial successes in the valley, winning the Battles of Cool Spring on July 17–18 and Second Kernstown on July 24. But months and months of constant campaigning took its toll on him and on his officers and men. Things started to go seriously downhill for Early when Union major general Philip Sheridan defeated him decisively at the September 19 Battle of Opequon, also known as Third Winchester.

After a disastrous defeat at Waynesboro in central Virginia on March 2, 1865, Lee reluctantly relieved Early of his command. The Civil War ended when Lee surrendered to Grant on April 9, 1865, at Appomattox Courthouse in Virginia. John Brown Gordon, who was the final commander of the Confederate Second Corps, took part in the formal surrender ceremonies.

Jubal Early lived until 1890. He never got over the Civil War. When the war ended, Early, the epitome of the unreconstructed Confederate loyalist, vowed that he would never live under Yankee rule, and went west to try to keep the rebellion going.

"As soon as I was in a condition to travel, I started on horseback for the Trans-Mississippi Department to join the army of Gen. Kirby Smith, should it hold out," Early wrote in his autobiography, "with the hope of at least meeting an honorable death while fighting under the flag of my country."

Early embarked on a long, arduous journey from Virginia to Texas, only to learn along the way that Smith had surrendered his command. Early made it to the Lone Star State in August, where he spent nearly four months devising a way to escape to Mexico. On December 27, he boarded a ship at Galveston, which stopped at Nassau and Bimini in the Bahamas, and Cuba before arriving in Veracruz.

Early eventually settled in Mexico City and began work on his memoirs. He hoped that a war would break out between French-ruled Mexico and the United States so that he could once again fight the hated Yankees. When Early was convinced that that unlikely scenario would not materialize, he decided to move his self-imposed exile into Canada.

He made it to Canada—with a brief stop in Havana—in August of 1866, living in Niagara, close to the American border. He then moved to Toronto, where he self-published his memoir of the last year of the war. For the next three years Early worked on a longer war memoir in Canada. He returned to the United States in 1869, and lived out his days in a hotel in downtown Lynchburg, Virginia.

He resumed the practice of law, but spent the bulk of his time lecturing and writing on the Civil War. As the first president of the Southern Historical Society, his priorities were burnishing Robert E. Lee's legend and arguing that the Southern cause was just.

The Confederate troops who died in the war "gave their lives for what they not only believed to be, but what I insist was a just and righteous cause," Early said in 1889 in a typical "Lost Cause" speech. "That cause was lost, but that did not prove that it was wrong, for the history of the world abounds with instances in which might has proved more powerful than right."

Jubal Anderson Early died on March 2, 1894, at age seventy-seven, following a fall down a flight of stairs in Lynchburg.

———

Two of Early's division commanders, Robert Emmet Rodes and Stephen Dodson Ramseur, were killed in action in the fall of 1864. Rodes perished at Winchester on September 19, after being hit in the back of the head by a Union artillery shell. He was thirty-five years old.

Ramseur died at the Battle of Cedar Creek on October 19, 1864. "He fell at his post fighting like a lion at bay," Early said of his twenty-seven-year-old general.

John C. Breckinridge fought with Early until Winchester, then commanded the Department of Southwestern Virginia. He left the Confederate army in January of 1865 to take the post of secretary of war in the waning days of the Confederate States of America. Breckinridge organized the evacuation of Richmond on April 2, and, when the war ended, helped Jefferson Davis escape. Breckinridge, under indictment for treason, made his way to Florida, took a boat to Cuba, and went into exile in England, on the Continent, and, later, in Canada, where he, along with Jubal Early, settled in Toronto.

Taking advantage of a general amnesty, John C. Breckinridge came home to Lexington, Kentucky, in February of 1869. The former vice president of the United States practiced law in Louisville, and became vice president of the Elizabethtown, Lexington, Big Sandy Railroad Company. In public speeches he spoke out for reconciliation. Breckinridge died in Lexington at age fifty-four on May 17, 1875.

John Brown Gordon, who, when the war ended, was perhaps Lee's most trusted lieutenant, went back into private business in Georgia after the war. In 1868 he ran unsuccessfully as the Democratic candidate for governor. Following that defeat, Gordon began a successful political career. He was elected as a Democrat to the U.S. Senate in 1873, where he became a voice for reconciliation between North and South.

Gordon was reelected to the Senate in 1879 and served until May of 1880, when he resigned to go once again into private business. Gordon was elected governor of Georgia in 1886, served two terms, and returned to the U.S. Senate in 1891. He became the first president of the United Confederate Veterans in 1889. John Brown Gordon died in Miami at age seventy-one on January 9, 1904. His memoir, *Reminiscences of the Civil War*, was published that same year.

Tiger John McCausland, on Early's orders, burned every building in the small city of Chambersburg, Pennsylvania, on July 30, 1864, after the town fathers would not come up with the $100,000 in gold or $500,000 in greenbacks

John Brown Gordon became a voice for reconciliation during Reconstruction. He was elected to the U.S. Senate and to the governorship of his home state of Georgia. *Credit: Library of Virginia*

he demanded. Early said the demand and punishment were in retaliation for the destruction caused by David Hunter in the Shenandoah Valley.

McCausland went on to serve under Early until he was relieved of his command. Refusing to take part in the surrender at Appomattox, McCausland led his two hundred men through the Union lines to Lynchburg, where he disbanded the unit and headed to his boyhood home in the Great Kanawha Valley of West Virginia.

He was not warmly received because of what had happened in Chambersburg. So McCausland went into exile for two years in Canada, England, France, and Mexico. After returning to West Virginia in 1867, McCausland enjoyed great financial success in a series of farming and business ventures for the next sixty years. He died of a heart attack in his sleep at his home in Pliney, West Virginia, in his ninetieth year on January 27, 1927.

Early's other top cavalry commander, Bradley Tyler Johnson, also took part in the burning of Chambersburg. He went on to serve with Early in the Shenandoah, then was sent to Salisbury, North Carolina, in December 1864, to command a Confederate prison camp. When the war ended Johnson moved to Richmond, where he practiced law. Johnson became active in the Virginia Democratic Party, attending the 1872 National Convention as a delegate, and three years later, winning a seat in the Virginia Senate.

Johnson moved to Baltimore in 1883, where he lectured and wrote about the war. He died in Amelia, Virginia, between Richmond and Appomattox, at age seventy-three on October 5, 1903.

Harry Gilmor, the Maryland Confederate cavalry raider, was captured by the Yankees in February 1865 in Hardy County, West Virginia, where he and his men were trying to disable the B&O Railroad lines. Gilmor was held in the Fort Warren Union prisoner of war camp on George's Island in Boston Harbor until July 24, 1865. He moved to New Orleans after his release, married, had three children, wrote his memoirs, and then returned to Maryland.

Gilmor served as a colonel in the Maryland National Guard and as Baltimore city police commissioner from 1874 to 1879. He died at age fifty in Baltimore on March 4, 1883, from complications related to war wounds.

John Singleton Mosby, the infamous Confederate guerrilla leader who broke with Early, disbanded his rangers on April 21, 1865, but did not surrender until the end of June. He received a pardon from General Grant, and moved to Warrenton, Virginia, in Fauquier County, where he practiced law, and—to the consternation of some old friends—joined the Republican Party.

Mosby served as U.S. consul to Hong Kong from 1878 to 1885. After coming home, he briefly worked as a land agent in Colorado. From 1904 to 1910 he was an assistant attorney for the U.S. Department of Justice. Mosby died in Warrenton on May 30, 1916, at age eighty-two.

Lew Wallace, his reputation restored following Early's flight from Washington, went on to become a member of the military commission that tried the Lincoln conspirators in 1865. He also served as the president of the court-martial

that tried Capt. Henry Wirz, the commandant of Andersonville, the notori-
ous Confederate prison. With his conviction in October 1865, Wirz became
the only Confederate soldier convicted and executed for war crimes committed during the Civil War.

Pres. Rutherford B. Hayes, who fought under Hunter in the Shenandoah
Valley, named Wallace governor of the territory of New Mexico, a position
he held from 1878 to 1881. Pres. James Garfield appointed Lew Wallace
U.S. minister to Turkey, where he served from 1881 to 1885.

Lew Wallace is best known for his literary endeavors, most notably his
second novel, *Ben-Hur: A Tale of the Christ*, which was published in November of 1880. *Ben-Hur* went on to become one of the bestselling books of the
nineteenth century. Wallace spent seven years researching and writing his
story of Jesus Christ told through the eyes of a young Jewish nobleman
called Judah Ben-Hur. The book was made into movies in 1907, 1925 (starring Ramon Navarro), and 1959. The latter, starring Charlton Heston, won
eleven Academy Awards and is regarded as a cinematic classic.

"In composing his books he had the peculiar habit of writing first upon a
slate, then copying the lines on paper," Wallace's *New York Times* obituary
noted, "and afterward recopying and pruning his composition until it met
with his approval. It used to be said that frequently he wrote but one line a
day, and then scratched that out within the next twenty-four hours."

Wallace died in his seventy-eighth year on February 15, 1905, in Crawfordsville, Indiana. His two-volume, eight-hundred-page autobiography was
published the following year.

Wallace's tormentor, Henry Halleck, was relieved of his office as the
Union army's chief of staff on April 19, 1865, shortly after the end of the war
and assigned to command the newly formed Richmond-based Military Division of the James. At the end of August Halleck became commander of the
Military Division of the Pacific in San Francisco. Old Brains Halleck died on
January 9, 1872, one week short of his fifty-seventh birthday, while serving as
commander of the Division of the South in Louisville, Kentucky.

Edwin McMasters Stanton stayed on as secretary of war under Pres. Andrew Johnson following Lincoln's assassination. Johnson pushed for Stanton's resignation in August 1867 after the two vehemently disagreed on
reconstruction policies. When Stanton refused to leave office, Johnson sus-
pended him, but Congress, which had asserted its power over the hiring and
firing of cabinet members, overrode that action in January 1868.

President Johnson tried to fire Stanton again the next month, but the secretary of war again fought the order. That led to Congress's impeachment of Johnson. When that effort failed, Stanton resigned as secretary of war, and returned to private life. When Ulysses S. Grant became president in 1869, he appointed Stanton, a strong supporter, to the U.S. Supreme Court. Edwin Stanton died five days before his fifty-fifth birthday, on December 24, 1869, four days after the Senate had confirmed the appointment, but before he joined the Supreme Court.

Black Dave Hunter's stained Civil War record seemed not to hamper his brief late- and postwar military career. He served in the honor guard at the funeral of Abraham Lincoln and accompanied the president's body back to Springfield, Illinois. Hunter then was named president of the military commission trying the conspirators of Lincoln's assassination and conducted the trial from May 8 to July 15, 1865. That commission also included three other Union officers who fought at the Battle of Monocacy and its environs: Lew Wallace, Brig. Gen. Albion P. Howe, and Lt. Col. David R. Clendenin of the Eighth Illinois Cavalry.

David Hunter retired from the army in July 1866. He died in 1886 at the age of eighty-one.

Clendenin, who had served heroically at Monocacy, mustered out of the Union army in July of 1865. Two years later he rejoined the United States army as a major with the Eighth Cavalry. Clendenin served until he retired from the military as a colonel in 1891. He died in Oneida, Illinois, on March 5, 1895.

Franz "the Flying Dutchman" Sigel resigned his army commission in May 1865 to edit a German-language newspaper in Baltimore. He moved to New York City in 1867, where he held a series of government jobs, lectured, and published and edited another German newspaper. Sigel died at age seventy-seven on August 21, 1902, in New York, and is buried in Woodlawn Cemetery in the Bronx.

James Ricketts, the Union military hero of the Battle of Monocacy, joined Maj. Gen. Philip Sheridan's army in the Shenandoah Valley following Early's retreat from Washington in mid-July of 1864. Ricketts was shot through the chest at the October 19 Battle of Cedar Creek while temporarily commanding the Sixth Corps.

He recovered rapdily and took command of the division again in April of 1865 just before the war ended. Ricketts retired from the army in January 1867 and moved to Washington, where he died on September 22, 1887, at age seventy.

Horatio Wright commanded the Sixth Corps for most of the last Shenandoah Valley Campaign against Jubal Early, and at the subsquent end of the siege of Petersburg. He went on to command the Army of Texas from July 1865 until August of the following year, then moved into army engineering, becoming chief engineer in 1879. In that position, he directed the completion of the Washington Monument. Wright retired in 1884 and died in Washington, D.C, in his seventy-ninth year on July 2, 1899. He is buried in Arlington National Cemetery.

Alexander McDowell McCook served in the U.S. Army until he retired in 1895. His posts included acting inspector general, aide-de-camp to Gen. William T. Sherman, and commander of the Infantry and Cavalry School at Fort Leavenworth. The year after he retired, McCook was named U.S. representative to the coronation of Czar Nicholas II of Russia. McCook died at age seventy-two in Dayton, Ohio, on June 12, 1903.

Montgomery Meigs served in the honor guard at Abraham Lincoln's funeral in April 1865. He remained quartermaster general of the army until retiring from the military in 1882. Following his retirment, Meigs designed and built the ornate Pension Building (now the National Building Museum) in Washington, D.C.

He died in Washington on January 2, 1892, at age seventy-five, and was buried with high military honors at Arlington National Cemetery. Meigs himself had come up with the idea on June 15, 1864, that Arlington (the plantation home of Robert E. Lee) become the site of the nation's newest official national cemetery.

Christopher Augur stayed in the army until he retired in 1885. He spent nearly all of that time commanding military departments in the West, directing action against Indian tribes. He died at age seventy-six in Washington, D.C., on January 16, 1898.

Abraham Lincoln's political nadir came late in August 1864, when he wrote what became known as his "blind memorandum" to his cabinet. The memorandum, which Lincoln asked his cabinet members to open after the November election, was tantamount to an admission of defeat. In it, Lincoln called on his cabinet to "co-operate with the President elect, as to save the Union between the election and the inauguration. . . ."

Lincoln's political fortunes changed 180 degrees on September 3, when he—and the nation—received word that Sherman had taken Atlanta. The good war news continued throughout the rest of the summer and into the fall as Sheridan racked up victories over Early in the Shenandoah Valley.

Reproduction of a Civil War artillery piece at the partially reconstructed Fort Stevens today in residential Northwest Washington, D.C. *Credit: Michael Keating*

Lincoln defeated his Democratic challenger, Gen. George McClellan, in the November election, winning 212 out of the 233 electoral votes in outpolling McClellan by a smaller margin of 2.2 million votes to 1.8 million.

Fort Stevens, where Lincoln came under fire on July 11 and 12, 1864, no longer exists. Its remnants, including a rebuilt parapet, remain at Thirteenth and Quakenbush Streets in Northwest Washington. That site is not far from the Walter Reed Army Medical Center, which was built on the land where Early's troops had set up their skirmish lines outside Fort Stevens. The spot where the Confederate sharpshooter fired at Lincoln is inside the Walter Reed grounds and marked with a plaque.

A three-ton boulder sits on the spot where Lincoln stood on the Fort Stevens parapet. It contains a bronze bas-relief with the words "Lincoln Under Fire at Fort Stevens, July 12, 1864," and a depiction of the surgeon Crawford being shot, with Lincoln at his side and Horatio Wright urging Lincoln to get down. Four large cannon balls found on the battlefield sit at the marker's base, along with a reproduction of a Civil War cannon.

The area of the city in which the fighting occurred around the fort, which was mostly open farmland in 1864, began being developed for housing at the start of the twentieth century. Today the area is almost completely urbanized, and little if anything remains of the fields of battle.

The one-acre graveyard about a mile north of the fort where forty Union soldiers who perished in the fighting are buried became a government-owned Battleground National Cemetery in 1867. The cemetery, today known as the Battlefield National Cemetery, is located at 6625 Georgia Avenue and is administered by the National Park Service. Thought to be the second smallest national cemetery, it contains memorial pillars representing the Twenty-fifth New York Volunteer Cavalry, the 122nd New York Volunteer Infantry, Company K of the 150th Ohio National Guard, and the Ninety-eighth Pennsylvania Volunteer Infantry.

The remains of seventeen unidentified Confederate troops who died in the fighting around Fort Stevens were buried at Grace Episcopal Church in Silver Spring. Those remains were moved to a mass grave site when the church was forced to relocate because of construction of a new trolley line in 1896. The new church and cemetery are at the corner of Georgia Avenue and Grace Church Road about a mile west of downtown Silver Spring.

Falkland, the Silver Spring, Maryland, home of Postmaster Montgomery Blair, which Early's troops burned to the ground, was rebuilt after the war. In 1958 it was demolished to make way for the Blair Shopping Center. Silver Spring, the home of Francis P. Blair in which Early set up his headquarters, was razed that same year.

The Battle of Monocacy took place on roughly 1,600 acres of privately owned farms and other smaller residential parcels. Veterans, primarily from the north, made pilgrimages to the site periodically in the years after the war. A large commemoration took place there on July 9, 1889, the twenty-fifth anniversary of the battle. Union veterans from Vermont, Ohio, Illinois, New York, New Jersey, and Pennsylvania met in Baltimore and took a special train to Monocacy that day, where they formed a national association to raise funds for a battlefield monument. A similar effort took place at Monocacy fifteen years later on July 9, 1904.

The movement to build one monument never came to fruition. But in the next eleven years separate monuments were erected commemorating three northern units—the Fourteenth New Jersey (1907), the Sixty-seventh, Eighty-seventh, and 138th Pennsylvania (1908), and the Tenth Vermont Infantry Regiments (1915). In 1914, the United Daughters of the Confederacy

The Fourteenth New Jersey Volunteer Infantry Regiment memorial, erected on the Monocacy Battlefield in 1907. *Credit: Michael Keating*

installed a stone marker honoring the Confederate veterans who fought and died there.

Glenn Worthington, who as a boy witnessed the battle from the cellar of his family farm, led a movement in 1928 to have Congress create a National Military Park on the site. On June 21, 1934, Pres. Franklin D. Roosevelt signed a congressional resolution authorizing fifty thousand dollars for the development of the Monocacy National Military Park.

It took more than forty years, but on October 1, 1976, Congress finally appropriated the funds to acquire the land. By 1980 the National Park Service was in charge of the battlefield of 1,587 acres. Interstate 270 was built soon thereafter, running through the Thomas and Worthington Farms, the sites of the big field battle between Gordon's division and Ricketts's Sixth Corps men. Route 355, as it did then, also bisects the battlefield.

In July of 1991, the National Park Service opened the Monocacy National Battlefield to the public. The old Gambrill Mill just south of Monocacy Junction was converted into a small visitor center. Ground was broken for a new visitor center on March 24, 2006.

Some seventy years earlier, on September 18, 1937, Col. Judson Spofford of Boise, Idaho, was buried at Arlington National Cemetery in Washington. Spofford, who served with Ricketts's Sixth Corps, was believed to be the last Union survivor of the Battle of Monocacy.

No record has surfaced noting the date of the death of the last Confederate survivor of Monocacy, the "battle that saved Washington."

Union Order of Battle
The Battle of Monocacy,
July 9, 1864

(The names in bold played the most important roles in the battle.)

Middle Department and Eighth Army Corps, Maj. Gen. Lew Wallace, commanding

First Separate Brigade, Brig. Gen. **Erastus B. Tyler,** commanding
First Potomac Home Brigade (five companies), Capt. Charles J. Brown
Third Potomac Home Brigade, Col. Charles Gilpin
Eleventh Maryland Infantry Regiment, Col. William T. Landstreet
144th Ohio Infantry Regiment (three companies), Col. A. L. Brown
149th Ohio Infantry Regiment (seven companies), Col. A. L. Brown
Baltimore Light Artillery (six guns), Capt. **Frederick W. Alexander**

Cavalry, Lt. Col. David R. Clendenin, commanding

Eighth Illinois Cavalry Regiment, Lt. Col. **David R. Clendenin**
159th Ohio Mounted Infantry Regiment (detachment), Capt. Edward H. Leib

Detachment of Mixed Cavalry, Maj. Charles H. Wells
Loudoun (Virginia) Rangers

Sixth Army Corps
Third Division, Brig. Gen. **James B. Ricketts,** commanding
First Brigade, Col. **William S. Truex,** commanding
  Fourteenth New Jersey Infantry Regiment, Lt. Col. Caldwell K. Hall
  106th New York Infantry Regiment, Capt. E. M. Paine
  151st New York Infantry Regiment, Col. W. Emerson
  Eighty-seventh Pennsylvania Infantry Regiment, Lt. Col. James A. Stahle
  Tenth Vermont Infantry Regiment, Col. William W. Henry

Second Brigade, Col. Matthew R. McClennan, commanding
  Ninth New York Heavy Artillery, Col. **William H. Seward Jr**.
  110th Ohio Infantry Regiment, Lt. Col. Otto H. Brinkley
  122nd Ohio Infantry Regiment (detachment), Lt. Col. Charles J. Gibson
  126th Ohio Infantry Regiment, Lt. Col. Aaron W. Ebright
  138th Pennsylvania Infantry Regiment, Maj. Lewis A. May

Source: National Park Service, Monocacy National Battlefield

APPENDIX 2

Confederate Order of Battle The Battle of Monocacy, July 9, 1864

(The names in bold played the most important roles in the battle.)

Army of the Valley, Lt. Gen. Jubal A. Early, commanding

Breckinridge's corps, Maj. Gen. John C. Breckinridge, commanding
Gordon's division, Maj. Gen. **John B. Gordon**, commanding
Evans's brigade, Brig. Gen. Clement A. Evans, commanding
  Thirteenth Georgia Infantry Regiment, Col. J. H. Baker
  Twenty-sixth Georgia Infantry Regiment, Col. Edmund M. Atkinson
  Thirty-first Georgia Infantry Regiment, Col. John H. Lowe
  Thirty-eighth Georgia Infantry Regiment, Maj. Thomas H. Bomar
  Sixtieth Georgia Infantry Regiment, Capt. Milton Russell
  Sixty-first Georgia Infantry Regiment, Col. John H. Lamar
  Twelfth Georgia Infantry Battalion, Capt. J. W. Anderson

Consolidated Louisiana Brigade, Brig. Gen. Zebulon York, commanding
Hay's brigade (Early's division), Col. William R. Peck
  Fifth Infantry Regiment, Maj. Alexander Hart
  Sixth Louisiana Infantry Regiment, Lt. Col. Joseph Hanlon
  Seventh Louisiana Infantry Regiment, Lt. Col. Thomas M. Terry
  Eighth Louisiana Infantry Regiment, Capt. Louis Prados
  Ninth Louisiana Infantry Regiment, Lt. Col. John J. Hodges

Stafford's brigade (Johnson's division), Col. Eugene Waggaman, commanding
  First Louisiana Infantry Regiment, Capt. Joseph Taylor
  Second Louisiana Infantry Regiment, Lt. Col. Michael A. Grogan
  Tenth Louisiana Infantry Regiment, Lt. Col. Henry D. Monier
  Fourteenth Louisiana Infantry Regiment, Lt. Col. David Zable
  Fifteenth Louisiana Infantry Regiment, Capt. H. J. Egan

Terry's brigade, Brig. Gen. William Terry, commanding
  Second, Fourth, Fifth, Twenty-seventh, Thirty-third Virginia Consolidated
    Infantry Regiments

(Stonewall brigade), Col. John H. S. Funk
  Twenty-first, Twenty-fifth, Forty-second, Forty-fourth, Forty-eighth, Fiftieth
    Virginia Consolidated Infantry Regiments

(Jones's brigade), Col. Robert H. Dungan
  Tenth, Twenty-third, Thirty-seventh Virginia Consolidated Infantry
    Regiments, Lt. Col. Samuel H. Saunders

Breckinridge's division, Brig. Gen. John Echols, commanding
Echols's brigade, Col. George Smith Patton
  Twenty-second Virginia Infantry Regiment, Col. George Smith Patton
  Twenty-fifth Virginia Infantry Regiment
  Twenty-third Virginia Infantry Battalion, Lt. Col. Clarence Derrick
  Twenty-sixth Virginia Infantry Battalion, Lt. Col. G. M. Edgar

Wharton's brigade, Brig. Gen. Gabriel C. Wharton
  Thirtieth Virginia Infantry Battalion, Maj. Peter J. Otey

Forty-fifth Virginia Infantry Regiment, Lt. Col. Edwin H. Harman
Fifty-first Virginia Infantry Regiment, Col. Augustus Forsberg

Smith's brigade, Col. Thomas Smith
Thirty-sixth Virginia Infantry Regiment
Sixtieth Virginia Infantry Regiment, Col. Beuhring Hampden Jones
Forty-fifth Virginia Infantry Battalion, Maj. Blake Lynch Woodson

Early's divisions
Rodes's division, Maj. Gen. **Robert E. Rodes,** commanding
Grimes's brigade, Brig. Gen. Bryan Grimes
Second North Carolina Infantry Battalion
Thirty-second, Forty-third, Fifty-third, Forty-fifth North Carolina
    Infantry Regiments

Cook's brigade, Brig. Gen. Phillip Cook
Fourth, Twelfth, Twenty-first, Forty-fourth Georgia Infantry Regiments

Cox's brigade, Brig. Gen. William R. Cox
First North Carolina Infantry Regiment, Col. H. M. Brown
Second North Carolina Infantry Regiment, Col. J. P. Cobb
Third North Carolina Infantry Regiment, Col. S. D. Thurston
Fourth North Carolina Infantry Regiment, Col. J. H. Wood
Fourteenth North Carolina Infantry Regiment, Lt. Col. W. A. Johnston
Thirtieth North Carolina Infantry Regiment, Col. F. M. Parker

Battle's brigade, Col. Charles Pickens
Third Alabama Infantry Regiment
Fifth Alabama Infantry Regiment, Lt. Col. E. L. Hobson
Sixth Alabama Infantry Regiment
Twelfth Alabama Infantry Regiment, Col. Charles Pickens
Sixty-first Alabama Infantry Regiment

Ramseur's division, Maj. Gen. Stephen Dodson Ramseur, commanding
Lilley's brigade, Brig. Gen. Robert D. Lilley
Thirteenth Virginia Infantry Regiment, Maj. Charles Thomas Crittenden
Thirty-first Virginia Infantry Regiment, Col. John Stringer Hoffman
Forty-ninth Virginia Infantry Regiment, Capt. William D. Moffett

Fifty-second Virginia Infantry Regiment, Col. Augustus Forsberg
Fifty-eighth Virginia Infantry Regiment, Col. Francis Howard Board

Johnston's brigade, Brig. Gen. Robert D. Johnston
Fifth North Carolina Infantry Regiment, Col. John W. Lea
Twelfth North Carolina Infantry Regiment, Lt. Col. W. S. Davis
Twentieth North Carolina Infantry Regiment, Col. Thomas F. Toon
Twenty-third North Carolina Infantry Regiment, Col. Charles C. Blacknall

Lewis's brigade, Brig. Gen. William G. Lewis
Sixth North Carolina Infantry Regiment, Lt. Col. S. M. Tate
Twenty-first North Carolina Infantry Regiment, Maj. William J. Pfohl
Fifty-fourth North Carolina Infantry Regiment, Lt. Col. Anderson Ellis
Fifty-seventh North Carolina Infantry Regiment, Col. Archibald C.
  Goodwin

Chief of Artillery, Brig. Gen. Armistead L. Long
Artillery: Lt. Col. J. Floyd King

Nelson's battalion, Lt. Col. William Nelson
Milledge's Georgia Battery, Capt. John Milledge
Amherst Virginia Artillery, Capt. Thomas J. Kirkpatrick
Fluvanna Virginia Artillery, Capt. John L. Massie

Braxton's battalion, Lt. Col. Carter Braxton
Alleghany Virginia Artillery, Capt. John C. Carpenter
Stafford Virginia Artillery, Capt. Raleigh L. Cooper
Lee Virginia Artillery, Capt. W. W. Hardwicke

McLaughlin's battalion, Maj. William McLaughlin
Lewisburg Virginia Artillery, Capt. Thomas A. Bryan
Wise Legion Artillery, Capt. W. M. Lowry
Monroe Virginia Artillery, Capt. George B. Chapman

Cavalry, Maj. Gen. Robert Ransom, commanding
McCausland's brigade, Brig. Gen. **John McCausland**
Fourteenth Virginia Cavalry Regiment, Col. James Cochran
Sixteenth Virginia Cavalry Regiment, Col. Milton J. Ferguson

Seventeenth Virginia Cavalry Regiment, Lt. Col. W. C. Tavenner
Twenty-second Virginia Cavalry Regiment, Col. Henry Bowen

Johnson's brigade, Brig. Gen. Bradley T. Johnson
First Maryland Cavalry Battalion
Eighth Virginia Cavalry
Twenty-first Virginia Cavalry
Twenty-second Virginia Cavalry Battalion
Thirty-fourth Virginia Cavalry Battalion
Thirty-sixth Virginia Cavalry

Imboden's brigade, Brig. Gen. John Imboden, Col. George Smith
Eighteenth Virginia Cavalry
Twenty-third Virginia Cavalry
Sixty-second Virginia Mounted Infantry
Unauthorized Virginia Cavalry Battalion

Parts of the following cavalry units were at Monocacy; the remainder stayed
behind in southwest Virginia. All of Vaughn's cavalry were dismounted.

Vaughn's brigade, Brig. Gen. John C. Vaughn
Twelfth and Sixteenth Tennessee Cavalry Battalions
Sixteenth Georgia Cavalry Regiment
First Tennessee Cavalry Regiment, Col. Carter
Thirty-ninth (or Thirty-first) Tennessee Mounted Infantry Regiment, Maj.
  Robert McFarland
Forty-third and Fifty-ninth Tennessee Mounted Infantry Regiments,
  Captain Aiken
Thomas's Legion, Maj. William W. Stringfield

Sources: National Park Service, Monocacy National Battlefield; Benjamin
Franklin Cooling, *Jubal Early's Raid on Washington, 1864* (Nautical &
Aviation Publishing, 1989)

Notes

This book is aimed at the general reader, as well as those who have a keen interest in the Civil War. These endnotes are intended for readers in the latter category, as well as for anyone else with a desire to know the sources I consulted to tell this story.

I gratefully acknowledge the secondary sources that have covered some of the ground in this book, especially Benjamin Franklin Cooling's *Jubal Early's Raid on Washington, 1864* (1989) and *Monocacy: The Battle That Saved Washington* (2000), Glenn H. Worthington's pioneering 1932 memoir/history, *Fighting for Time: The Battle of Monocacy*, and Civil War military history scholar Edwin C. Bearss's report written for the National Park Service, *The Battle of Monocacy* (2003).

Using those volumes as a road map, I went to as many primary-source materials as I could find. I focused mainly on letters, diaries, journals, and memoirs from those who took part in these events.

The most valuable primary source, by far, is the compilation of Civil War official records—reports, orders, and correspondence—from both sides put together by the U.S. Government Printing Office in 1880. The collection's official title is *The War of the Rebellion: A Compilation of the Official Records of the Union and Confederate Armies Prepared Under the Direction of the Secretary of War by Bvt. Lieut. Col. Robert N. Scott, Third U.S. Artillery.* It is commonly referred to—as we do in the Notes—as the *O.R.*

The *O.R.* is available in a 128-volume bound edition, on a CD-ROM, and online in two forms: in PDF form (photographs of the actual pages) at the Cornell University "Making of America" site (http://cdl.library.cornell.edu/moa/browse.monographs/waro.html) and transcribed at the "ehistory" site maintained by Ohio State University (http://ehistory.osu.edu/uscw/search/index_advanced.cfm?OR=1).

PROLOGUE

3. A "rebel occupation of Washington for however brief a time": George C. Gorham, *Life and Public Services of Edwin M. Stanton* (Houghton, Mifflin, 1899), p. 165.

3. With Washington "in the hands of the enemy": Quoted in David Homer Bates, *Lincoln in the Telegraph Office* (The Century, 1907), p. 255.

ONE

For an excellent summary of the history of the Monocacy River and the Monocacy River Valley, see Edmund F. Wehrle, "Catoctin Mountain Park: A Historic Resource Study," National Park Service, March 2000. Also see: Helen C. Roundtree and Thomas E. Davison, *Eastern Shore Indians of Virginia and Maryland* (University of Virginia Press, 1977); T. J. C. Williams and Folger McKinsey, *History of Frederick County* (Regional Publications, 1967); Grace L. Tracey and John P. Dern, *Pioneers of Old Monocacy: The Early Settlement of Frederick County, Maryland* (Genealogical Publications, 1987); and Robert J. Brugger, *Maryland: A Middle Temperament, 1634–1980* (Johns Hopkins University Press, 1988).

7. By 1860, on the eve of the Civil War: Census figures cited in John H. Schildt, *Drums Along the Monocacy* (Antietam Publications, 1991), p. 19.

9. the (most likely apocryphal). . . poem "Barbara Frietschie": See Marc Leepson, *Flag: An American Biography* (Thomas Dunne Books, 2005), pp. 113–16.

10. "Our troops were wildly welcomed": "Domestic Intelligence: The Rebel Invasion of Maryland," *Harper's Weekly* (September 22, 1862).

11. When he reached White's Ford: Lee's report to Secretary of War George Randolph, October 14, 1862, *O.R.* 19, p. 51.

11. "The results of this expedition": *O.R.* 19, p. 54.

TWO

13. "It is well that war is so terrible": Comment to James Longstreet during the Battle of Fredericksburg. See Justin Wintle, ed., *Dictionary of War Quotations* (Free Press, 1989), p. 286.

14. "Lee, with the capital of the Confederacy": Ulysses S. Grant, *Personal Memoirs* (C. L. Webster, 1886); Bartleby.com, 2000. www.bartleby.com/1011, Chapter XLVII, paragraph 1.

17. "Sigel is merely a book soldier": Cecil D. Eby Jr., ed., *Yankee in the Civil War: The Diaries of David Hunter Strother* (University of North Carolina Press, 1998), pp. 222, 229.

19. "I am ashamed to belong to such an army": Letter dated June 29, 1864. Richard R. Duncan, ed., *Alexander Neil and the Last Shenandoah Valley Campaign: Letters of an Army Surgeon to His Family, 1864* (White Mane, 1996), p. 39.

19. "If Hunter can possibly get to Charlottesville": *O.R.* 37, part 1, p. 24.

20. In Staunton, his men: Hunter's dispatch was dated August 8, 1864. *O.R.* 37, Part 1, p. 96.

21. "Both the Institute and the College were well rummaged": J. O. Humphries Diary, Part 2, June 1–18, 1864, VMI Archives.

22. The burning "was done by order of Genl. Hunter": *William G. Watson Memoirs*, Part 1, January–June 16, 1864, VMI Archives, Manuscript No. 037.

22. One Staunton newspaper described Hunter's: *Staunton Republican Vindicator*, July 22, 1864. See William G. Thomas, "Nothing Ought to Astonish Us: Confederate Civilians in the 1864 Shenandoah Valley Campaign" in Gary W. Gallagher, ed., *The Shenandoah Valley Campaign of 1864* (University of North Carolina Press, 2006), p. 231.

22. Hunter, said CSA general John Brown Gordon: John B. Gordon, *Reminiscences of the Civil War* (Charles Scribner's Sons, 1904), pp. 302–3.

22. "This does not suit many of us": Quoted in T. Harry Williams, *Hayes of the Twenty-Third: The Civil War Volunteer Officer* (Knopf, 1965), p. 194.

22. "The troops," Union private Frank Reader wrote: Frank S. Reader Diary, June 13, 1864. Quoted in Richard R. Duncan, *Lee's Endangered Left: The Civil War in Western Virginia Spring of 1864* (Louisiana University Press, 1998), p. 234.

THREE

24. Although he spent four years there and graduated in 1837: For details on Early's life before the Civil War, see Early's introduction in his *Autobiographical Sketch and Narrative of the War Between the States* (Lippincott, 1912); Charles S. Osborne, *Jubal: The Life and Times of Jubal A. Early, CSA* (Algonquin, 1992), pp. 1–54; and Millard Kessler Bushong, *Old Jube: A Biography of General Jubal A. Early* (White Mane), 1990.

24. "I was not a very exemplary soldier": Early, *Autobiographical Sketch*, p. xvii.

24. "It was generally conceded by officers": Ibid., p. xxii.

25. "I experienced a decided improvement": Ibid., p. xxiii.

25. They had four children between 1850 and 1864: See Osborne, op. cit., pp. 31 and 485. The children—Joseph, Florence, Robert, and Jubal L.—all took Early's surname.

25. "When the question of practical secession": Early, *Autobiographical Sketch*, p. vii.

26. . . . the man Robert E. Lee, in 1864, called: Quoted in the *Mobile Advertiser* (September 15, 1864). See also Gary W. Gallagher's introduction in Jubal A. Early, *A Memoir of the Last Year of the War of Independence* . . . (University of South Carolina Press, 2001), p. x.

26. He had a distinctive, rasping, high-pitched voice: Henry Kyd Douglas, *I Rode with Stonewall* (University of North Carolina Press, 1940), p. 295.

26. Early's "appearance was quite striking": Gen. G. Moxley Sorrel, *Recollections of a Confederate Staff Officer* (Neale Publishing, 1905), p. 56.

26. ... "a person who would be singled out in a crowd": The *Richmond Whig* (October 31, 1984). Also see Bushong, op. cit., p. 187.

26. "I was quite erect and trim": Early, *Autobiographical Sketch*, p. xxv.

27. He had a "caustic, biting tongue": Robert Stiles, *Four Years Under Marse Robert* (Neale Publishing., 1904), p. 189.

28. He "hates his staff like blazes": V. Dabney to Dr. George W. Bagby, Virginia Historical Society, *Bagby Family Papers* (Mss1 B1463 b, Section 72). Virginius Dabny (1835–94), a lawyer, served as a CSA staff officer throughout the war. His grandson and namesake, the historian, author, and journalist Virginius Dabney (1901–95), was the editor of the *Richmond Times-Dispatch* from 1936 to 1969 and received the Pulitzer Prize for editorial writing in 1948.

28. He "received with impatience and never acted upon": Douglas, op. cit., p. 33.

28. "Arbitrary, cynical, with strong prejudices": Douglas, op. cit., p. 33. Douglas, who wrote his memoir in 1899, borrowed his description of Early nearly verbatim from the Southern partisan writer Edward A. Pollard's characterization of Early on page 477 in Pollard's 1871 book, *The Early Life, Campaigns, and Public Services of Robert E. Lee* . . . (E. B. Treat & Co.).

28. "Do you think if the Gates of Hell were opened": Early letter to Thomas Carter, December 13, 1866, Virginia Historical Society, *Lee Family Papers* (Mss1151 b67, Box 68). Early reportedly once said of Plymouth Rock and the Yankees: "If that rock had landed on them, we would never had had the damned, hell-fired war." Quoted in David E. Johnston, *The Story of a Confederate Boy in the Civil War* (Glass & Prudhomme, 1914), p. 188.

28. "An old bachelor, he had during the war the reputation of being a woman hater": Edward A. Pollard, *The Early Life, Campaigns, and Public Services of Robert E. Lee* . . . (E. B. Treat., 1871), p. 476.

28. African slaves, Early wrote in the preface: Early, *A Memoir of the Last Year of the War for Independence*, pp. xxv–xxvi.

30. ... famously called slavery "a moral and political evil": In a letter to his wife on December 27, 1857, from Fort Brown, Texas. Quoted, among other places, in Edward Lee Childe, *The Life and Campaigns of General Lee* (Chatto and Windus, 1875), p. 26.

31. "Being a graduate of the West Point Military Academy": Robert E. Lee to J. A. Early, November 22, 1865, Virginia Historical Society, *Early Family Papers* (Mss1 EA765b, Section 4, Folder 5).

31. "Of all the generals who made for themselves a reputation": Douglas, op cit., p. 33.

FOUR

33. "The maintenance of western Virginia": Lee to Davis, Jan. 27, 1864. See Clifford Dowdey, ed., *The Wartime Papers of Robert E. Lee* (Da Capo, 1961), p. 662.

33. "Since I withdrew General Breckinridge": O.R. 37, part 1, pp. 757–58.

34. On June 1 Lee implored Gen. Grumble Jones: Lee to Jones, June 1, 1864, *Robert Edward Lee Headquarters Papers, 1850–1876,* Virginia Historical Society (Mss3 L515 a).

34. He "will do us great evil": *Wartime Papers of Robert E. Lee,* p. 767.

34. He told Davis that he saw: *Wartime Papers of Robert E. Lee,* pp. 774–75.

35. . . . that one biographer called "a plan of great boldness": John Esten Cooke, *A Life of Robert E. Lee* (D. Appleton, 1871), p. 349. Cooke was a well-known novelist, poet, and biographer of Stonewall Jackson and Lee. He served as a captain in J. E. B. Stuart's cavalry.

35. "My first object is to destroy Hunter": O.R. 37, part 1, p. 762.

35. "I was directed to move," he said: Early, *Autobiographical Sketch,* p. 371.

35. "Success in the Valley," Lee wrote to Jefferson Davis: *Wartime Papers of Robert E. Lee,* pp. 782–83.

36. Of the Virginia contingent, nearly 30 percent: See Aaron Sheehan-Dean, "Success Is So Blended with Defeat: Virginia Soldiers in the Shenandoah Valley" in Gallagher, ed., *The Shenandoah Valley Campaign of 1864,* op. cit., p. 267.

36. "Constant exposure to the weather": Early, *Autobiographical Sketch,* p. 372.

36. Early characterized Rodes: Ibid., p. 427.

37. Ramseur—whom his biographer called: Gary W. Gallagher, *Stephen Dodson Ramseur: Lee's Gallant General* (University of North Carolina Press, 1985).

39. "The struggle between devotion to my family on the one hand": Gordon, *Reminiscences,* op. cit., pp. 3–4.

40. "General Early, hearing of her constant presence": Ibid., p. 319.

41. Gordon, who had no military training, "had the natural instincts": Douglas Southall Freeman, *Lee's Lieutenants: A Study in Command* 1 (Scribner's, 1970), p. 251.

41. "Gordon always had something pleasant to say to his men": John H. Worsham, *One of Jackson's Foot Cavalry: His Experience and What He Saw During the War, 1861–1865* (Neale Publishing, 1912), p. 228.

42. By the end of the war, Gordon "earned the reputation": Writing in the introduction to Gordon's *Reminiscences,* op. cit., p. xix.

43. The former vice president had a "striking and noble presence": Edward Alfred Pollard, *Lee and His Lieutenants* (J. S. Morrow, 1867), p. 620.

44. Breckinridge was "one of the finest looking men I ever saw": Alfred Seelye Roe, *The Ninth New York Heavy Artillery: A History of its Organization, Services in the Defenses of Washington . . .* (self-published, 1899), p. 318.

44. Though "frequently petulant to others": William Barksdale Myers to Gustavus Adolphus Myers, July 23, 1864, Virginia Historical Society, *Myers, Gustavus Adolphus Papers, 1812–1866* (VHI Mss2M9895).

45. "My feet were so sore": John O. Casler, *Four Years in the Stonewall Brigade* (Morningside, 1971), p. 224.

46. "Strike as quick as you can": O.R. 37, part 1, p. 766.

FIVE

47. "Much to the surprise of the men": Worsham, op. cit., p. 229.

48. "We laid down that night believing that the next day would bring a battle": Charles T. O'Ferrall, *Forty Years of Active Service* (Neale Publishing, 1904), p. 107.

48. "It was then and still is incomprehensible to me": John B. Gordon, *Reminiscences,* p. 300.

48. "It was not known where he was retreating": Early, *A Memoir of the Last Year . . . ,* p. 47.

49. "My command had marched sixty miles": Early, *Autobiographical Sketch*, p. 379.

49. "I knew," Early said: Ibid., p. 378.

50. "All the gateways of the Shenandoah Valley—its roads, passes, gaps— were standing wide open": Lew Wallace, *Lew Wallace: An Autobiography* 2 (Harper & Brothers, 1906), p. 702.

50. Hunter and his men went through many "hardships and privations" on the way to Charleston: O.R. 37, part 1, p. 123.

50. Hunter's army marched day and night: Alexander Neil letters, op. cit., pp. 37–39.

51. "Day intensely hot and dusty": Entry for June 26, 1864, Thomas Feamster Diary, Container 1, *Feamster Family Papers, 1794–1967*, Library of Congress, Manuscript Division.

51. As they filed past the Confederate army hero's grave: Douglas, op. cit., p. 292.

51. Every soldier "pulled off his ragged cap": I. G. Bradwell, "Early's Demonstration Against Washington in 1864," *Confederate Veteran* (October 1914), p. 438.

52. The cable, Early later explained: Early, *Autobiographical Sketch*, p. 382.

52. "I think I can maintain our lines here": Robert E. Lee to Jefferson Davis, June 26, 1864, *The Wartime Papers of Robert E. Lee*, p. 807.

53. "Pickett's division, about 6,000 infantry": O.R. 37, part 1, p. 644.

53. "Lee has sent Doles' and Kershaw's brigades": Ibid.

54. On June 30 at New Market, Early cabled Lee: O.R. 51, part 2, p. 1,028.

55. . . . many of them "felt perfectly at home": Worsham, op cit., p. 232.

55. The Flying Dutchman's "stampede" from Martinsburg: Charles G. Halpine letter to James Gordon Bennett, July 12, 1864, Charles G. Halpine, *Papers of Charles G. Halpine, 1811–1889*, Huntington Library.

55. "All of Sigel's operations from the beginning of the war": Grant to Maj. Gen. Henry W. Halleck, July 7, 1864, John Y. Simon, ed., *The Papers of Ulysses S. Grant, 11: June 1–August 15, 1864* (Southern Illinois University Press, 1984), p. 185.

56. . . . Siegel evacuating Martinsburg "after very light skirmishing": Early, *A Memoir of the Last Year* . . . , p. 55.

57. The food was "divided among the men": Worsham, op. cit., p. 233.

57. "Some say that Breckinridge and Pickett": O.R. 37, part 2, p. 4.

57. "The enemy that attacked Harper's Ferry": O.R. 37, part 1, p. 176.

58. "I find from various quarters statements": O.R. 37, part 1, p. 695.

58. Earlier in the war Southern sympathizers had turned out: "Maryland, My Maryland" was written by James Ryder Randall, a Maryland native who was living in Louisiana when the Civil War broke out. Sung to the traditional tune of "O Tannenbaum," the nine-stanza "Maryland, My Maryland" was popular throughout the South during the Civil War. It was not adopted as the Maryland official state song until 1939.

58. "We crossed the Potomac at Shepherdstown": John G. Young Diary, entry for July 9, 1864, Collection No. 1076, North Carolina State Archives.

58. "I took off my clothing, made a bundle": Worsham, op. cit., pp. 233–34.

59. It "was a desperate thing to do": Douglas, op. cit., pp. 292–93.

59. "My father gave me verbally the contents of his letter": Capt. Robert E. Lee, *Recollections and Letters of General Robert E. Lee* (Broadfoot Publishing, 1988), p. 131. Rob Lee, Lee's youngest son, enlisted in the Rockbridge Artillery as a private in 1862, then spent the rest of the war as a captain serving under his brother Custis Lee, who was aide-de-camp to Confederate president Jefferson Davis.

59. The secret letter, Early said, informed him: Early, *Autobiographical Sketch*, p. 385.

59. "That night," Early said: Ibid.

59. . . . Confederate troops not to harm "unarmed and defenseless" civilians in the North: General Order No. 73, issued June 27, 1863, O.R. 27, part 3, p. 943.

59. . . . in reaction to what he called "deplorable accounts of plundering and confusion": O.R. 37, part 2, p. 592.

61. They "would go into the people's houses in the country": Allen Sparrow Diary, quoted in Kathleen Ernst, *Too Afraid to Cry: Maryland Civilians in the Antietam Campaign* (Stackpole, 1999), pp. 214–15.

61. Confederate troops, another local man wrote in his diary: *Diary of Jacob Englebrecht*, July 11, 1864 (Frederick, Maryland: C. Burr Artz Library). Also see Richard R. Duncan, "Maryland's Reaction to Early's Raid in 1864: A Summer of Bitterness," *Maryland Historical Society Magazine* (Fall 1969), pp. 254–56.

61. "Neither foe nor friend escaped": Chapl. E. M. Haynes, *A History of the Tenth Regiment, Vermont Volunteers, with Biographical Sketches* . . . (Tenth Vermont Regimental Association, 1870), p. 101.

SIX

63. Garrett told Wallace: Lew Wallace, *An Autobiography* 2, op. cit., p. 699.

64. That fight turned out to be the July 9 Battle of Monocacy: Ibid., p. 697.

64. Lewis Wallace—known universally as Lew: The standard work on Wallace's life is Robert E. Morsberger and Katharine M. Morsberger, *Lew Wallace: Military Romantic* (McGraw-Hill, 1980). Wallace's two-volume *Autobiography* was written decades after the fact and contains many liberally recreated quotes.

65. Before long, he shaped them into a Zouave unit: The name "Zouave" came from a regiment of the French colonial army made up of fierce warriors from the Kabyli tribe who lived in the hills of Algeria and Morocco. The French Zouaves made their reputation during the Crimean War of 1854–56. During the Civil War, American Zouave units fought on both sides of the conflict.

65. "This is my native state": Wallace, *Autobiography* I, p. 260.

66. "His deep, flashing eye": Catherine Merrill, *The Soldier of Indiana in the War for the Union* (Merrill, 1869), quoted in Morsberger, op. cit., p. 56.

66. The spoils of the battle included "seven officers' marquees": "The Battle of Romney," *Harper's Weekly* (July 6, 1861), p. 423.

67. When one partisan Republican correspondent: See, among others, Edward G. Longacre, *General Ulysses S. Grant: The Soldier and the Man* (Da Capo, 2006), p. 137.

67. As Wallace noted in his autobiography: According to the U.S. Departments of Defense and Veterans Affairs, some 10,600 Americans were killed and wounded in the American Revolution; some 6,800 in the War of 1812;

and 5,900 in the Mexican War, making a total of some 23,300—versus some 24,000 casualties at Shiloh.

67. "Somebody in the dark gave me a push": Wallace, *Autobiography* I, p. 465.

68. "Time and care had told upon him": Wallace, *Autobiography* 2, p. 670.

70. "So great is my confidence in Stanton's judgment": Quoted in "Edward Mc-Masters Stanton," *Ohio History Central: An Online Encyclopedia of Ohio* (Ohio Historical Society, 2005); http://www.ohiohistorycentral.org/entry.php?rec=356.

70. Lew Wallace described Stanton at their first meeting: Wallace, *Autobiography* 2, p. 671.

71. . . . whom one Union officer called "the marplot [someone who ruins a plan by meddling] of the war": Thomas W. Hyde, *Following the Greek Cross or Memories of the Sixth Army Corps* (University of South Carolina Press, 2005), pp. 169–70.

71. Halleck "is in a perfect maze": Gideon Welles, *Diary of Gideon Welles* 2 (Houghton Mifflin, 1911), p. 70.

72. Halleck has the "habit of looking at people": Wallace, *Autobiography* 2, pp. 570–71.

72. "The department, as I am painfully aware": General Order No. 15, March 22, 1864, published in *The New York Times* (March 24, 1864).

72. "Rebels and traitors," he announced: Quoted in Morsberger, op. cit., p. 134.

72. "Great battles are to be scented far off ": Lew Wallace to Susan Wallace, April 24, 1864, Wallace Collection, William Henry Smith Memorial Library, Indiana Historical Society, Indianapolis. Also see Morsberger, op. cit., p. 138.

SEVEN

73. "The truth is I did not care to have my absence": Wallace, *Autobiography* 2, p. 711.

74. "The enemy (Jubal Early) appeared at Harper's Ferry last Saturday": W. A. Croffut, ed., *Fifty Years in Camp and Field: Diary of Major-General Ethan Allen Hitchcock, U.S.A.* (G. P. Putnam's Sons, 1909), p. 463.

75. On July 8 Welles railed in his diary about the "profound ignorance": Welles, *Diary*, op. cit., p. 69.

75. The Flying Dutchman, Grant said: O.R. 37, part 2, p. 15.

76. Grant told Halleck that a Confederate deserter: O.R. 37, part 2, p. 33.

76. Assistant Secretary of War Charles A. Dana: Charles A. Dana, *Recollections of the Civil War* (D. Appleton, 1898), p. 228.

76. An "intelligent deserter," Dana's dispatch said: O.R. 37, part 2, p. 34.

76. "Some accounts, probably exaggerated": O.R. 37, part 2, p. 59.

77. Halleck on July 5 advised Grant to send "a large dismounted cavalry force" to Washington immediately: Gen. Ethan Allen Hitchcock wrote in a July 28 diary entry that Halleck told him that Hitchcock's stern Stonewall Jackson speech had caught Lincoln's attention and impelled the president to ask Grant to send troops to Washington. No other source corroborates Hitchcock's claim that he was the one who convinced Lincoln of the danger to the capital or the general's claim, in that same diary entry, that he believed that his "earnest intervention" with Lincoln "saved this city from capture by Early's army."

77. "Early, in command of two divisions": O.R. 37, part 2, p. 60.

77. "We want now to crush out and destroy": Ibid.

77. Wallace, writing in an after-action report a month later: O.R. 37, part 1, p. 193.

78. Putting together a force to make a stand at Monocacy: Wallace, *Autobiography* 2, p. 705.

78. The unit's commander, Wallace said: Wallace, *Autobiography* 2, p. 721.

78. "Here ended the good time we had": Frederick W. Wild, *Memoirs and History of Capt. F. W. Alexander's Baltimore Battery of Light Artillery U.S.V.* (Press of the Maryland School for Boys, 1912), p. 118.

79. Halleck for the first time on July 6: O.R. 37, part 2, p. 79.

80. "Presently the General said: "'Very well, tell General [Horatio] Wright'": George R. Agassiz, ed., *Meade's Headquarters, 1863–65: Letters of Col. Theodore Lyman from The Wilderness to Appomattox* (The Atlantic Monthly Press, 1922), p. 184. Lyman (1833–97) was born in Waltham, Massachusetts, graduated from Harvard in 1855, and served as a volunteer aide-de-camp on Meade's staff from September 2, 1863, to April 20, 1865. After the war, he

served one term (1883–85) as an Independent Republican in the U.S. House of Representatives.

81. "We are on the Steamship *Columbia*": William Burroughs Ross's letter, July 7, 1864. See Bernard A. Olsen, ed., *Upon the Tented Field* (Historic Projects, 1993), p. 252.

81. . . . which the eminent Civil War historian James McPherson called: Ibid., p. 9.

81. "A large force of veterans has arrived": O.R. 37, part 2, p. 100.

81. "Every house along the road displayed the national flag": Osceola Lewis, *History of the One hundred and thirty-eighth Regiment, Pennsylvania Volunteer Infantry* (Wills, Iredell & Jenkins,1866), p. 113.

82. "I hear a train in the direction of Baltimore": Wallace, *Autobiography* 2, p. 735.

82. "He was tall, broad-shouldered, with a campaign complexion": Ibid., p. 736.

83. Ricketts "was slightly above the average height": Ibid., p. 752.

84. "Instead of strengthening me here": Ibid., p. 755.

EIGHT

86. "On July 4," Mosby wrote: Charles Wells Russell, ed., *The Memoirs of Colonel John S. Mosby* (Little Brown, 1917), p. 275.

87. "Most of the men went into the dry-goods business": Maj. John Scott, *Partisan Life with Col. John S. Mosby* (Harper & Brothers, 1867), p. 241.

87. "I found Mosby with two pieces of artillery": O.R. 37, part 1, p. 219.

88. "I will obey any order you will send me": Quoted in Jeffrey D. Wert, *Mosby's Rangers* (Simon & Schuster, 1990), p. 178.

88. "I had work of the utmost importance for him": Wallace, *Autobiography* 2, p. 718.

88. Clendenin "accepted the proposal": Ibid., p. 719.

89. "The heat was very oppressive": Abner Hard, *History of the Eighth Cavalry Regiment Illinois Volunteers, During the Great Rebellion* (Morningside, 1996), p. 295.

89. "Though out of my department": O.R. 37, part 1, p. 194.

89. "The enemy are pressing us": O.R. 51, part 1, p. 1,171.

89. "The conduct of both officers and men": O.R. 37, part 1, p. 213.

90. That night he sent a cable to his aide: O.R. 37, part 2, p. 110.

90. "The enemy was coming": Wallace, *Autobiography* 2, p. 725.

91. "Young men, if you should be captured fighting": See Glenn H. Worthington, *Fighting for Time: The Battle of Monocacy* (Burd Street Press, 1985), pp. 168–73. The story has a happy ending. The young men and women survived and the two engaged couples were married, according to Worthington, whose book, the first extended history of the Battle of Monocacy, originally was published in 1932.

92. Wallace met up with Tyler: Ibid., p. 739.

92. The "rebels," he said "are jubilant this morning": O.R. 51, part 1, p. 1,174.

92. "Our [command] had quite a severe little fight": Letter dated July 26, 1864. Reprinted in Edward B. Williams, ed., *Rebel Brothers: The Civil War Letters of the Truehearts* (Texas A&M University Press, 1995), p. 201.

92. "Since the arrival of Gen. Lew Wallace": "The Raid," *The New York Times*, (July 9, 1864), p. 1.

93. . . . Early's main force was on the move: O.R. 37, part 1, p. 180.

93. "Who was Howe?": Wallace, *Autobiography* 2, p. 740.

93. Wallace himself confirmed what Early was up to: Ibid., p. 742.

94. It was "the twilight hour, not yet dusk": Ibid., p. 746.

94. "Breckenridge, with a strong column": O.R. 37, part 2, p. 127.

94. At 10:30 on July 8 he sent a telegram to Grant: O.R. 37, part 2, p. 119.

NINE

97. "It was a beautiful day in this beautiful country": Worsham, op. cit., p. 235.

97. The morning of July 9 "dawned with a halo on sunshine": W. T. McDougle, "Account of Monocacy," *National Tribune* (February 21, 1884). The *National Tribune*, a newspaper for Civil War veterans, was published by the first

great American veterans' service organization, the Grand Army of the Republic, beginning in 1877. The paper was a forerunner of the *Stars and Stripes*.

98. "Everywhere I read the promise": Wallace, *Autobiography* 2, p. 756.

99. Jubal Early was not on the scene: For a detailed recounting of Early's time
in Frederick that morning, see B. Franklin Cooling, *Monocacy: The Battle That
Saved Washington* (White Mane, 2000), pp. 97–99.

99. Early then wrote out an order: See Worthington, op. cit., pp. 104–5.

100. We "bought what we wanted & paid for it": Jedediah Hotchkiss to Sara
A. Hotchkiss, July 15, 1864, Jedediah Hotchkiss Collection, Reel 4, Manuscripts Division, Library of Congress.

100. We "had approached within one hundred and fifty yards of a squad":
Chaplain E. M. Haynes, op. cit., p. 91.

101. A history of Pennsylvania's Civil War volunteer forces: Samuel P. Bates,
History of Pennsylvania Volunteers, 1861–65 (B. Singerly, 1869), p. 639.

101. The official Union war records note that: O.R. 37, part 1, p. 274.

102. "The enemy, in considerable force under General Lew Wallace": Early,
Reminiscences, p. 387.

102. The covered bridge, Glenn Worthington wrote: Worthington, op. cit.,
p. 59.

103. Alexander's howitzer "took up its cry": Wallace, *Autobiography* 2, p. 759.

103. "We could not see their guns": Wild, op. cit., p. 124.

103. The noise overhead, Wallace said: Wallace, *Autobiography* 2, p. 763.

104. McCausland's dismounted cavalrymen "started forward": Ibid., pp. 768–71.

105. "We received a murderous volley": Margaretta Barton Colt, *Defend the
Valley: A Shenandoah Family in the Civil War* (Orion Books, 1994), p. 330.

105. Worthington described McCausland's troops: Worthington, op. cit., p. 120.

106. As soon as McCausland crossed the Monocacy: Early, *Autobiographical
Sketch*, p. 387.

106. artillery fire that Wallace described as "terrible": Wallace, *Autobiography*
2, p. 777.

107. The rebel troops "indulged in no foolishness": Worthington, op. cit., pp.
124–25.

107. It said: "Hurry up your troops": *O.R.* 51, part 1, p. 1,177.

107. Wallace said he "felt a thrill of gratification": Wallace, *Autobiography* 2, p. 765.

108. "My object," he said, "was to release the guard": Ibid., p. 788.

108. "Members of the company procured sheaves of wheat": Roe, *The Ninth New York Heavy Artillery*, p. 128.

109. The men of the Twenty-third "made a dash for the blockhouse": V. E. Turner and H.C. Wall, "History of the Twenty-Third Regiment" in Walter Clark, *Histories of the Several Regiments and Battalions from North Carolina in the Great War 1861–'65* (Nash Brothers, 1901), pp. 245–46. Also see Edwin C. Bearrs, *The Battle of Monocacy: A Documented Report* (Monocacy National Battlefield, 2003), p. 69.

109. "Every time I raised my head": Daniel B. Freeman, "A Day's Skirmish," *National Tribune* (March 18, 1897). Also see Paul Mathless, ed., *Voices of the Civil War: Shenandoah 1864* (Time-Life Books, 1998), p. 61, and Worthington, op. cit.

TEN

112. "The men took off blankets, oilcloths, etc.,": Worsham, op. cit., pp. 235–36.

112. Gordon's men "stopped to remove their shoes": Worthington, op. cit., p. 129.

112. General "Gordon sat on his horse": Bradwell, op. cit., p. 439.

113. "There was Gordon": Worsham, op. cit., pp. 237–38.

113. Gordon . . . he found himself "separated from all other Confederate infantry": Gordon, *Reminiscences*, p. 310.

113. . . . Ricketts's men . . . spotted the initial movements of Evans's Georgians men "advancing on us": Writing in the *National Tribune*, April 15, 1886.

113. "Wait boys," he said: Quoted in Edwin M. Haynes, *A History of the Tenth Regiment Vermont Volunteers with Biographical Sketches* (Tuttle, 1894), p. 194. Also see Cooling, op. cit., p. 149.

114. "We could not see a Yankee on our part of the line": G. W. Nichols, *A Soldier's Story of His Regiment* (Continental, 1961), reprinted in Mathless, ed., op. cit., p. 63.

114. Gordon's attack, he said in his autobiography: Early, *Autobiographical Sketch*, p. 388.

115. "The whole field was in wheat": Worthington, op. cit., p. 132.

115. "We did not know of the presence on the field": Quoted by Wallace in his *Autobiography* 2, p. 771. Wallace recounted an accidental meeting he and Gordon had at the White House during the McKinley administration (1897–1901) when Gordon was a U.S. senator from Georgia. They had a conversation about Monocacy, Wallace said. "Among other things, General Gordon said he had long wished to know me," Wallace said, "and in explanation stated that I was the only person who had whipped him during the war." Wallace said he found Gordon "remarkably frank and communicative, and a most delightful conversationalist. He took away with him my profoundest respect."

116. Maj. Peter Vredenburgh of the Fourteenth New Jersey said: Letter dated July 12, 1864, reproduced in Olsen, op. cit., p. 253.

116. They were "hours of suspense, anxiety": Interviewed in the *Frederick Post*, July 9, 1914. Also see Cooling, op. cit., pp. 147–48.

116. Wild saw wounded Union troops: Wild, op. cit., p. 127.

116. He came upon a line of dead Union soldiers: Joseph T. Durkin, ed., *Confederate Chaplain: A War Journal of Rev. James B. Sheeran* (Bruce, 1960), p. 984.

117. "My hope, already faint, began shriveling": Wallace, *Autobiography* 2, p. 791.

119. Those were the last words Lew Wallace wrote in his autobiography: Lew Wallace died on February 15, 1905, while at work on his autobiography, which was completed by his wife, Susan, with the help of Mary Hannah Krout. The book was published in 1906.

ELEVEN

121. "What have you heard about battle": O.R. 37, part 1, p. 138.

121. He had just that minute received word: Ibid.

121. "A dispatch, not signed by Lew Wallace": O.R. 37, part 1, p. 134.

122. "I fought the enemy at Frederick Junction": O.R. 37, part 1, p. 144.

122. The Union retreat, Wallace wrote: O.R. 37, part 1, pp. 191–92.

122. Ramseur's men "were endeavoring to surround us": Wild, op. cit., p. 129.

123. Wallace in his after-action report said he ordered "the bridge to be held": O.R. 37, part 1, p. 197.

124. "I attempted to rally my men": O.R. 37, part 1, p. 218.

124. "When the final order was given to retire": Frederick William Seward, ed., *William H. Seward: An Autobiography from 1801–1834, with a Memoir of His Life, and Selections from His Letters* 1, pp. 230–31.

125. "To say that the men and horses were exhausted": Hard, op. cit., p. 301.

125. "The pursuit was soon discontinued": Early, *Autobiography*, p. 388.

126. Echols "asked me to what command I belonged": W. G. Duckett, "My Capture and Escape," in Roe, *The Ninth New York Heavy Artillery*, p. 307.

126. As the young former schoolteacher fled the final Confederate charge: Roe, *A Sketch of the Battle*, p. 128.

126. Alfred Roe described seeing "the burning stubble of the battlefield": Roe, *The Ninth New York Heavy Artillery*, pp. 314–15.

127. "But so great was his suffering": Worthington, op. cit., pp. 158–59.

128. . . . they saw "the gastly forms" of "Yanks killed in the fight": Diary entry dated July 9, William Williams Stringfellow Collection 1091, North Carolina State Archives, Raleigh, North Carolina.

128. Terry's brigade set up "in an orchard near the road": Worsham, op. cit., pp. 239–40.

128. . . . many of the latter "groaning & shrieking with pain": Williams, ed., op. cit., *Rebel Brothers*, p. 201.

129. The first shot crushed his ankle joint: Writing in the *National Tribune*, April 15, 1886.

130. "Imagine, if you can, the sight that greeted the eye": Quoted in the Frederick *Post*, July 9, 1914, the fiftieth anniversary of the battle.

130. We "had plenty of Uncle Sam's coffee": James Hutcheson, "Saved the Day at Monocacy," *Confederate Veteran*, February 1915, p. 77. Also see Benjamin Franklin Cooling, *Jubal Early's Raid on Washington, 1864* (Nautical & Aviation, 1898), p. 78.

130. "There was too many of them for us": Lisa Saunders, ed., *Ever True: A Union Private and His Wife: The Civil War Letters of Private Charles McDowell, New York Ninth Artillery* (privately published, 2003), p. 66.

130. Ricketts's division, the general wrote in his after-action report: O.R. 37, part 1, p. 204. Wallace listed the dead, wounded, and missing by unit in the same volume on pages 200–203.

130. . . . the Fourteenth New Jersey, the "Monocacy Regiment": Casualty figures cited in Waterman, ed., op. cit., p. 255.

131. Of the Fourteenth New Jersey's fifteen officers: Figures cited by Worthington, op. cit., p. 145, based on the speech given by Maj. John C. Patterson at the unveiling of the Fourteenth New Jersey monument at the Monocacy Battlefield in 1908.

131. Zebulon York's Consolidated Louisiana Brigade "lost fully one half": Terry L. Jones, ed., *The Civil War Memoirs of Captain William J. Seymour: Reminiscences of a Louisiana Tiger* (Louisiana State University Press, 1991), p. 137.

131. Clement A. Evans's Georgians, who "had displayed such splendid courage": Bradwell, op. cit., p. 439.

131. "I regret to state that my loss was heavy": O.R. 37, part 1, p. 352.

131. Wallace's losses—which he called "heavy": O.R. 37, part 1, p. 199.

131. "The Confederate victory," John Brown Gordon wrote: Gordon, op. cit., p. 313.

131. "Orders have been given to collect the bodies": O.R. 37, part 1, p. 200.

132. "Does General Ord report to me": O.R. 37, part 2, p. 215.

132. Stanton replied that Wallace was to report to Ord: Ibid.

132. The outcome at Monocacy, Wallace later told his son: Wallace, *Autobiography* 2, p. 808.

132. "For want of sufficient powder": Douglas, op. cit., p. 294.

TWELVE

134. Grant ordered General Ord that day: O.R. 37, part 2, p. 158.

134. Union general Henry Hayes Lockwood in Baltimore put out the order that day: O.R. 37, part 2, p. 180.

134. "The state of affairs in Baltimore is terrible": O.R. 37, part 2, p. 187.

134. When Alexander's Baltimore Artillery Battery arrived home: Wild, op. cit., p. 133.

134. The "rebel cavalry" are "infesting" the area: O.R. 37, part 2, p. 186.

134. "I was now where I knew pretty much every one": Harry Gilmor, *Four Years in the Saddle* (Harper & Brothers, 1866), p. 191.

136. Franklin, Early pointed out: Early, *Autobiography*, p. 394.

136. "The whole brigade engaged in feasting": George W. Booth, *Personal Reminiscences of a Maryland Soldier in the War Between the States, 1861–1865* (Press of Fleet, McGinley, 1898). Also see Mathless, ed., op. cit., p. 67.

137. "There was not time enough": Gordon, *Reminiscences*, p. 316.

137. "The panic here is heavy and increasing": O.R. 37, part 2, p. 213.

138. "It was an anxious Sunday throughout the North": John G. Nicolay and John Hay, *Abraham Lincoln: A History* 9 (The Century, 1890), p. 165. John Milton Hay (1838–1905), a native of Salem, Indiana, and the German-born John Nicolay (1832–1901) lived in the White House and served loyally as Lincoln's personal secretaries and confidants. Nicolay devoted much of his life after Lincoln's death to cowriting, with Hay, what would become an influential ten-volume biography of Lincoln, as well as an edition of Lincoln's collected works. Hay became a journalist after the Civil War, but returned to government service in 1897 as ambassador to the United Kingdom. Hay went on to serve as secretary of state under Presidents William McKinley and Theodore Roosevelt from September 1898 to his death in July 1905.

138. "Send forward to Baltimore": O.R. 37, part 2, p. 188.

138. "I have been defeated": O.R. 37, part 2, p. 174.

139. . . . the Georgetown Pike—the present-day Route 355: Route 355 today is called Urbana Pike in Frederick County, Frederick Road and Rockville Pike

in Montgomery County, Maryland, and Wisconsin Avenue in Washington, D.C. The road parallels Interstate 270, which goes through the Worthington and Thomas Farms on the Monocacy Battlefield.

139. "On the morning of July 10th we marched early": Worsham, op. cit., p. 241.

139. McCausland's men faced "hard and severe skirmishing": Thomas Feamster Diary, op. cit., entry for Sunday, July 10, 1864.

140. After arriving in Rockville, Early "occupied the Clerk's office of the Court-house": *Baltimore Sun*, July 16, 1864, reprinted in *The New York Times*, July 21, 1864.

140. "By latest accounts": O.R. 37, part 2, p. 173.

140. Grant reported to Meade early that morning: O.R. 37, part 2, p. 158.

140. "The war fever is once more at high heat": Ely Parker to William R. Rowley, July 9, 1864, *William R. Rowley (1824–1886) Papers*, SC 1306, Abraham Lincoln Presidential Library and Museum. Ely Samuel Parker (1828–95) was a Seneca Indian from Indian Falls, New York. Parker met Ulysses S. Grant while working as a civil engineer for the federal government. He tried to join the Union army when the Civil War began, but initially was denied a commission, most likely because he was an Indian. Parker persevered and in 1863 became a captain of engineers and was assigned as one of Grant's staff officers. Parker became Grant's military secretary and was at Grant's side when Robert E. Lee surrendered at Appomattox. Parker stayed in the army until 1869, reaching the brevet rank of brigadier general. President Grant appointed Parker Commissioner of Indian Affairs that same year.

141. Grant's aide-de-camp, Gen. Horace Porter, said in his war memoir: Horace Porter, *Campaigning with Grant* (The Century, 1897), p. 236. Porter (West Point class of 1860), the son of one-time Pennsylvania governor David Rittenhouse and the grandson of Revolutionary War general Andrew Porter, served as U.S. ambassador to France from 1897 to 1905. He received the Medal of Honor in 1902 for gallantry at the September 20, 1863, Battle of Chickamauga. His Medal of Honor citation reads: "While acting as a volunteer aide, at a critical moment when the lines were broken, rallied enough fugitives to hold the ground under heavy fire long enough to effect the escape of wagon trains and batteries."

141. "There was no commotion at General Grant's head-quarters": Charles Carleton Coffin, *Four Years of Fighting: A Volume of Personal Observations with the Army and Navy from the First Battle of Bull Run to the Fall of Richmond* (Ticknor and Fields, 1866), pp. 386–87.

142. There were breathless reports that the Union troops put up a feeble fight at Monocacy: See, for example, the *Richmond Dispatch* of July 16, which reported: "The fight at Monocacy bridge, our informant says, was just no fight at all. It was a big run, and if the Yankees lost one thousand men, most of them must have broken their necks running. There wasn't a soldier with Wallace who fired more than once. They found the rebels getting around them in all directions, and, using discretion, took to their heels. The one hundred days men . . . didn't seem disposed to hurt anybody. Some of them didn't know which end of [the] cartridge went in first, and the general impression among them was that the regulation mode of getting the ramrod out of a gun was to blow it up."

142. Richmond "is in great excitement and joy": J. B. Jones, *A Rebel War Clerk's Diary at the Confederate States Capital* 2 (J. B. Lippincott, 1866), p. 248.

142. . . . a city "wild with excitement over the Northern news": *James M. Holloway Papers*, Mss1H7286a 92–110, Virginia Historical Society, Richmond.

143. Speaking of the "present emergency," Lincoln told Grant: *O.R.* 37, part 2, p. 155.

143. "Did my best to get general [Grant] to go to Washington": Martin E. Sumner, ed., *The Diary of Cyrus B. Comstock* (Morningside, 1987), p. 279.

144. Grant—who on July 9 had wired Halleck: Grant to Maj. Gen. Henry W. Halleck, July 9, 1864, John Y. Simon, ed., *The Papers of Ulysses S. Grant 11: June 1–August 15, 1864*, op. cit., p. 199.

144. "I think on reflection it would have a bad effect": *O.R.* 37, part 2, p. 156.

144. "We have no forces here for the field": *O.R.* 37, part 2, p. 157.

THIRTEEN

145. Washington . . . grew into the nation's fourteenth largest city: According to the official U.S. Census of 1860 New York City, including Brooklyn, was by far the nation's most populous city, with more than one million residents in

1860. Philadelphia was second with some 565,000. The largest Southern cities in 1860 were New Orleans (some 170,000) and Richmond, with just under 38,000 residents.

146. Whitman estimated that from late 1862 to February of 1866 he made "600 visits or tours": Walt Whitman, *Memoranda During the War* (Indiana University Press, 1962), pp. 55–56. Also see Martin G. Murray, "Traveling with the Wounded: Walt Whitman and Washington's Civil War Hospitals," *Washington History: The Magazine of the Historical Society of Washington, D.C.,* Fall/Winter 1996–97.

147. But the city had a profusion of barrooms and brothels and several crime-ridden neighborhoods: Margaret Leech, *Reveille in Washington, 1860–1865* (Time-Life Books, 1980), p. 15.

147. The stunning defeat at Manassas "left no longer room to doubt": Report dated December 10, 1861, O.R. (Volume. 5), part 1, p. 679.

149. "The soldiers camped here at this time were mostly German": Quoted in William V. Cox, "The Defenses of Washington: General Early's Advance on the Capital and the Battle of Fort Stevens, July 11 and 12," *Records of the Columbia Historical Society, Washington, D.C.* 4 (1901), p. 138.

151. Acting Ordnance Sergeant Spink, Alexander reported: O.R. 37, part 2, p. 83.

151. "The armament was insufficient, the ordnance supplies limited": Benjamin P. Thomas, ed., *Three Years with Grant: As Recalled by War Correspondent Sylvanus Cadwallader* (Knopf, 1956), p. 226.

152. . . . a group of soldiers that Lew Wallace called: Wallace, *Autobiography* 2, p. 701.

152. . . . the Invalid Corps consisted of "experienced soldiers": Capt. J. W. De Forest, November 30, 1865, O.R. 5, Series 3, part 1, p. 543.

153. The next day they reported to brigade headquarters: David Herbert Donald, ed., *Gone for a Soldier: The Civil War Memoirs of Private Alfred Bellard* (Little, Brown, 1975), p. 270.

154. Gideon Welles, the navy secretary, wrote in his journal that day: Welles, op. cit., Volume 2, p. 71.

154. Men, that day, "stood in groups on street corners": Frank Wilkeson, *Turned Inside Out: Recollections of a Private Soldier in the Army of the Potomac*

(University of Nebraska Press, 1997), pp. 209–10. Wilkeson, the son of *New York Times* war correspondent Samuel Wilkeson (1817–89) and the nephew of the famed suffragist Elizabeth Cady Stanton, ran away from his Buffalo, New York, home and joined the Union army on March 26, 1864, eighteen days after his sixteenth birthday. He served with the Eleventh Battery of New York Light Artillery and fought in Grant's Wilderness Campaign. Wilkeson reenlisted on June 25, 1864, in Washington and was appointed a second lieutenant in the Fourth U.S. Artillery.

155. "Bands of music, bodies of infantry and little clouds of cavalry": *Chicago Evening Journal,* July 20, 1864. Also see J. Cutler Andrews, *The North Reports the Civil War* (University of Pittsburgh Press, 1955), p. 591.

155. "Excitement in the city," Pliny Fiske Sanborne: *Diary of Pliny Fiske Sanborne: Civil War Chaplain: June 7–August 15, 1864,* transcribed copy in the Eleanor S. Brockenbrough Library at the Museum of the Confederacy, Richmond, Virginia. The Christian Commission relief organization formed in November 1861. By the end of war the commission had sent some five thousand volunteers to help Union chaplains in their work with soldiers in the field and to lend a hand in field hospitals.

FOURTEEN

157. Halleck relayed an order from U. S. Grant: *O.R.* 40, part 3, p. 106.

158. "We had become too much accustomed to sudden movements": George T. Stevens, *Three Years in the Sixth Corps* (S. R. Gray, 1866), p. 371.

159. "We could not tell where we were going": Hyde, op. cit, p. 221.

159. "When leaving . . . made a great deal of noise": *O.R.* 40, part 3, p. 124.

159. It was "an all-night march from the dust of Petersburg": Writing in the Veterans Column in the Fayetteville, N.Y., *Weekly Recorder,* February 12, 1891.

159. "Enjoyed a shower, the first we have experienced in forty days": William S. Tyler, ed., *Recollections of the Civil War . . . by Mason Whiting Tyler* (G. P. Putnam's Sons, 1912), p. 246.

160. "The trip, taken together, was a rather pleasant one": James M. Greiner, et. al., eds., *A Surgeon's Civil War: The Letters and Diary of Daniel M. Holt, M.D.* (Kent State University Press, 1994), p. 219.

161. . . . a day that Henry H. Atwater of the U.S. Military Telegraph Corps called "one of the hottest": Quoted in David Homer Bates, op. cit., p. 253.

162. The "panic-stricken people from Rockville, Silver Spring, Tennallytown, and the other Maryland villages": Noah Brooks, *Washington in Lincoln's Time* (The Century, 1895), p. 173.

162. Farmers "living in the path of the coming enemy": Frederick William Seward, ed., op. cit., p. 232.

162. "I can give you but a faint idea of the panic": John H. Brinton, *Personal Memoirs of John H. Brinton, Civil War Surgeon, 1861–1865* (Southern Illinois University Press, 1996), p. 279.

163. Washington, *New York Herald* correspondent Sylvanus Cadwallader said: Thomas, ed., *Three Years with Grant*, op. cit., p. 227.

163. "Never has danger so menaced us before": E. Harman to Abraham Lincoln, Monday, July 11, 1864, Library of Congress, Abraham Lincoln Papers, Series 1, General Correspondences, 1833–1916.

163. "If the rebels make an attack on the Forts at all": *The Diary of Horatio Nelson Taft, 1861–1865*, Volume 3, Manuscript Division, Library of Congress (January 1, 1864–May 30, 1865).

163. When he entered the city, Dana said, he also found the citizens: Dana, op. cit., p. 229.

163. ". . . accompanied by appropriate medical supplies for the care of the wounded": Writing in *The Washington Post*, July 8, 1906.

164. The city's "large secession element": Albert Gallatin Riddle, *Recollections of War Times: Reminiscences of Men and Events in Washington, 1860–1865* (G. P. Putnam's Sons, 1895), pp. 291–92. Riddle (1816–1902), who served one term in the House (1861–63), subsequently was a U.S. consul in Cuba, then returned to practice law in Washington in 1864. After the war he worked with the government's prosecution of John H. Surratt, one of John Wilkes Booth's accomplices in the murder of President Lincoln. On July 10, 1864, Riddle was drafted into a local militia company and ordered to muster the following day. He reported for duty on the morning of July 11, but could not find the unit. He and two other civilians took a carriage to Fort Stevens, but did not take part in the fighting there.

164. Noah Brooks reported that Union troops confiscated a half-sewn Confederate flag: Brooks, op. cit., p. 176.

165. "We have five times as many generals as we want": O.R. 37, part 2, p. 196.

166. "There was no head to the whole": Dana, op. cit., pp. 230–31.

166. He "discovered the fact that the only troops on the north of Washington": O.R. 37, part 1, p. 230.

167. ... described by the commander of Fort Stevens, Lt. Col. John N. Frazee: O.R. 37, part 1, p. 245.

167. "On the roof in the blazing sun": Bates, op. cit., pp. 253–54.

167. "The Rebels are upon us": Welles, Diary, op. cit., 2, pp. 72–73.

167. The alarmed Stanton "directed that all orderlies": Brinton, op. cit., p. 279.

168. "I became a member of a naval brigade": Simon Newcomb, The Reminiscences of an Astronomer (Houghton, Mifflin, 1903), pp. 339–40.

168. Young second lieutenant Frank Wilkeson, assigned to Fort Totten: Wilkeson, op. cit., p. 212.

169. The next morning, Monday, July 11, according to Bellard: Donald, ed., op. cit., p. 271.

169. One Union soldier called the assemblage a collection: Quoted in Walter Clark, ed., Histories of the Several Regiments and Battalions from North Carolina in the Great War, 1861–1865 2 (Broadfoot, 1982), p. 123. Also see Cooling, Monocacy, op. cit., p. 187.

169. "President Lincoln stood upon the wharf ": Stevens, op. cit., p. 372.

169. "At the landing we were met": James H. Croushore, ed., A Volunteer's Adventures: A Union Captain's Record of the Civil War (Louisiana State University Press, 1946), p. 161.

170. "Please stop Gen. Wright's movement up the Potomac": O.R. 37, part 2, p. 209.

170. The heat "was appalling," Lieutenant Colonel Hyde remembered: Hyde, op. cit., p. 222.

170. We found the citizens of Washington "in a state of great and not surprising consternation": Aldace F. Walker, The Vermont Brigade in the Shenandoah Valley, 1864 (The Free Press Association, 1869), p. 28.

171. "All sorts of rumors—vague and ridiculous": Holt, op. cit., p. 220.

171. "The attempt to capture Washington had thrown the population into a state": Writing in the Fayetteville, N.Y., *Weekly Observer*, July 3, 1890.

171. He saw "the 19th Corps pass the city from Louisiana via City Point": *Diary of Plinly Fiske Sanborne*, op. cit., entry for July 11, 1864.

172. "The enemy are reported advancing toward Tennallytown": Edwin M. Stanton to Abraham Lincoln, Sunday, July 10, 1864, Abraham Lincoln Papers at the Library of Congress.

172. "The President concluded to desert his tormentors today": Michael Burlingame and John R. Turner Ettlinger, eds., *Inside Lincoln's White House: The Complete Civil War Diary of John Hay* (Southern Illinois University Press, 1999), p. 221.

172. "His tall form must have been a conspicuous target": Bates, op. cit., p. 253.

172. At the telegraph office he sketched a diagram: Ibid.

FIFTEEN

173. Among the regimental commanders: Virginian George Smith Patton graduated from VMI in 1852, and then studied law. He set up a law practice in Charleston, in what is now West Virginia, where he organized the Kanawha Riflemen Militia Company. Patton took that unit into the Confederate army in 1861; a year later it was renamed the Twenty-second Virginia. One of six brothers who served in the Civil War, he was severely wounded and briefly taken prisoner at the Battle of Scary Creek, but recovered and fought courageously for two more years. Col. George Smith Patton died on September 24, 1864, from a gunshot wound at the Third Battle of Winchester.

175. First, as Early put it in his autobiography: Early, *Autobiographical Sketch*, pp. 390–91.

175. Many of Early's men, as John Worsham noted in his war memoir: Worsham, op. cit., p. 243.

175. . . . what Union prisoner of war W. G. Duckett called the "almost suffocating" heat: Writing in Roe, *The Ninth New York Artillery*, p. 308.

176. "We were nearer to the national capital": Gordon, *Reminiscences*, p. 314.

176. "I believe," Charles T. O'Ferrall of the Twenty-third Virginia Cavalry: O'Ferrall, op. cit., p. 110.

176. All along the march from Monocacy "our guards had jokingly told us": Roe, *The Ninth New York Heavy Artillery*, p. 315.

177. "Many of Early's men were bloated with extravagant notions": Baltimore *Sun*, July 16, 1864, reprinted in *The New York Times*, July 21, 1864.

177. "Our army is very anxious to enter Washington City:" Diary entry for July 11, 1864, William Williams Stringfellow Collection, op. cit.

177. "Long before we came in sight of the defenses": Bradwell, op. cit., p. 439.

177. "I did not arrive in front of the fortifications until after noon": Early, *Autobiographical Sketch*, p. 393.

177. "Before us were the tremendous and almost impregnable fortifications of the city": Seaton Gales, "Experiences with the Army of Virginia—Campaign of 1864," *Our Living and Our Dead* (journal), (February 25, 1874); also see Mathless, op. cit., p. 65.

178. Rode's men also saw "a cloud of dust": Early, *Autobiographical Sketch*, p. 390.

178. "The enemy were shelling the road at this point": Worsham, op. cit., p. 241.

181. "We may," Lee said, "assume that a corps or its equivalent": O.R. 37, part 2, p. 595.

181. Men of the Ninety-eighth, 102nd, and 139th Pennsylvania Veteran Volunteers: O.R. 37, part 1, p. 276.

181. . . . Thomas H. Scott of the 122nd New York characterized as "a desperate engagement": Writing in the Fayetteville, N.Y., *Weekly Observer*, July 3, 1890.

182. The fighting "occurred chiefly on the skirmish line": Writing in *The Washington Post*, July 8, 1906.

182. "We had quite a sharp fight": Brinton, op. cit., p. 284.

182. "Could see the line of pickets of both armies": Welles, op. cit. 2, p. 72.

183. There "was not a dissenting opinion": Gordon, *Reminiscences*, pp. 324–25.

184. "After interchanging views with them": Early, *Autobiographical Sketch*, p. 392.

184. Washington, he told Grant in a cable that morning: O.R. 37, part 2, p. 222.

184. "Nothing can possibly be done here toward pursuing or cutting off the enemy": O.R. 37, part 2, p. 223.

SIXTEEN

187. "The President is in very good feather this evening": Hay, op. cit., p. 221.

187. "Even with the sound of hostile guns in his ears": Nicolay and Hay, op. cit., p. 167.

187. "The President has been a good deal incredulous": Welles, op. cit., 2, p. 69.

188. "The awful fighting in the Wilderness and at Cold Harbor": Brooks, op. cit., p. 173.

188. "All familiar with him will remember the weary air": F. B. Carpenter, *The Inner Life of Abraham Lincoln: Six Months at the White House* (University of Nebraska Press, 1995), p. 217. Francis Bicknall Carpenter, a New York–born artist who specialized in portraits, wrote his reminiscences in 1866. His most famous painting, *The First Reading of the Emancipation Proclamation*, was based on the six months of access Carpenter was given to President Lincoln at the White House from February to July of 1864.

189. "No element of Mr. Lincoln's character": Quoted in Joshua Wolf Shenk, *Lincoln's Melancholy: How Depression Challenged a President and Fueled His Greatness* (Houghton Mifflin, 2005), p. 4.

189. Lincoln "was a sad looking man": Quoted in F. B. Carpenter, op cit., p. 323.

190. "War, at the best, is terrible": Roy P. Basler, ed., *Abraham Lincoln: His Speeches and Writings* (World Publishing, 1946), pp. 751–52.

190. . . . the president asked him "if he would kindly send word over to the White House": Brooks, op. cit., p. 160.

191. "The immense slaughter of our brave men chills and sickens us all": Welles, op. cit., 2, pp. 44, 73.

191. "An accumulation of disheartening difficulties": Gideon Welles, "The Opposition to Lincoln in 1864," *Atlantic Monthly* (March 1878), p. 387.

192. Washington's "capture and possession for a day would have been disastrous": L. E. Chittenden, *Recollections of President Lincoln and His Administration* (Harper & Brothers, 1891), p. 423. A great-grandson of Thomas Chittenden, Vermont's first governor, Lucius Chittenden (1824–1900), a lawyer and fervent antislavery advocate, came to Washington in February 1861 as a delegate to the failed Washington Peace Conference. He was appointed register of the U.S. Treasury—an accounting-keeping post—in March and served in that position until August of 1864. Chittenden accompanied his wife and children by train to Baltimore on July 10, 1864, then returned to Washington and witnessed the fighting at Fort Stevens on July 11.

193. "The parapets," he saw, were "lined with troops": Early, *Autobiographical Sketch*, p. 392.

194. "The enemy has been close to Fort Stevens": O.R. 37, part 2, p. 208.

194. "I do not consider it advisable to make any advance": Ibid.

194. During a day that dawned "bright and glorious": Stevens, op. cit., p. 374.

194. Confederate cavalry, Frank Wilkeson at nearby Fort Totten remembered: Wilkeson, op. cit., p. 214.

194. "Long practice" had made the Eleventh Vermont's "officers and men entirely familiar": Walker, op. cit., p. 28.

195. The Union skirmish line that day, Alfred Bellard reported, "was on a range of hills": Stevens, op. cit., p. 271.

195. "The noise of the encounter on the 12th was great:" Roe, *The Ninth New York Heavy Artillery*, p. 319.

195. "The pseudo-soldiers who filled the trenches around the Fort": Walker, op. cit., p. 29.

196. The "big guns boomed": Writing in the "Veterans Column" in the Fayetteville, New York, *Weekly Recorder*, February 12, 1891.

196. The Confederate fire "was so hot that in the little time": Chittenden, op. cit., pp. 416–17.

197. "Labored all day in hospital and grounds": Sanbourne, *Diary*, op. cit., entry for July 12, 1864.

197. "It is a wonder that more men were not wounded or killed": Writing in "The Veterans Column," of the Fayetteville, N.Y., *Weekly Recorder*, July 19, 1888.

SEVENTEEN

199. Lincoln's "interest in the progress of affairs was intense and ardent": Nicolay and Hay, op. cit., p. 172. The presidential secretaries also pointed out that the engagement at Fort Stevens was "witnessed by the president of the United States on one side and on the other by General Breckinridge, the candidate [and former vice president] who had received the suffrages of the seceding States in 1860."

199. Amid the firing on Monday, according to Hay: Burlingame and Ettlinger, eds., op. cit, p. 221.

201. "Grabbing the president by the arm": Alexander Woolcott, "Get Down, You Fool!" *Atlantic Monthly* (February 1938), p. 170.

201. Inside the fort, Welles wrote in his journal that night: Welles, op. cit. 2, p. 75.

201. In a letter to his wife dated July 14, Bull wrote: Reprinted in John Henry Cramer, *Lincoln Under Enemy Fire* (Louisiana State University Press, 1948), p. 27.

201. "President Lincoln and his wife drove up to the barracks": Stevens, op. cit., p. 375.

202. Lincoln, Reyburn said, "watched the conflict from the ramparts": *Washington Post*, July 8, 1906.

202. Lt. Col. Thomas Hyde of Wright's staff, writing in his 1894 war memoir: Hyde, op. cit., p. 223.

202. The president, he said, was "frequently cautioned by the commanding officer": George A. Armes, *Ups and Downs of an Army Officer*, self-published (1900), p. 115.

203. A Confederate bullet, the history recounts: James L. Bowen, *History of the Thirty-Seventh Regiment Mass. Volunteers in the Civil War of 1861–1865* (Clark W. Bryan, 1884), p. 352.

203. Lincoln "stood, apparently unconscious of danger": Nicolay and Hay, op. cit., p. 173.

203. Lincoln, Wright recalled six years after the fact, "evinced a remarkable coolness": Stevens, op. cit., (1870 edition), p. 377.

204. After asking Lincoln to come down from the parapet: Cox, "Defenses of Washington," op. cit., p. 155.

204. "I saw [the attack] coming and thought we were 'gone up'": Douglas, op. cit., p. 295.

EIGHTEEN

205. England's newspaper of record, *The Times* of London, reported that Early's "operations": *Times* of London, July 28, 1864, reprinted in *The New York Times*, August 12, 1864.

206. The "remainder of the night," General Wheaton said: O.R. 37, part 1, p. 277.

206. At "about dark" that night, Early said: Early, *Autobiographical Sketch*, p. 394.

206. "The President," John Hay wrote in his diary on Wednesday, July 13: Burlingame and Ettlinger, ed., op. cit., p. 222.

206. Grant, directing things a hundred miles away outside Richmond: O.R. 37, part 2, p. 222.

206. "The gray dawn spread over the landscape widely extended in sight": O.R. 37, part 1, p. 259.

207. Meig's "irregulars" . . . "were withdrawn from the fortifications": Dana, op. cit., p. 232.

207. Jackson's men charged Lowell's advance guard: Lowell's report of July 13, 1864, 2:30 p.m., quoted in Edward W. Emerson, *Life and Letters of Charles Russell Lowell* (Houghton, Mifflin 1907), p. 456.

207. . . . the Massachusetts men "charged upon them gallantly": Charles A. Humphries, *Field, Camp, Hospital and Prison: In the Civil War, 1863–1865* (Press of Geo. H. Ellis, 1918), pp. 149–50.

208. . . . that he saw "traces of rebel occupation five or six miles from Washington": Brooks, op. cit., p. 178.

209. Wright had assured Augur the night before: O.R. 37, part 1, p. 265.

209. Everybody, presidential secretaries Nicolay and Hay later wrote: Nicolay and Hay, op. cit., p. 173.

207. "They are making, I remarked, for Edward's Ferry": Welles, op. cit., 2, p. 76. Early and his men actually crossed the Potomac at White's Ferry. The ferryboat that shuttles cars across the Potomac today at the spot where Early crossed on July 14, 1864, is named the *Jubal Early*.

210. He had learned from Lincoln's "own lips": Brooks, op. cit., p. 177.

210. Early "should have on his heels, veterans, Militiamen, men on horseback": O.R. 37, part 2, pp. 300–310.

210. Halleck, in jest, said to Mrs. Lincoln: Carpenter, op. cit., p. 301.

NINETEEN

211. I "do not exaggerate in the least": John Y. Simon, ed., *The Papers of Ulysses S. Grant, 11: June 1–August 15, 1864*, op. cit., pp. 230–31.

212. The army chief, Dana told Rawlins the next night: Ibid., p. 244.

213. "I have always wondered at Early's inaction throughout the day": Cadwallader, op. cit., p. 227.

214. Early "passed the night of the 10th within five miles of Washington": Chittenden, op. cit., p. 423.

214. "Had Stonewall Jackson been in command of that force": Nelson A. Miles, *Serving the Republic: Memoirs of the Civil and Military Life of Nelson A. Miles* (Harper & Brothers, 1911), pp. 72–73.

214. Presidential secretaries Nicolay and Hay, in their biography of Lincoln, accused Early: Nicolay and Hay, op. cit., pp. 170–71.

215. The mercurial Horace Greeley . . . also believed Early could have "taken the city": Horace Greeley, *The American Conflict: A History of the Great Rebellion in the United States of America, 1860–'65 . . . 2* (O. D. Case, 1866), p. 605.

215. "Natural obstacles alone prevented our taking Washington": Stephen Dodson Ramseur to Ellen Richmond Ramseur, July 15, 1864, folder 9, Stephen Dodson Ramseur Papers, Southern Historical Collection, Wilson Library, University of North Carolina, Chapel Hill. Also see Gary W. Gallagher, *Stephen Dodson Ramseur: Lee's Gallant General,* op. cit., p. 130.

215. On "Monday [July 11] we went up to the fortifications, & within 6 miles of the President's House": Jedediah Hotchkiss to Sara A. Hotchkiss, July 15, 1864, Jedediah Hotchkiss Collection, Reel 4, Manuscripts Division, Library of Congress.

215. The Confederates "found the enemy's works of a very formidable character": O.R. 43, part 1, p. 1,021.

216. If "the invasion of Maryland was designed to create a diversion from Grant's army": Brooks, op. cit., p. 177.

216. The journalist and author Edward A. Pollard (1818–72): Edward A. Pollard, *The Lost Cause: A New Southern History of the War of the Confederates* (E. B. Treat, 1866), p. 536

216. Early, Roe wrote in 1890, "personally told me": Roe, *The Ninth New York Heavy Artillery,* pp. 319–20. Alaric the First (circa 370–410), a Visigoth king, conquered and sacked Rome in the year of his death, an event that hastened the fall of the Western Roman Empire.

217. Grant spoke of "the gravity of the situation": Grant, *Personal Memoirs,* op. cit., p. 522.

218. The "men were almost completely exhausted": O.R. 37, part 1, p. 1,021.

218. . . . Early said that on leaving Monocacy on July 10 he had hoped: Early, *A Memoir of the Last Year of the War,* op. cit., p. 60.

219. It "was hoped," Lee wrote to his secretary of war, James A. Seddon, on July 19: Dowdey, ed., *The Wartime Papers of Robert E. Lee,* op. cit., p. 822.

219. "I have been asked," Davis said in a September 23, 1864, speech: Transcribed from the Macon *Telegraph,* September 24, 1864, see *The Papers of Jefferson Davis* 11: September 1864–May 1865 (Louisiana State University Press, 2003), p. 63.

220. "There has been some criticism on the part of some": Quoted in the *Winchester Times Extra,* June 7, 1889.

220. "The exhaustion of our force": Jefferson Davis, *The Rise and Fall of the Confederate Government* 2 (D. Appleton, 1881), p. 530.

221. "General Early could not have held Washington": Fitzhugh Lee, *General Lee* (D. Appleton, 1894), pp. 351–52.

221. In his official report written a year after the war's end: O.R. 36, part 1, p. 28.

221. "Whether the delay caused by the battle [of Monocacy]": Grant, *Personal Memoirs*, op. cit., p. 522.

222. "Many in the North saw [Early's] raid": James McPherson, author interview, January 10, 2006.

222. "Had Wallace failed to intercept Early": Writing in Francis H. Kennedy, ed., *The Civil War Battlefield Guide*, 2nd edition (Houghton Mifflin, 1998), p. 308.

222. Grant "had been planning some important offensive operations": Porter, op. cit., p. 237.

222. . . . . he had "the bulk of the Rebel Army" besieged: Grant to J. Russell Jones, July 5, 1864, John Y. Simon, ed., *The Papers of Ulysses S. Grant 11: June 1–August 15, 1864*, op. cit., p. 175.

223. In a telegram Grant wrote to Halleck from City Point four days later: Grant to Maj. Gen. Henry W. Halleck, July 9, 1864, Ibid., p. 197.

223. Lee's "strategy in sending Early down the Shenandoah": Thomas L. Livermore, "The Generalship of the Appomattox Campaign," in *Papers of The Military Historical Society of Massachusetts: The Shenandoah Campaigns of 1862 and 1864 and the Appomattox Campaign of 1865* 6 (The Military Historical Society of Massachusetts, 1907), p. 461.

EPILOGUE

226. "As soon as I was in a condition to travel, I started on horseback": Early, *Autobiographical Sketch*, p. 468.

226. The Confederate troops who died in the war "gave their lives": Speaking June 6, 1889, at Confederate Memorial Day ceremonies at Stonewall Cemetery in Winchester, Virginia. Quoted in the *Winchester Times Extra*, June 7, 1889.

227. "He fell at his post fighting like a lion at bay": Jubal Early, "Winchester, Fisher's Hill, and Cedar Creek," essay in *Battles and Leaders of the Civil War* 4, p. 529.

230. "In composing his books he had the peculiar habit of writing": *The New York Times*, February 16, 1905.

Bibliography

BOOKS

Memoirs, Diaries, Letters

Agassiz, George R., ed. *Meade's Headquarters, 1863–1865: Letters of Colonel Theodore Lyman from the Wilderness to Appomattox*. Atlantic Monthly Press, 1922.

Baker, George E., ed. *The Works of William H. Seward*. Vol. 4. Houghton, Mifflin, 1890.

Basler, Roy P. *Abraham Lincoln: His Speeches and Writings*. World Publishing, 1946.

Bates, David Homer. *Lincoln in the Telegraph Office: Recollections of the United States Military Telegraph Corps During the Civil War*. The Century, 1907.

Bates, Samuel P. *History of Pennsylvania Volunteers, 1861–5, Prepared in Compliance with Acts of the Legislature*. B. Singerly, 1869.

Beale, Howard K., ed. *The Diary of Edward Bates, 1859–1866*. Da Capo, 1971.

Bowen, James L. *History of the Thirty-Seventh Regiment Mass. Volunteers, in the Civil War of 1861–1865*. Clark W. Bryan, 1884.

Brinsfield, John W., ed. *The Spirit Divided: Memoirs of Civil War Chaplains: The Confederacy*. Mercer University Press, 2006.

Brinton, John H. *Personal Memoirs of John H. Brinton, Civil War Surgeon: 1861–1865*. Southern Illinois Press, 1996.

Brooks, Noah. *Washington in Lincoln's Time*. The Century, 1895.

Burlingame, Michael, and John R. Turner Ettlinger, eds. *Inside Lincoln's White House: The Complete Civil War Diary of John Hay*. Southern Illinois University Press, 1999.

Carpenter, F. B. *The Inner Life of Abraham Lincoln: Six Months at the White House*. University of Nebraska Press, 1995.

Casler, John O. *Four Years in the Stonewall Brigade*. Morningside, 1971.

Chittenden, L. E. *Recollections of President Lincoln and His Administration*. Harper & Brothers, 1891.

Coffin, Charles Carleton. *Four Years of Fighting: A Volume of Personal Observations with the Army and Navy from the First Battle of Bull Run to the Fall of Richmond*. Ticknor and Fields, 1866.

Colt, Margaretta Barton. *Defend the Valley: A Shenandoah Family in the Civil War*. Orion Books, 1994.

Croffut, William A., ed. *Fifty Years in Camp and Field: Diary of Major-General Ethan Allen Hitchcock*. Putnam, 1909.

Dana, Charles A. *Recollections of the Civil War: With the Leaders at Washington and in the Field in the Sixties*. D. Appleton, 1898.

Davis, Jefferson. *The Rise and Fall of the Confederate Government*. Vol. 2. D. Appleton, 1881.

De Forest, John William. *A Volunteer's Adventures: A Union Captain's Record of the Civil War*. Louisiana State University Press, 1946.

Donald, David Herbert, ed. *Gone for a Soldier: The Civil War Memoirs of Private Alfred Bellard*. Little, Brown, 1975.

Douglas, Henry Kyd. *I Rode with Stonewall*. University of North Carolina Press, 1940.

Dowdy, Clifford, and Louis H. Manarin, eds. *The Wartime Papers of Robert E. Lee*. Little, Brown, 1961.

Duncan, Richard, ed. *Alexander Neil and the Last Shenandoah Valley Campaign: Letters of an American Surgeon to his Family, 1864*. White Mane, 1996.

Durkin, Joseph T., ed. *Confederate Chaplain: A War Journal of Rev. James B. Sheeran*. Bruce, 1960.

Early, Jubal Anderson. *Autobiographical Sketch and Narrative of the War Between the States*. J. B. Lippincott, 1912. (Electronic edition: http://docsouth.unc.edu/early/menu.html)

Early, Jubal Anderson. *Lieutenant General Jubal Anderson Early, C.S.A., Narrative of the War Between the States*. Da Capo, 1989.

Early, Jubal Anderson, and Gary W. Gallagher. *A Memoir of the Last Year of the War for Independence in the Confederate States of America, Containing an Account of the Operations of His Commands in the Years 1864 and 1865*. University of South Carolina Press, 2001.

Eby, Cecil D. Jr., ed. *Yankee in the Civil War: The Diaries of David Hunter Strother*. University of North Carolina Press, 1998.

Emerson, Edward Waldo. *The Life and Letters of Charles Russell Lowell*. University of South Carolina Press, 2005.

Esten, John. *Wearing of the Gray: Being Personal Portraits, Scenes, and Adventures of the War*. Louisiana State University Press, 1997.

Gilmor, Harry. *Four Years in the Saddle*. Harper & Brothers, 1866.

Gordon, John Brown. *Reminiscences of the Civil War*. Charles Scribner's Sons, 1904. (Electronic edition: http://docsouth.unc.edu/gordon/menu.html)

Grant, Ulysses S. *Personal Memoirs*. C. L. Webster, 1885–86. (Electronic edition: www.bartleby.com/1011/)

Greiner, James M., Janet L. Coryell, and James R. Smither, eds. *A Surgeon's Civil War: The Letters and Diary of Daniel M. Holt, M.D.* Kent State University Press, 1994.

Hard, Abner. *History of the Eighth Cavalry Regiment, Illinois Volunteers, During the Great Rebellion*. Morningside Bookshop, 1996.

Haynes, Chaplain E. M. *A History of the Tenth Regiment, Vermont Volunteers with Biographical Sketches.* . . . Tenth Vermont Regimental Association, 1870; reprint published by Tuttle, 1894.

Humphries, Charles A. *Field, Camp, Hospital and Prison: In the Civil War, 1863–1865*. Press of Geo. H. Ellis, 1918.

Hunton, Eppa. *Autobiography of Eppa Hunton*. William Byrd Press, 1933.

Hyde, Thomas W. *Following the Greek Cross or Memories of the Sixth Army Corps*. University of South Carolina Press, 2005.

Johnson, Robert U., and Clarence C. Buell, eds. *Battles and Leaders of the Civil War*. 4 vols. The Century, 1887.

Jones, J. B. *A Rebel War Clerk's Diary at the Confederate States Capital*. Vol. 2. J. B. Lippincott, 1866.

Jones, Terry L., ed. *The Civil War Memoirs of Captain William J. Seymour: Reminiscences of a Louisiana Tiger*. Louisiana State University Press, 1991.

Laas, Virginia Jeans, ed. *Wartime Washington: The Civil War Letters of Elizabeth Blair Lee*. University of Illinois Press, 1991.

Lee, Captain Robert E. *Recollections and Letters of General Robert E. Lee*. Broadfoot, 1988.

Lee, Fitzhugh. *General Lee*. D. Appleton, 1894.

Lewis, Osceola. *History of the One hundred and thirty-eighth Regiment, Pennsylvania Volunteer Infantry*. Wills, Iredell & Jenkins, 1866.

Mathless, Paul, ed. *Voices of the Civil War: Shenandoah, 1864*. Time-Life Books, 1998.

McDonald, Archie P., ed. *Make Me a Map of the Valley: The Civil War Journal of Stonewall Jackson's Cartographer*. Southern Methodist University Press, 1973.

Miles, Nelson A. *Serving the Republic: Memoirs of the Civil and Military Life*. Harper & Brothers, 1911.

Moore, Frank, ed. *The Rebellion Record: A Diary of American Events with Documents, Narratives, Illustrative Incidents, Poetry, Etc*. D. Van Nostrand, 1868.

O'Ferrall, Charles T. *Forty Years of Active Service*. Neale Publishing, 1904.

Olsen, Bernard A., ed. *Upon the Tented Field*. Historic Projects, 1993.

Pelka, Fred, ed. *The Civil War Letters of Colonel Charles F. Johnson, Invalid Corps*. University of Massachusetts Press, 2004.

Porter, Horace. *Campaigning with Grant*. The Century, 1897.

Riddle, Albert Gallatin. *Recollections of War Times: Reminiscences of Men and Events in Washington, 1860–1865*. G. P. Putnam's Sons, 1895.

Roe, Alfred S. *Monocacy: A Sketch of the Battle*. Toomey Press, 1997.

Roe, Alfred Seelye. *The Ninth New York Heavy Artillery: A History of Its Organization, Services in the Defenses of Washington. . . .* Self-published, 1899.

Russell, Charles Wells, ed. *The Memoirs of Colonel John S. Mosby*. Little, Brown, 1917. (Electronic edition: http://docsouth.unc.edu/mosby/mosby.html)

Saunders, Lisa, ed. *Ever True: A Union Private and His Wife: Civil War Letters of Private Charles McDowell, New York Ninth Heavy Artillery*. Heritage Books, 2004.

Scott, Major John. *Partisan Life with Col. John S. Mosby*. Harper & Brothers, 1867.

Sears, Stephen W., ed. *The Civil War Papers of George B. McClellan: Selected Correspondence, 1860–1865*. Ticknor & Fields, 1989.

Seward, Frederick W. *Reminiscences of a War-Time Statesman and Diplomat, 1830–1915*. G. P. Putnam's Sons, 1916.

Seward, Frederick William, ed. *William H. Seward: An Autobiography from 1801–1834. With a Memoir of His Life, and Selections from His Letters*. 3 vols. Derby Miller, 1891.

Sheridan, Philip. *Civil War Memoirs*. Bantam, 1991.

Simon, John Y., ed. *The Papers of Ulysses S. Grant*. Southern Illinois University Press, 1992.

Sorrel, Moxley. *Recollections of a Confederate Staff Officer*. Neale Publishing, 1905. (Electronic edition: www.civilwarancestor.com/sorrel.htm)

Staudenraus, P. J., ed. *Mr. Lincoln's Washington: The Civil War Dispatches of Noah Brooks*. Yoseloff, 1967.

Stevens, George T. *Three Years in the Sixth Corps: A Concise Narrative of Events in the Army of the Potomac, from 1861 to the Close of the Rebellion, April 1865.* S. R. Gray, 1866.

Stiles, Robert. *Four Years Under Marse Robert.* Neale Publishing, 1904. (Electronic edition: http://docsouth.unc.edu/stiles/stiles.html)

Sumner, Merlin E., ed. *The Diary of Cyrus B. Comstock.* Morningside, 1987.

Thomas, Benjamin P., ed. *Three Years with Grant: As Recalled by War Correspondent Sylvanus Cadwallader.* Knopf, 1956.

Tyler, William S., ed. *Recollections of the Civil War by Mason Whiting Tyler.* G. P. Putnam's Sons, 1912.

Walker, Aldace F. *The Vermont Brigade in the Shenandoah Valley, 1864.* The Free Press Association, 1869.

Wallace, Lew. *An Autobiography.* Harper, 1906.

Welles, Gideon. *Diary of Gideon Welles, Secretary of the Navy Under Lincoln and Johnson.* 3 vols. Houghton Mifflin, 1911.

Wild, Frederick W. *Memoirs and History of Capt. F. W. Alexander's Baltimore Battery of Light Artillery U.S.V.* Press of the Maryland School for Boys, 1912.

Wilkeson, Frank. *Turned Inside Out: Recollections of a Private Soldier in the Army of the Potomac.* University of Nebraska Press, 1997.

Williams, Edward B., ed. *Rebel Brothers: The Civil War Letters of the Truehearts.* Texas A&M University Press, 1995.

Worsham, John H. *One of Jackson's Foot Cavalry: His Experience and What He Saw During the War, 1861–1865.* Neale Publishing, 1912. (Electronic edition: http://docsouth.unc.edu/worsham/menu.html)

BOOKS

Selected Secondary Sources

Acken, J. Gregory, ed. *Inside the Army of the Potomac: The Civil War Experience of Captain Francis Adams Donaldson.* Stackpole, 1998.

Andrews, J. Cutler. *The North Reports the Civil War*. University of Pittsburgh Press, 1955.

Bearss, Edwin C. *The Battle of Monocacy: A Documented Report*. Monocacy National Battlefield, 2003.

Boomhower, Ray E. *The Sword and the Pen: A Life of Lew Wallace*. Indiana Historical Society, 2005.

Carwardine, Richard. *Lincoln: A Life of Purpose and Power*. Knopf, 2006.

Catton, Bruce. *The Army of the Potomac: A Stillness at Appomattox*. Doubleday, 1953.

Clark, Walter, ed. *Histories of the Several Regiments and Battalions from North Carolina in the Great War, 1861–1865*. Broadfoot, 1982.

Cooke, John Esten. *A Life of Gen. Robert E. Lee*. D. Appleton, 1871. (Electronic edition: http://manybooks.net/authors/cookejoh.html)

Cooling, Benjamin Franklin. *Jubal Early's Raid on Washington, 1864*. Nautical & Aviation Publishing, 1989.

Cooling, B. Franklin. *Monocacy: The Battle That Saved Washington*. White Mane Publishing, 1997.

Cooling, Benjamin Franklin III. *Symbol, Sword and Shield: Defending Washington During the Civil War*. White Mane, 1991.

Cramer, John Henry. *Lincoln Under Enemy Fire: A Complete Account of His Experiences During Early's Attack on Washington*. Louisiana State University Press, 1948.

Decker, Harry L., ed. *To Commemorate the 100th Anniversary of the Battle of Monocacy*. Frederick County Civil War Centennial, 1964.

Duncan, Richard E. *Lee's Endangered Left: The Civil War in Western Virginia, Spring of 1864*. Louisiana State University Press, 1998.

Eckert, Ralph Lowell. *John Brown Gordon: Soldier, Southerner, American*. Louisiana State University Press, 1993.

Epstein, Daniel Mark. *Lincoln and Whitman: Parallel Lives in Civil War Washington*. Ballantine, 2004.

Ernst, Kathleen A. *Too Afraid to Cry: Maryland Civilians in the Antietam Campaign*. Stackpole, 1999.

Evans, Clement A., ed. *The Confederate Military History: A Library of Confederate States History Written by Distinguished Men of the South*. Confederate Publishing, 1899.

Foote, Shelby. *The Civil War: A Narrative: Red River to Appomattox*. Vintage, 1974.

Freeman, Douglas Southall. *Lee's Lieutenants: A Study in Command*. Scribner's, 1970.

Freeman, Douglas Southall. *R. E. Lee: A Biography*. Scribner's, 1934.

Furgurson, Ernest B. *Freedom Rising: Washington in the Civil War*. Knopf, 2004.

Gallagher, Gary W. *Jubal A. Early, the Lost Cause and Civil War History: A Persistent Legacy*. Marquette University Press, 1995.

Gallagher, Gary W., ed. *Lee and His Army in Confederate History*. University of North Carolina Press, 2001.

Gallagher, Gary W., ed. *Lee the Soldier*. University of Nebraska Press, 1996.

Gallagher, Gary W., ed. *The Shenandoah Valley Campaign of 1864*. University of North Carolina Press, 2006.

Gallagher, Gary W. *Stephen Dodson Ramseur: Lee's Gallant General*. University of North Carolina Press, 1985.

Gallagher, Gary W., ed. *Struggle for the Shenandoah: Essays on the 1864 Valley Campaign*. Kent State University Press, 1991.

Goldsborough, E. Y. *Early's Great Raid and the Battle of Monocacy*. Historical Society of Frederick County, 1989.

Goodwin, Doris Kearns. *Team of Rivals: The Political Genius of Abraham Lincoln*. Simon & Schuster, 2005.

Gorham, George G. *Life and Public Services of Edwin M. Stanton*. Vol. 2. Houghton, Mifflin, 1899.

Harris, William C. *Lincoln's Last Months*. Belknap Press, 2004.

Jackson, William T. *New Jerseyans in the Civil War: For Union and Liberty*. Rutgers University Press, 1925.

Judge, Joseph. *Season of Fire: The Confederate Strike on Washington*. Rockbridge Publishing, 1994.

Klement, Frank L. *The Limits of Dissent: Clement L. Vallandigham and the Civil War.* Fordham University Press, 1998.

Klement, Frank L. *Lincoln's Critics: The Copperheads of the North.* White Mane, 1999.

Krick, Robert E. L. *Staff Officers in Gray: A Biographical Register of the Staff Officers in the Army of Northern Virginia.* University of North Carolina Press, 2003.

Leech, Margaret. *Reveille in Washington, 1860–1865,* Time-Life Books, 1980.

Lepa, Jack H. *The Shenandoah Valley Campaign of 1864.* Macfarland, 2003.

Longacre, Edward G. *General Ulysses S. Grant: The Soldier and the Man.* Da Capo, 2006.

Longacre, Edward G. *Lincoln's Cavalrymen: A History of the Mounted Forces of the Army of the Potomac, 1861–1865.* Stackpole Books, 2000.

Marszalek, John F. *Commander of All Lincoln's Armies: A Life of General Henry A. Halleck.* Harvard University Press, 2004.

Martin, David G., ed. *The Monocacy Regiment: A Commemorative History of the Fourteenth New Jersey Infantry in the Civil War, 1862–1865.* Longstreet House, 1987.

Marvel, William. *Mr. Lincoln Goes to War.* Houghton Mifflin, 2006.

McKee, Irving. *"Ben-Hur" Wallace: The Life of General Lew Wallace.* University of California Press, 1947.

Morris, Roy. *The Better Angel: Walt Whitman in the Civil War.* Oxford University Press, 2000.

Morsberger, Robert E., and Katharine M. Morsberger. *Lew Wallace: Militant Romantic.* McGraw-Hill, 1980.

Nicolay, John G., and John Hay. *Abraham Lincoln: A History.* Vol. 9. The Century, 1890.

Osborne, Charles C. *Jubal: The Life and Times of General Jubal A. Early, CSA.* Louisiana State University Press, 1998.

Perret, Geoffrey. *Ulysses S. Grant: Soldier & President.* Random House, 1997.

Pinsker, Matthew. *Lincoln's Sanctuary: Abraham Lincoln and the Soldiers' Home.* Oxford University Press, 2003.

Pollard, Edward A. *The Early Life, Campaigns, and Public Services of Robert E. Lee.* . . . E. B. Treat, 1871.

Pollard, Edward A. *The Lost Cause: A New Southern History of the War of the Confederates.* E. B. Treat, 1866.

Rhodes, James Ford. *History of the Civil War, 1861–1865.* Macmillan, 1917. (Electronic edition: www.bartleby.com/252)

Rolle, Andrew. *The Lost Cause: The Confederate Exodus to Mexico.* University of Oklahoma Press, 1965.

Sandburg, Carl. *Abraham Lincoln: The War Years.* Vol. 3. Harcourt, Brace, 1930.

Scharf, John Thomas. *History of Maryland.* 3 vols. Tradition Press, 1967.

Scharf, J. Thomas. *History of Western Maryland: Being a History of Frederick, Montgomery, Carroll, Washington, Allegany, and Garret Counties from the Earliest Period to the Present Day.* . . . Family Line Publications, 1995.

Schildt, John W. *Drums Along the Monocacy.* Antietam Publications, 1991.

Sears, Stephen W. *George B. McClellan: The Young Napoleon.* Ticknor & Fields, 1988.

Shenk, Joshua Wolf. *Lincoln's Melancholy: How Depression Challenged a President and Fueled His Greatness.* Houghton Mifflin, 2005.

Siepel, Kevin H. *Rebel: The Life and Times of John Singleton Mosby.* Thomas Dunne Books, 1983.

Stuart, Brian. *Campaigning with the 17th Virginia Cavalry Night Hawks at Monocacy.* Night Hawk Press, Washington, 2005.

Tracey, Grace L., and John P. Dern. *Pioneers of Old Monocacy: The Early Settlement of Frederick County Maryland, 1721–1743.* Clearfield, 2001.

Tucker, Spencer C. *Brigadier General John D. Imboden: Confederate Commander in the Shenandoah.* University Press of Kentucky, 2002.

Vandiver, Frank Everson. *Jubal's Raid: General Early's Famous Attack on Washington in 1864.* University of Nebraska Press, 1992.

Wallace, General Lew. *The Story of the Making of Ben-Hur: A Tale of the Christ.* Random House, 1959.

Weber, Jennifer L. *Copperheads: The Rise and Fall of Lincoln's Opponents in the North*. Oxford University Press, 2006.

Welsh, Jack D. *Medical Histories of Confederate Generals*. Kent State University Press, 1999.

Wert, Jeffrey D. *Mosby's Rangers*. Simon & Schuster, 1990.

Williams, Harry T. *Hayes of the Twenty-third: The Civil War Volunteer Officer*. University of Nebraska Press, 1994.

Williams, T. J. C., and Folger McKinsey. *History of Frederick County, Maryland*. Regional Publications Company, 1967.

Winslow, Cossoul Watson. *The Military and Civil History of the County of Essex, New York*. J. Munsell, 1869.

Wolcott, Walter. *The Military History of Yates County, New York*. Express Book and Job Printing House, 1895.

Worthington, Glenn H. *Fighting for Time: The Battle of Monocacy*. Burd Street Press, 1985.

ARTICLES, REPORTS, COLLECTIONS

Bernard, John Gross Barnard. *A Report on the Defenses of Washington, to the Chief of Engineers, U. S. Army, Corps of Engineers, Corps of Engineers, Professional Paper No. 20*. U.S. Government Printing Office, 1871.

Biography of Thomas Feamster, Feamster Family Papers, 1794–1967. Manuscript Division, Library of Congress.

Bradwell, I. G. "Early's Demonstration Against Washington in 1864." *Confederate Veteran* (October 1914).

Bradwell, I. G. "Early's March to Washington in 1864." *Confederate Veteran* (May 1920).

Brown, James Earl. "Life of Brigadier General John McCausland." *West Virginia History* (July 1943).

Colyer, Henry I. *Correspondence of Henry I. Colyer, 1862–1865*. Huntington Library.

Cooke, John Esten. "The Battles of Virginia." *The Old Guard* (December 1867).

Cox, William V. "The Defenses of Washington: General Early's Advance on the Capital and the Battle of Fort Stevens, July 11 and 12." *Records of the Columbia Historical Society, Washington, D.C.* 4 (1901).

Duncan, Richard R. "Maryland's Reaction to Early's Raid in 1864: A Summer of Bitterness." *Maryland Historical Magazine* (Fall 1969).

Early Family Papers, 1764–1956. Virginia Historical Society.

Feis, William B. "A Union Military Intelligence Failure: Jubal Early's Raid, June 12–14, 1864." *Civil War History* (September 1990).

Garrett, Robert. *Robert Garrett Family Papers, 1778–1925.* Library of Congress.

Golladay, V. Dennis. "Jubal Early's Last Stand." *Virginia Cavalcade* (Summer 1970).

Halpine, Charles G. *Papers of Charles G. Halpine, 1811–1889.* Huntington Library.

Hatcher, Charles S. *Recollections of the Civil War, 1861–1865.* Library of Virginia Archives and Manuscript Room.

Holloway, James Montgomery. *Papers, 1861–1905.* Virginia Historical Society.

Hutcheson, James A. "Saving the Day at Monocacy." *Confederate Veteran* (February 1915).

Jubal Anderson Early Papers. Earl Gregg Swem Library. College of William and Mary.

"*The Late Rebel Raid.*" *Harper's Weekly,* Issue 07/30, 1864.

Lee Family Papers, 1810–1914. Virginia Historical Society.

Lee, Robert E. *Correspondence with Jefferson Davis, 1862–1865.* Library of Virginia, Archives and Manuscripts Room.

Lee, Robert E. *Headquarters Papers, 1850–1876.* Virginia Historical Society.

Lewis, Thomas A. "There in the Heat of July, Was the Shimmering Capitol." *Smithsonian* (July 1988).

Lew Wallace Collection, 1799–1972. Indiana Historical Society.

Lincoln, Abraham. *Papers of Abraham Lincoln, 1774–1948.* Manuscript Division, Library of Congress.

McMurran, Joseph. "Diary, 1864, May 4–August 17." Library of Virginia, Archives and Manuscripts Room.

McPherson, James. "No Peace Without Victory, 1861–1865." *The American Historical Review*. Volume 109, Issue 1, 2004.

"Monthly Record of Current Events." *Harper's New Monthly Magazine* (September 1864).

Myers, Gustavus Adolphus. *Papers, 1812–1866*. Virginia Historical Society.

Nicolay, John G. *Papers of John G. Nicolay, 1811–1943*. Manuscript Division, Library of Congress.

Point Lookout, Md., Prison Camp, Records, 1863 January 2–1864 June. William L. Clements Library, the University of Michigan, Schoff Civil War Collections.

Rowley, William Reuben. *Papers, 1862–1892*. Abraham Lincoln Presidential Library and Museum.

Schmitt, Martin F. "An Interview with General Jubal A. Early in 1889." *Journal of Southern History* 11, no. 4 (November 1945).

Stephens, Gail. "Battle of Monocacy Timeline (May 13–August 1864)." Monocacy National Battlefield, Interpretive File.

Stringfellow, William Williams. *Diary*. North Carolina State Archives, Collection 1091.

Swift, Gloria Baker, and Gail Stephens. "Honor Redeemed: Lew Wallace's Military Career and the Battle of Monocacy." *North and South Magazine* (January 2001).

Swisher, James K. "Unreconstructed Rebel: Jubal Early." *Military History* (February 2001).

Taft, Horatio Nelson. *Diary of Horatio Nelson Taft, 1861–1865*. Manuscript Division, Library of Congress.

U.S. Department of the Interior. National Park Service. National Capital Region. "A Historic Resources Study: The Civil War Defenses of Washington, Parts I and II" (2004).

U.S. War Department. *The War of the Rebellion: A Compilation of the Official Records of the Union and Confederate Armies*. Vol. 70., U.S. Government Printing Office, 1880–1901. (Electronic editions: http://ehistory.osu.edu/uscw/search/index_advanced.cfm?OR=1, http://cdl.library.cornell.edu/moa/browse.monographs/waro.html)

Venable, Charles Scott. *Papers*. Manuscripts Department, Library of the University of North Carolina at Chapel Hill, Southern Historical Center.

Wehrle, Edmund F. "Catoctin Mountain Park: A Historic Resource Study." National Park Service (March 2000).

Welles, Gideon. "The Opposition to Lincoln in 1864." *Atlantic Monthly* (March 1878).

Wright Family Correspondence, 1856–1869. Library of Virginia, Archives and Manuscripts Room.

Young, John G. *Diary*. North Carolina State Archives Collection (1076).

Index

Boldface page numbers refer to pages with illustrations.

Virginia Military Institute (VMI), 18, 21, 51
Virginia Secession Convention, 25–26
Vredenburgh, Maj. Peter, 116, 118

Wade, Benjamin Franklin, 212
Walker, Lt. Col. Aldace F., 170, 194–95, 195, 213
Wallace, David, 64
Wallace, Brig. Gen. Lew, 50, 63, 63–64, 64–68, **65**, 68, 70–72, 73–74, 77–79, 79, 81, 82–83, 83–84, 85, 88–90, 90, 91, 92–93, 93–94, 97, 98–99, 100, 101, 101–3, 103–6, 106–7, 107–8, 115, 117–18, 118–19, 121, 121–22, 122, 123, 125, 128, 132, 133, 137, 138, 140, 142, 143, 144, 152, 213, 229–30, 231
Wallace, Susan Elston, 64, 72
War of 1812, 216
Washington, 142, 145–47, 216
    defense of, 147–51, **151**, 151–54, 154–55, 157–60, 161, 161–65, 165–66, 166–68, 168–71, 171–72
    Early's march on, 126, 132, 134, 137, 138, 139–40, 140–42, 142–44, 144, 164–65, 173–75, 175–79, 179–83, 183–85, 188, 188, 192, 193, 193–98, 204, 205–6, 213–17, 217, 217–22, 222–24
    Early's retreat, 206, 208, 209–10, 225–26
    See also Battle of Monocacy; Civil War Defenses of Washington
Washington, George, 7, 29, 145, 160
Washington, Martha Custis, 29
Washington Daily National Intelligencer, 199
Watson, William G., 22
Waynesboro, Battle of, 225
Welles, Gideon, 71–72, 75, 154, 157, 167, 182–83, 187–88, 191–92, 201, 209–10

Wells, Maj. Charles H., 91
Wells, Maj. Levi, 139
Wheaton, Brig. Gen. Frank, 181, 206
Whitman, George, 146
Whitman, Walt, 146–47
Whitney, Henry Clay, 189
Whittier, James Greenleaf, 9
Wild, Frederick W., 78–79, 116, 134, 122–23
Wilderness Campaign, Battle of the, 16, 17–22, 29, 36, 39, 83, 157, 188, 190, 200
Wilderness Campaign, Grant's, 15–22, 83, 190
Wilke, Lt, 109–10
Wilkeson, Frank, 154–55, 168–69, 194, 198
Wilkins, Andrew, 197
Williamsburg, Battle of, 26–27
Wirz, Henry, 230
Wisewell, Col. Moses N., 166
Wood, Capt. John Taylor, 53
Woolcott, Alexander, 199, 201
Worsham, Pvt. John, 42, 47–48, 55, 58–59, 97, 112, 128, 129–30, 139, 175, 178, 179
Worthington, Glenn, 102, 105–6, 107, 112–13, 116, 127, 235
Worthington, Harry, 127
Worthington, John, 127
Worthington Farm, 97, 103, **104**, 105–6, 111–13, 127, 236
Wren, Porter, 115–16
Wright, Maj. Gen. Horatio, 80, 157–60, **158**, 165, 169–70, 178, 193–94, 195, 200, 201, 202, 203, 203–4, 206, 210, 212, 215, 232, 233

York, Brig. Gen. Zebulon, 44, 111, 131
York's Consolidated Louisiana Brigade, 113, 131
Young, Sgt. Maj. John G., 58